Pi
wl
w

NOTES AS VICE PRESIDENT
1928–1929

CHARLES GATES DAWES

Notes as
VICE PRESIDENT
1928–1929

BY
CHARLES G. DAWES

WITH ILLUSTRATIONS

BOSTON   1935

LITTLE, BROWN, AND COMPANY

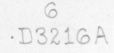

175493

ILLUSTRATIONS

NOTES AS VICE PRESIDENT
1928–1929

CHAPTER I

Evanston, Illinois, June 27, 1928.

I HAVE finally determined to keep some notes while I occupy my present office. Contemporaneous comment on facts is almost always the most valuable. What one may write after an event is a recollection of it — not an observation. One's recollections, too, may be confused by later events.

However, since I have been neglectful in writing during the first three years of my service as Vice President, a natural desire to make some permanent record of it will lead me in the first part of this new journal to comment upon the past and the present together.

My experiences in this office I have found far from uninteresting and unimportant. The superficial attitude of indifference which many public men assume toward the office of Vice President of the United States is easily explained. It is the office for which one cannot hope to be a candidate with sufficient prospects for success to justify the effort involved in a long campaign. One's political availability for nomination to the position cannot be determined until the nominating convention has in effect decided upon the head of the ticket.

Geographic considerations — sectional political situations which continually change, combined with the controlling fact that the nomination for the vice-presidency must fit into a picture dominated by the Presidential nominee — make early quest for the office too dangerous to attract public men of sufficient stature to justify a serious aspiration for it. Nevertheless it is regarded at its real value by public men, whatever may be their assumed attitude. To-day we see the majority leader of the Senate nominated for the vice-presidency by the Republican Party, and the minority leader in a receptive mood at the Democratic National Convention at Houston, which has just assembled. (June 26, 1928.)

The office is largely what the man in it makes it — which applies to all public offices. The fact that the Vice President in the Senate Chamber cannot enter into debate is considered a disadvantage, yet for that reason he is removed from the temptation to indulge in the pitiable quest of that double objective so characteristic of many Senate speeches — the placating of general public opinion and of an opposing local constituency at the same time. For his prestige as a presiding officer, it is to his advantage that he neither votes nor speaks in the Senate Chamber. Outside the Senate Chamber, his position as Vice President gives him a hearing by the general public as wide as that accorded any Senator, other things being equal. If he lacks initiative, courage, or ideas, he of course will be submerged; but that is true also of a Senator or any other parliamentary member.

Whatever may be said to the contrary, as anyone discovers who occupies the office, the people hold it in great respect. While I shall serve eight months more as Vice President and may make future mistakes, I see the prospect of closing my public career at least without discredit. The occupancy of a public office, unless decorated with public respect, is a curse to anyone.

Evanston, June 27, 1928.

Listened over the radio to the proceedings of the Democratic National Convention at Houston, and heard the speech of the Permanent Chairman, Joseph T. Robinson. He is a man of great ability, of high character, of industry and of exceptional qualities as a leader of men. His courage is that of a lion. He never deceives and his decisions are quick but sound. His ideals are high and he deserves to be rewarded with the best his party can give. It seems to-night that he will be nominated to succeed me in office, and I may say here that if he is elected, the place will not submerge him. I regard him as a statesman of high rank.

This recalls my recent visit with another friend just before leaving Washington — Dwight W. Morrow, our Ambassador to Mexico. I remained over a day to meet him. He was staying at the White House, and after the meeting there of the Arlington Memorial Bridge Association, of which the President and the Vice President are among the members, Dwight and I met at General Pershing's office in the War Department. From his letters to me and from the press I knew already that he was making great progress. I knew that within a few months of his stay in Mexico he had created a new status of peace and mutual understanding between

the two great American republics, and that he had
brought about a settlement of the apparently insoluble
oil controversy. But as I listened to his own narrative
and came to appreciate how complete is his understanding with Calles, and the degree of co-operation he is
receiving from him, I felt that, if he is spared, he will
have contributed during his term of office more to the
cause of peace and good will among the nations of the
Western Hemisphere than any other man of his generation.

What he said of Calles was especially interesting. He
tells me that Calles is determined to retire. "I could
stay in power thirty-five years as did Diaz, if I would
sink to his level," he quoted Calles as saying. It is evident that he has won Calles as he has won everybody
ever associated with him. He practises the highest
diplomacy — which, after all, largely consists of plain
and truthful statement, and, when in conferences with
foreign officials, of never making or receiving propositions without the consideration of the limitations upon
their power to act as determined by their respective
domestic public sentiments.

Morrow is genuine. His nature is a sympathetic one.
He is a friend to the weak and humble. He is natural.
He is generous in every way. He is a modest man and
never affected. Added to these endearing qualities are
his great mental ability and culture, which so set them
off. He is naturally industrious and of course is greatly
overworking himself. He weighs twenty pounds less
than when he left for Mexico. Last year, when he was
considering the suggestion of the President that he go

to Mexico, he stopped off at Evanston to talk it over with me. I strongly advised him to accept the place. He replied that of all his friends and family, his wife and I were the only ones who took this view.

I said in effect to him something like this: "Knowing you as I do, you are going to take the place and are delighted to do so. You are very fortunate, because to a man of your constructive genius, any public task but a difficult one would be unattractive. To hold a public place is nothing; to accomplish in it is everything. You have achieved great business success and prestige, but work during the war gave you, as it did me, a new perspective. You will never be satisfied until you have tried your wings in the higher atmosphere of difficult public service. The position in Mexico, to take which might ruin the ordinary diplomat of so-called 'high class', will make you. You cannot afford to take an easier diplomatic position of higher rank.

"But this opportunity is providential. It involves great difficulties and an apparently hopeless outlook for cordial relations; and thus gives you a task commensurate with your unusual abilities — the first demand of the thoroughbred. Again, every conventional mind in the country which does not visualize you as your friends know you will regard you as making a sacrifice. That, and the importance to our nation of your success, means that if you achieve success you will get full credit for it — something of which a public servant is rarely assured.

"And, lastly, it will be a place of joy to you, because in going, you are doing your duty to your President and to your country, possessing qualifications which few men have for this particular service."

Besides the oil settlement, Dwight is concerning himself with the matter of other property rights of Americans, with the Church property, and with the status of the foreign debt; and lastly, of greatest importance to Mexico, with the balancing of the Mexican budget. Calles apparently has been quick to realize in Morrow an invaluable adviser. I have no doubt that he will be as influential with Obregón, the next President, as with Calles.

Evanston, June 28, 1928.

The first portion of these "contemporaneous notes" is destined to be largely memoirs, for there runs constantly through my mind the thought of experiences during the last four years which are worth recording. During my inactive summer, at least, what I write will be more of the recent past than of the immediate present.

During the last two years my name has been constantly mentioned in connection with the Republican nomination for the presidency. From the beginning I stated I would not be a candidate for the nomination, and as soon as my friend Governor Lowden indicated that he would be a receptive candidate, I announced myself for him. This pledge of assistance I have kept to the best of my ability.

Evanston, June 29, 1928.

For the last year many articles commenting on me and my alleged prospects have appeared in the press.

As a rule articles written under such circumstances about anyone either overpraise or overcondemn. As a candidate before the people for the vice-presidency and since that time, I have fared well enough, but such articles enable me to realize that public impressions of one who is a temporary factor in political contests are largely based upon a constant reiteration of such incidents as make interesting reading from a newspaper standpoint.

And these reflections lead me to comment for the first time on my speech in 1921 before the Congressional Committee investigating the A.E.F. which helped put an end in this country to the official effort to blacken American military achievement for political and partisan purposes.

The effectiveness of a speech depends largely on the circumstances under which it is delivered, and the existing public state of mind — not alone upon the competency and sincerity of the speaker. As to the latter, as Chief of Supply Procurement of our army in France, upon the particular subject of the supply of the A.E.F. I could qualify.

For the two greatest years of my life, bearing heavy responsibilities in a great and continuing military emergency, I had represented in France our army and government in innumerable conferences with the officials of Allied armies and governments — in some of which were representatives of the politician type whom I came greatly to detest.

Where one was right and the supplies for men in action were involved, there was no time for conventionalities or "unlimited debate." The latter is not considered "a safeguard of liberty" when men are fighting in its cause. Action, then, is everything — words nothing except as they lead immediately to it.

I came out of the war a postgraduate in emergency conferences. This particular Congressional Committee was attacking a work in France for which I was chiefly responsible — the department of the administrative staff of the A.E.F., of which I was the head, having gathered, in the Allied and neutral countries of Europe, supposed to be largely stripped of supplies, over 10,-000,000 of the 17,000,000 ship tons of military supplies which our army used in France — the submarine warfare and ship shortage creating the critical situation under which we labored.

When I was called before the Committee I had devoted no time to preparation. On this particular subject I needed none. On the morning of my arrival at Washington I walked alone for an hour or so in the Capital Park, waiting for the time at which the Committee was to assemble. As I thought over the work we had done in France, my indignation that it should be attacked steadily increased, and I suddenly decided that so far as I could bring it about either the Committee or I would go out of business — that after all it was not my work which was being attacked but that of the splendid army our country had sent to France — that it was not at the service of particular men that mud was being slung but at the glorious banner of American achievement — that we, coming home, were now only meeting that which had confronted our great war President and his Secretary of War, who had been faithful to our army — a pitiful, detestable effort to exploit political and partisan purposes through our recent national calamity. The Congressional Committee which I was to confront had visited France after the armistice to "investigate the American Expeditionary Forces." Within two days from the time when General Pershing was to take the ship for his return to the United States from the war, with his headquarters files packed in over one hundred boxes, this Committee endeavored to prevent his departure in order that they might investigate him there in Paris with attendant publicity. Failing in this, they had summoned Judge Parker, the head of the Liquidating Commission of the War Department, then functioning in Paris. The Judge, whose industry in thorough preparation and the mastery of details was famous, was ready for them. He appeared before them anxious for the fray, with three boxes of documents, each one of which required the services of two soldiers to carry.

Believing that the Committee wanted pertinent facts, he had come loaded with them. The first question asked him was in the usual form: "Why was this large number of airplanes burned by the army in France after the war instead of being salvaged?" The Judge reached into his boxes and his answer consumed something over an hour. The Committee suddenly realized what they were up against and, to the great disappointment of the Judge, promptly adjourned with the statement to him that his answer had been so complete and satisfactory that they were justified in assuming that all of the business on which he was called to testify, had been completed properly and in the best interests of the United States.

Only a week or so before my appearance, when Charles M. Schwab was a witness before this same Committee, their brutal and unjustified reflections upon his integrity had broken him down in tears.

I had no reason to hold the Committee in high esteem.

What is referred to as the "Hell and Maria" speech consumed about seven hours in its delivery and three sessions of the Committee; and was delivered after the first hour to "standing room only." It was not chiefly denunciation, but painstaking statement of pertinent facts. It was not reported coherently in any part except by the newspaper correspondents who gathered in large numbers as reports came to them as to what was going on. The Committee stenographers were unable to take me when I spoke rapidly — which is a trouble I experience with all reports of my extempore addresses.

Only the first two pages of the printed official report of the examination, transcribed before I really got into action, bore any resemblance to what I said. The newspaper writers present, however, projected over the country the substance of the speech. It accomplished its purpose. It might have done so without profanity, but this is doubtful.

The Committee went out of business shortly thereafter and the political muckraking of American achieve-

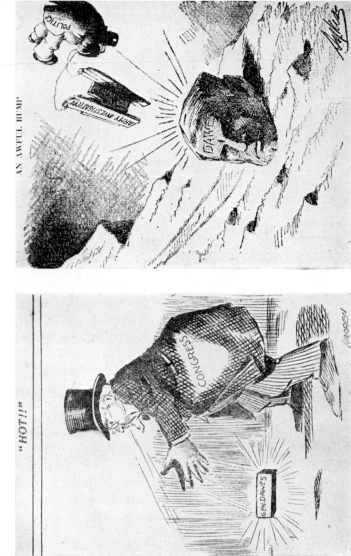

Cartoons on "Hell and Maria" Speech

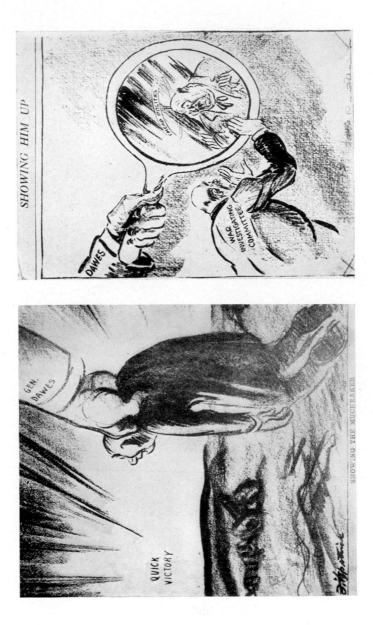

SHOWING HIM UP

SHOWING THE MUCKRAKER

MR. DAWES TESTIFIES BEFORE THE CONGRESSIONAL
WAR INVESTIGATION COMMITTEE

"What Was That?"

ment in the war ceased generally throughout the country.

Evanston, July 1, 1928.

Senator Curtis, the Republican nominee for Vice President, answered my telegram of congratulation saying that I knew whether he ought to be congratulated or not. Curtis is certainly qualified to make a fine presiding officer.

Hoover triumphed in his fight for the nomination through ability, inherent merit and persistence in organized effort. He is a man of courage and character. I have always admired him, having come to know him, his attitudes and his methods, through official association with him during the first year of the American budget, and in France during the post-armistice period of the war. The attacks upon him during the prenomination campaign only strengthened him. The justified association in the public mind of a man's name with real accomplishment in the public service, and for humanity, is always his best protection against the tongue of slander.

Every attack upon Hoover only emphasized and called attention to his merits instead of distracting attention from them. I have not always agreed with him, but have appreciated his courage in standing by his convictions. Dean Swift's saying, "Censure is the tax a man pays to the public for being eminent", certainly applies in this case.

Nothing infuriates the chronic nonconstructive parliamentary critics so much as the onward march of a man and his steady acquisition of power and influence through success in difficult administrative positions. In proportion as he achieves results through constructive action the virulence of minority criticism increases.

And it may be added — the smaller a minority becomes the more virulent it usually is; for the subconscious sense of the futility of its efforts adds to its bitterness and fury.

I owe Hoover one great debt of gratitude. At the beginning of the war, when I was seeking a commission as Lieutenant Colonel of Engineers, he strongly urged me to come into his work instead, saying that "he knew of a hundred men any one of whom would make a better Lieutenant Colonel of Engineers." I had to agree with the truth of this, but told him that my friend John Pershing, just appointed Commander in Chief of the A.E.F., said he could find appropriate work for me in France if I could get a commission. So I declined with appreciation of his thought; but when at Atlanta with my regiment, the 17th Engineers, I was startled to receive a telegram from him reading: "Would you bear me implacable resentment if I asked the President to assign you to me?" I replied: "It would be unfair and cruel and I know you will not consider it."

It was certainly within his power to have prevented my going to France, but he was generous enough not to employ that power. I had the pleasure of co-operating with him as representing the supply service of the army when he came to France for his post-armis-

tice relief work, and among other things recommended
to him that brilliant officer James A. Logan, who became his first assistant and in that place laid the foundation of his enduring fame as unofficial adviser of the
United States on the Reparation Commission and one
of the controlling factors in creating the "First Committee of Experts Reparation Commission."

Evanston, July 3, 1928.

During the inactive summer months is an oppor-
tune time to recapitulate some of the happenings at the
time of my nomination in 1924, thereafter during the
campaign, and later in office. I was nominated for the
vice-presidency from the floor of the Convention unexpectedly to myself and contrary to the desire, and notwithstanding the efforts, of the Chairman of the Republican National Committee, who finally endeavored to
unite his followers for Hoover.

The situation was exactly similar to one which arose
relative to the vice-presidential nomination in the Republican National Convention in Philadelphia in 1900.
In the absence of a commitment by President McKinley as to a running mate — and in this more recent
convention, President Coolidge declined to interfere —
Senator Hanna, then Chairman of the Republican National Committee, started to organize resistance to the
move to nominate Roosevelt. Realizing the undesir-
ability of this action from the President's standpoint,
since it would place him in a false attitude, I strongly
urged Hanna to abandon this effort. Finding him determined, I then took the matter up with President Mc-

Kinley at Washington over the telephone, who, through
me, ordered Hanna to desist — which he did.

Secretary Cortelyou, who was at an extension telephone, made a stenographic record of my conversation
with the President and of the directions he asked me
to deliver to Senator Hanna. Secretary Cortelyou kept
these notes, and many years afterward gave them to
Charles S. Olcott, who wrote "The Life of William
McKinley" in the "American Statesmen" series. In
that book Olcott published them, and there anyone
interested may now read them. What happened I re-
corded in my journal contemporaneously, and I insert
it here.

Philadelphia, Pa., June 20, 1900.

Spent morning at hotel. At about noon was in Hanna's room
with H. C. Payne, Senator Burrows and others. Hanna was much
enraged at the fact that Quay had started a stampede for Roosevelt and he (Hanna) seemed about to line up the Administration
forces for Long. He said that if Roosevelt were "nominated by
Quay or Platt" that he would refuse to be Chairman of the National Committee, etc. Hanna and I had almost an altercation,
since I insisted with all my power that any interference on his
part for Long or anybody else would start a stampede in the West
for Roosevelt and thus he, Hanna, would be playing into Quay's
hands; that it was simply a trick of Quay's to take advantage of
the Roosevelt sentiment and make it appear that he was a factor
in it. Hanna was in such a state of mind that I arranged later to
have Cortelyou at one telephone and the President at another
(at the White House) so that I could talk with Cortelyou and
have the President hear what I said. Outlined the situation to them
and received an ultimatum from the President for Hanna which,
at the President's dictation, I copied and took to Hanna. It read
as follows: —

"The President's close friend must not undertake to commit the Administration to any candidate. It has no candidate. The convention must make the nomination. The Administration would not if it could. The President's close friend should be satisfied with his unanimous nomination and not interfere with the vice-presidential nomination. The Administration wants the choice of the Convention and the President's friends must not dictate to the convention."

· After the session of the convention, took this to Hanna. He had already called a conference at Bliss's rooms at the Stratford at 10:30 P.M. to "decide whether to make an effort to unite the Convention on some other candidate than Roosevelt for Vice President." Hanna said, however, that he would follow the President's instructions. Invited me to the conference to represent Dolliver. Saw Dolliver and Allison, who asked me to insist that the Administration should not interfere for Long. At conference were Hanna, Bliss, Lodge (representing Long), Spooner, H. C. Payne, Kerens and Burrows. After they had urged Hanna to interfere for a time — Hanna remaining silent — I spoke for Dolliver and Allison, insisting that Dolliver must not be interfered with in his right to test his strength upon an uninfluenced ballot. Lodge immediately spoke up and said that this settled it, and Roosevelt would be the candidate. Hanna immediately said that it settled the fact that there would be no interference. The conference then discussed the plan of uniting all candidates for Roosevelt, which was afterwards done later in the night; but I had to withdraw to answer a call by telephone from the White House (Cortelyou). As I left the room, Hanna whispered to me to tell the President that he would do exactly as he had requested. Was greatly relieved at this outcome, as nothing could have stopped the Roosevelt movement, and the only result of Hanna's interference would have been humiliation for him and embarrassment for the President.

It was largely, therefore, because of my intervention that Senator Hanna was spared the predicament in which Mr. Butler found himself at Cleveland when I was nominated. I do not criticize Mr. Butler and certainly had no reason to resent his attitude.

In the following campaign, while at first we differed on which issues should be urged before the public as predominant, he was most courteous and helpful. As a campaign manager he made a splendid success. His inherent honesty, his scrupulous care to keep the activities of his organization clean and beyond criticism, and his refusal to countenance irregularities of any kind made the Coolidge campaign a credit to the committee and to the party. To-day, when a former administration of the committee is subjected to criticism, no accusing word has been uttered against Mr. Butler or the campaign he managed.

He must always rank as one of the ablest of national chairmen, and his record serves now to lessen the effectiveness of the effort to pin upon his party — numbering millions of citizens in its membership — blame for that which was inexcusable, but nevertheless individual, error in the conduct of the preceding national committee.

My nomination occurred while I was at my old home at Marietta attending the Commencement of the college from which I graduated. There is one recollection I shall always treasure. It is of the gathering of thousands of the people of the town, the next day, to hear me speak briefly from the front porch of the old family home; and the church bells of the town were rung in honor of the occasion. Some people may claim that the vice-presidency does not amount to much, but just then it seemed to me the greatest office in the world.

The old proverb "A prophet is not without honor save in his own country" embodies a general truth with but occasional exceptions. The prophet in this case was one who had spent a more or less mischievous boyhood in the town, and his reflection was that the only explanation of the stirring scene was that those who really knew him then had for the most part departed this life.

Evanston, July 4, 1928.

The National Committee established headquarters in Chicago. I did not like its advice as to the issues which should be employed in the speaking campaign of which I was expected to bear the burden so far as activity at least was concerned. In my speech of acceptance I announced the constitutional issue precipitated by Senator La Follette as the dominant one. Chairman Butler was adverse to this course, feeling that the issue of economy should be the one to be stressed. I sent my speech before delivery to President Coolidge, who returned it without suggestion as to change, except that he substituted "an important issue" for "the predominant issue" as a caption to that portion of my address devoted to the La Follette position on the Constitution. From the time of delivery of the acceptance speech, before a throng estimated at over fifty thousand — reaching from our side porch at Evanston across the yard, road and park to Lake Michigan — until the end of the campaign, during which I traveled fifteen thousand miles in a special train and made one hundred and eight speeches,

I endeavored to keep that issue in the minds of the people.

(Extract from speech of Charles G. Dawes, delivered in Milwaukee, Wisconsin, September 11, 1924.)

In his platform, promulgated to the voters of Wisconsin, Mr. La Follette says: "We favor submitting to the people, for their considerate judgment, a constitutional amendment providing that Congress may by enacting a statute make it effective over a judicial veto."

His proposition is in effect that no inferior Federal court be allowed to set aside an Act of Congress on the ground that it is unconstitutional, and that Congress may set aside the verdicts of the Supreme Court itself, if it declares unconstitutional a law which Congress may have passed. This proposition is to abrogate the principle of three-fold division of power — executive, legislative, and judicial — which is the basis of our Constitution, and make the executive and judicial power subordinate to the legislative power.

It means that for our present form of government, we are to adopt another in which Congress will predominate.

The success of such a doctrine, which would mean that the Constitution would be stripped of authority, would be disastrous, and government would become the plaything of changing political parties, with demagogues in the saddle.

Its effects likewise would be disastrous to the rights of the states, to which are reserved such rights of government as are not specifically delegated to the Federal Government by the Constitution. It would bring disaster to the happiness, prosperity and peace of the American people as a whole if, in place of our stable, constitutional government, under which we have lived for one hundred and thirty-five years, we should establish a government by Congress. This would be practically equivalent to a government of free democracy, which history has proved is most futile and disastrous for the proper protection of a people.

CROWDS AT SPEECH OF ACCEPTANCE, EVANSTON, FOLLOWING OFFICIAL NOTIFICATION AS VICE-PRESIDENTIAL CANDIDATE ON THE REPUBLICAN TICKET

Under the Constitution, the courts are the guardians of the inalienable rights of the individual.

A bill of rights is a statement of those inalienable rights of the individual in which his government must protect him, and which any opposing power, within or without the government, must concede to him; such as the right to worship in the way his conscience may dictate; the right to own property; the right to peacefully pursue any proper avocation; the right to trial by jury, and such rights as protect him in the peaceful pursuit of happiness.

After ages of conflict, during which mankind has passed through martyrdom, all civilizations recognize an individual bill of rights. Indeed, the growth and establishment of bills of rights marks the growth and establishment of civilization.

The citizen formerly had to defend his individual bill of rights from the kings and princes and tyrants of the past. The Magna Charta was a bill of rights, and as Hamilton said, "It was forced from King John by the barons, sword in hand"; the "Petition of Right", exacted from Charles the First, and the "Declaration of Rights", drawn by the Lords and Commons in 1688 and exacted from the Prince of Orange, were bills of rights.

The bill of inalienable individual rights, the general recognition of which is the foundation of civilization, would be, under the La Follette proposition, at the mercy of Congress. It wickedly challenges the professed purpose of every civilized government to remove from the realm of public conflict those individual rights the reasonableness and necessity of which have been demonstrated by warfare as old as the world, and to establish which the blood of untold millions, throughout the ages, has been shed.

Since the inalienable rights of the individual are those which are always threatened by mob action, and since, in this country, it is government under our Constitution which is their only sure protection, I want to point out the difference between the rule of the people and the rule of the mob.

The fact that the ultimate judgment of the people is always sound and always just is the rock upon which representative constitutional government stands. History and all experience shows that in the process of forming ultimate judgment, public opinion passes through a series of changing and temporary phases.

What has destroyed free democracy in government in history is the fact that a temporary phase of public opinion would determine governmental attitude. This temporary phase being wrong, governmental action was taken, and then the ultimate right judgment of the people was too late to correct the mistake.

As some one has said, in the free democracy of Greece, Socrates was compelled to drink the hemlock one year, while a statue was raised to his memory the next year.

Under the constitutional government of the United States a system of checks and balances exists by which it is rendered certain that only the ultimate right and sound judgment of the people crystallizes into law.

That government whose policy is determined by the ultimate judgment of the people will permanently survive. The government whose actions are determined by the passing phases of popular opinion, as distinguished from ultimate opinion, will perish. The Constitution of the United States establishes the rule of the people, as distinguished from the rule of the mob. The difference between the demagogue and the statesman is that the demagogue appeals to the mob and the statesman to the sound judgment of the people.

Between the people and between the mob there is all the difference between daylight and darkness.

The audiences were enormous; the one at Lincoln, Nebraska, my old home and the residence of the Democratic nominee for the vice-presidency, Charles W. Bryan, being estimated at twenty-five thousand. At a rough calculation, I must have addressed three hundred and fifty thousand people, not including the radio audiences who listened in at most of the night addresses. It was a hard campaign. Sometimes I spoke eight or ten times a day from the rear platform of the train, where a "loud speaker" apparatus made it always possible to reach the crowd, which at times was as large as five thousand in number.

At Augusta, Maine, I discussed the Ku Klux Klan in answer to an address by the Democratic presidential nominee, John W. Davis. To mention the Ku Klux issue had been deemed inadvisable by Chairman Butler, and one of the officials of the Speakers' Bureau of the National Committee, who had heard it read, said the speech on that subject, if delivered, would lose us Indiana by a hundred and fifty thousand majority.

When I arrived at Augusta and it was learned that I was to mention the dread words "Ku Klux", the state committee was in a state of extreme apprehension which it took no pains to conceal. Under its orders, no Republican state candidate had been allowed to refer to the subject in his speeches. However, before an audience of six thousand people, I started my speech: "I first desire to speak . . . relative to the Ku Klux Klan. . . ."

Knowing that there can be no reaction to the right except a right reaction, I had no misgivings as to the reception of the speech by the public. It was the only argumentative statement on the Ku Klux subject made by a candidate during the campaign, according to my friend ex-Governor Hadley of Missouri.

Within three days the chairman of the Republican State Central Committee of Maine wired the National Committee at Chicago that, so far from injuring the Maine situation, he thought I had saved it.

He had also wired this to President Coolidge at Plymouth, where, on my return, the latter had asked me to stop. The President's only remark was that my Maine speech was a good one.

An amusing incident occurred at Plymouth further illustrating the taciturnity of the Coolidge family — the President's disinclination to waste words being the result of heredity, in my judgment. The President, Mrs. Coolidge, Colonel Coolidge, and I took lunch in the little dining room off the sitting room. During the lunch, Colonel Coolidge took no part in the conversation. In the sitting room afterwards he said nothing, but after a time he rose and left the room. The President and Mrs. Coolidge were sitting where they could see out of the window, and though I could not do so, I knew what was happening. About thirty newspapermen, waiting outside to tackle me, had waylaid the Colonel. The President rose abruptly, and with considerable impatience said "I asked him to say nothing." Mrs. Coolidge replied: "I don't think you need worry." When finally I met the newspaper phalanx outdoors, I asked them what they had said to the Colonel. "We asked him what you and the President were talking about, of course," they replied. "What did he say?" I asked. "My hearing ain't as good as it used to be" had been the Colonel's reply.

My statement in the Augusta, Maine, speech of August 23, 1924, as to the Ku Klux Klan was as follows: —

I first desire to speak, as Mr. Davis did yesterday, relative to the Ku Klux Klan. I agree with him that it has no proper part in this or any other campaign. But whether proper or not, unfortunately in this campaign a mobilization of radicalism under La Follette, the largest section of which, the Socialists, fly the red flag, is attacking the Constitution of the United States. I cannot agree, therefore, with his inference that its discussion diverts attention from those issues which the people must settle in November by their votes. It only emphasizes the greatest issue.

The questions of Mr. Pattengall, which appear in the press this morning, are the familiar trick questions of the ordinary politician. They are not the cause of the statement I am about to make.

Let me say at once that I recognize that the Ku Klux Klan in many localities and among many peoples represents only an instinctive groping for leadership, moving in the interest of law enforcement, which they do not find in many cowardly politicians and office holders. But it is not the right way to forward law enforcement.

Let us consider for a minute what happened in the State of Oklahoma. Governor Walton was some time ago elected governor of the state. In his campaign he had not preached the doctrine — so it seems to me at least — which was the proper one to be preached under the American flag. When he was elected, one of his carliest acts was to remove the President of the University of Oklahoma, a man who believed in the old-fashioned doctrines of the Constitution, to establish which our forefathers fought. He placed in that position a socialist who was likely to teach the young men of that state some new-fashioned doctrines which, to say the least, are not those of constitutional Americanism. He then loosed upon the State of Oklahoma a horde of hardened criminals from the penitentiary. Lax law enforcement prevailed in many places in the state. If there could be an excuse for law-abiding citizens to band themselves together in secret organizations for law enforcement, it existed in Oklahoma, and the Klan became a powerful organization. What happened then? Back stepped Governor Walton to the American flag — to which, it seems to me, he had not kept very close, up to that time — and called out the militia of the state. Then it was that those who had joined the Klan in the interest of law and order found themselves arrayed against their flag and the laws of Oklahoma. A situation akin to that of civil war existed and it was averted only by a few clearheaded men. And then what happened? There was the application of the only method by which our people can properly settle such differences — the procedure outlined by the Constitution and the laws of Oklahoma. Walton was removed from the governorship, a result made possible by the vote of the people — and quiet was restored under the orderly processes provided by the Constitution and the law.

Consider what happened in Williamson County, Illinois, where the town of Herrin is situated. A reign of lawlessness existed. It was marked by the terrible Herrin massacre. It was marked by a general breakdown in respect for law, which indicated that the officers of the County, including the sheriff, had been intimidated by lawbreakers into inaction. A thousand members of the Ku Klux Klan without disguises — they were brave men — marched to the office of Williamson County to protest against the lawlessness in that section. If a secret organization to uphold law and order is justifiable anywhere in our country, it was justified there. But what happened? Immediately the lawless element formed the Knights of the Flaming Circle, and thus both sides were afraid to go out at night, and a condition was created which actually culminated in civil war and the loss of life. And how, again, was peace established? By the only proper way, in the sending of the militia of the State of Illinois to the scene of the trouble, as provided by the law in such cases. The critical situation was settled by it without shedding a drop of blood, and the troops were quickly removed.

There is much in the Ku Klux Klan which appeals to the adventurous youth. I remember once, when traveling over Illinois speaking for law enforcement, the Constitution and the American flag, some of the American Legion men with me talked to other Legion men who had joined the Ku Klux Klan at one of the towns visited. These latter young men believed that they were acting in the interests of law enforcement. They told those who were with me what they were planning to do. They said: "There is a bootlegger in our county who is in cahoots with the sheriff and everybody knows it. Now, we are not going to hurt the man, but some night we are going for him and his still. We are going to gag him, carry him and the still up to the courthouse yard, and tie him to it so that the sheriff and the whole town will see them when they come down to their work in the morning." This may appeal to adventurous youth; but, my friends, government cannot last if that is the right way to enforce law in this country. Lawlessness cannot be met with lawlessness and civilization be maintained. What will happen if law is not enforced by government, but taken in hand by individuals and by minority organizations, is what happened some years ago on "Bloody Corner" in Chicago. Over one hundred murders were committed there in one year, and not one single murderer was brought to justice. The Black Hand was at work and the witnesses to the murders refused to testify against the murderers, because they felt their own lives were in danger if they did.

Now, society contains within itself the elements of its own self-purification. It has always been so, or civilization, which is an evolution, would not now exist.

After a time, in connection with these continuing murders, two new words crept into the press of the city of Chicago — the words "White Hand." In other words, the brothers, the fathers, and the friends of the murdered men sawed off their own shotguns and killed the murderers from behind the same corner, and thus peace was finally established at the cost of bloodshed and misery throughout that entire section of Chicago.

The same thing happens when minority organizations — whatever the high purpose they claim — whatever they may be called — take the law into their own hands. Force rises to meet force; lawlessness rises to meet lawlessness, and civilization commences to disintegrate into the savagery from which, through the ages, it has evolved.

Appeals to racial, religious, or class prejudice by minority organizations are opposed to the welfare of all peaceful and civilized communities. Our Constitution stands for religious tolerance and freedom. This happy country has never been through a religious war such as those which devastated Europe in the centuries past, and brought untold misery to millions of its inhabitants. We have progressed in civilization far beyond that possibility; but to inject religious and racial issues into politics is contrary to the welfare of all the people and to the letter and spirit of the Constitution of the United States.

Josiah Quincy was right when he said: "Society is never more certainly in the path of destruction than when it trusts itself to the guidance of secret societies."

I have told you why I am opposed to the Klan. Take what I say into your hearts and consciences and think it over calmly. However it may be with the mind, there is no acrimony in conscience.

Chicago, July 5, 1928.

During this visit to the President we talked over briefly the agricultural question. He was preparing to appoint a commission to make suggestions for agricultural relief measures.

I suggested that the commission should be so selected as to create public confidence in its economic and business competency, its impartiality as a body, and its constructive nonpartisanship, and that its value would depend upon its constructive ability. I suggested a committee of three: Owen D. Young (Democrat), representing industry; Frank O. Lowden (Republican), representing agriculture; and Professor Bullock of Harvard University, an economist.

At this time I had commenced some study of the agricultural question and had written Bullock for constructive suggestions. He replied admitting the unequal position of agriculture under the law as compared with industry, and then added: "I confess that I have no remedy which I am able to suggest." That seemed to me to be the proper attitude of mind toward the problem — an unusual attitude, too, for economists, who, as a class, are not humble but extremely opinionated.

Our Experts Committee, Reparations Commission, discovered this, and also that economists differ among
themselves as much as the less learned.

I felt that the conclusions of such a committee would
command public confidence and at least become the
basis of a nonpartisan, continuing search for sound legislative interpretation of certain principles, the recognition of which might remove from agriculture some
disadvantages it now endures under existing laws. I
believe if a Commission of such a standard of personnel had been named at that time, instead of one of a
more or less political complexion which the President
appointed, that at least we would be nearer now to
some sound constructive public consensus of opinion
as to a remedy for an admitted injustice. Its conclusions, certainly, would have removed from the present
situation much acrimonious discussion of admitted economic principles, and directed calmer attention to the
inherent faults or merits of specific suggestions.

The Reparation status before our Expert Committee
met at Paris well illustrates what results from six years
of political treatment of an economic problem.

(Extract from speech of Charles G. Dawes, delivered
at Augusta, Maine, August 23, 1924.)

American labor is too intelligent to be fooled by a certain brand
of nebulous clap-trap preached to them by a few leaders who want
to use them as a political asset, in a combination with socialists,
flying the red flag.

The benefits of trades-unions, honestly administered, are recognized not only by me, but by good citizens generally, whether in
or out of Trades-Unionism. It has elevated, protected and dignified

labor, and in so doing, it has been an element in the progress of our nation.

But why do so many politicians of both parties continue to regard the great, intelligent, honest, and conservative body of Trades-Unionism as if it were a puppet in the hands of a few socialist labor leaders and political demagogues?

Trades-Unionism stands loyally and solidly behind its good leadership, concerned with the real interests of the crafts and the real progress of labor; but it has never followed, and will never follow, the demagogue! When it selects labor leaders, it selects them for leaders of labor in the interest of labor, not as proprietors of its conscience or politics.

Let me state a great truth which no one understands better than those fine citizens, the upright labor leaders of the country and the great body of union labor: The worst enemies to unionism and the progress of labor are the small number of radical labor leaders who attack law-enforcing judges, and who, to the injury of law-abiding Trades-unionism, misrepresent the patriotic citizens belonging to it.

In Illinois and elsewhere, I have been denounced because I have opposed the kind of union tactics that have made building operations dangerous to human life in Chicago — where corrupt men have used their influence to extort vast sums from the contractors, and where the gunmen and the bomb-maker have been actively at work. Every laboring man knows of this condition in Chicago during the last four years — that there have been murders and bombing by the wholesale, that there has been extortion and jury-fixing, and that certain labor leaders have gone into politics in order to defeat law-enforcing judges. These leaders are a thorn in the side of honest unionism. Trades-Unionism, with a preponderant majority, does not approve these conditions. It abhors them as much as I do. When illegal violence is condoned and indifference to law is preached, what is the part of good citizenship, whether in or out of Trades-Unionism? Nobody knows better what that duty is than the patriotic membership of Trades-Unionism. It is not to lie down supinely under the whip of the labor demagogues, as so many political leaders and officeholders do, when law and order are attacked. It is to stand fearlessly against them. That is where the patriotic mass of union labor stands. It knows that its welfare, like the welfare of all our people, is bound up in the Constitution of the United States, in law enforcement, and the American flag.

I undertake to say that the few labor leaders who, in this campaign, are attempting to influence patriotic law-abiding union men into a political combination with socialists, flying the red flag, more than they endanger anything else are endangering their own leadership. Common American citizenship marches not behind the red flag, but under the Stars and Stripes, upholding the Constitution of the United States, to found which our forebears fought and died.

There is no more pitiful spectacle to-day, and none more significant of the danger of the times, than to see politicians cringing before the whip of a few bluffing labor leaders, undertaking to play politics in the name of patriotic men whose convictions on law enforcement and the Constitution they do not control, and who resent the idea that anyone should believe that they would let their honest opinions on elemental things be used as a political asset.

What pretext, except personal political advantage, have any labor leaders in attempting to bring the question of the open shop into politics? The Supreme Court of the United States has held that the right of employees in a body to bargain with their employers for the closed shop, is one of the inalienable rights of the individual under our Constitution. If a political party should place an open-shop plank in their platform, with a view to its crystallization into law, it would be striking at the Constitution just as much as the lawless labor leader who, in the interest of the closed shop, would order an American citizen assaulted as he went peacefully to his work. Questions like that of the open shop will always be at issue among good citizens, but these differences are not political. They are economic and must be adjusted between employer and employee — not by political parties.

CHAPTER II

Chicago, Illinois, July 6, 1928.

UNDER a government such as ours, and the method provided for the selection of the President, the man who occupies that office, in his temperament, attitudes, and characteristics, will well represent generally the inarticulate opinion of the public as to the kind of leadership the country needs at the time.

When Coolidge was elected President the world desired tranquillity — a reaction of its peoples from the excesses of war. That was the subconscious issue in the elections of 1924 in the United States, England and France. Where the victory of the conservative party associated itself in the public mind with a prospect of a tranquil future, the conservatives won, as they did in our country with Coolidge and in Britain with the Baldwin Government. Where, as in France, the attitude of the conservative party — dominated by Poincaré and his extreme nationalistic Ruhr policy — was regarded as conducive to increased controversy, Herriot and the left were victorious.

What first brought Calvin Coolidge to the favorable notice of our people generally was his action in the Boston police strike, which indicated courage in a period when growing lawlessness in the country had aroused public opinion.

Coolidge personifies to our people calmness, common sense with purpose, and splendid courage. The steadily increasing unreliability of nominal party majorities in Congress in upholding in legislation the platform policies which have won a party victory has tended to emphasize in the public mind that it is the President, possessing among other powers the right of veto, who must be relied upon after the election to guard in the Government the policies the public has approved.

The popularity of Coolidge, notwithstanding the opposition he has encountered from a Congress nominally Republican, is due to the fact that he, not it, best understood the people and they him. He is the product of his time.

The busybodies and mischief-makers, of which Washington has its full quota, flutter around those in public position like birds of ill omen, and have said much of unpleasant relations between Coolidge and myself; but I have paid little, if any, attention to them. And if Coolidge has, I am mistaken.

Nevertheless, the official relations of the President and Vice President lend themselves to the encouragement of misapprehensions which are easy to create. I have always sensed the inherent embarrassments involved in the plan of having the Vice President sit in the Cabinet, as Coolidge did under the Harding administration. After my election, not knowing how Coolidge felt about it, I wrote him stating my views on the subject.

This was done to relieve him — if he shared my views — of any embarrassment, if he desired to carry them out, notwithstanding the fact that he had accepted Harding's invitation. Again I did not want to do him the discourtesy of declining a possible invitation, and I thus avoided any necessity for such a course, however remote.

Chicago, July 10, 1928.

We are at the beginning of an unusual national campaign, one in which the results will be determined largely by the attitude of the public upon certain submerged issues, which the two platforms either do not radically differ upon, or do not mention. One thing is evident — that is that party lines are being drawn more loosely by our people than heretofore. Issues are not made by leaders or by platforms, but in the hearts and consciences of the people.

The prohibition issue is being forced to the front by a public interest which defies control by party managers. The result is already evident in a growing doubt as to the outcome of the election. The business situation in the country points to a coming business change. The credits of the country which, under natural laws, eventually grow beyond a proper proportion to the cash in which they are redeemable, give evidence in steadily increasing amounts of reaching that situation before many months. Will it, when reached, make nervous the depositing class, as used to happen in the days prior to the establishment of the Federal Reserve System with its large credit-creating potentiality? Will the American people, as they sometimes do during the closing of a period of prosperity, while it still persists suddenly turn over in bed — that is, wake up some morning changed from an optimistic to a pessimistic view of the future, as occurred in 1892, culminating in the panic of 1893? Such an action might mean political revolution, now as then. As the Bible has it: "Jeshurun waxed fat, and kicked." Since prosperity often begets folly and sometimes panic, these changes have their source in the instincts more than in the intelligence of the people. Their date cannot often be predicted with any certainty.

Yet there are some signs at present of the conditions which, in the past, have accompanied such changes in their first stages, and these signs contribute to the danger of prophesy in terms political.

Chicago, July 11, 1928.

Among the pleasant occasions of my past few years in Washington have been my occasional lectures at the Army War College on the military principles of supply in allied armies. I was situated in the army in a place which was related in supply problems to the activities of our army as a whole and to our allies considered as a whole. As Chief of Supply Procurement of the A.E.F., it was impossible for me not to become involved in a study of the devices which should be instituted to facilitate the fighting of the separate Allied armies as one army. When the Central Command under Foch was established, made possible only because the military situation involved all the Allies in the necessity of this action for self-preservation, I proposed to the Allies, under the authority and with the co-operation of Gen-

eral Pershing, a device for the unification of the supply
activities in the rear of the armies in the zone of the advance, to match the military unification of the front
under Foch, and conducted the negotiations which led
to its establishment and to its functioning during the
last four months of the war. This device being accepted
by the Governments, I became the member of the
A.E.F. of an Allied military board composed of one
officer from each of the five Allied armies, authorized
when in unanimous agreement to issue orders affecting
the supply service in the zone of the advance to the
General Staffs of the separate armies. This four months'
experience during the war made me something of an
authority on a subject of overwhelming importance in
allied warfare, but one not carried in any war college
course — that subject concerning itself with the science
of fighting allied armies as one army under one command.

To deliver these extempore lectures to a distinguished body of military experts at our Army War College, so many of whom were my old comrades in the
war, and to present to their keen intelligence and immediate comprehension and acceptance certain new
principles of allied warfare, the recognition and establishment of which only dire military emergency made
possible, brought to me that satisfaction which always
comes upon those rare occasions when one can impart
relevant information and constructive suggestions to
experts.

Everything of a military nature taught in a war college is a lesson learned in actual war experience. These

lessons which I taught were new only because extensive and prolonged allied warfare in an industrial age was new. The French, American and British armies in France in March, 1918, were suddenly faced with a great reverse which compelled the creation of a central command.

When Napoleon wrote his celebrated and universally accepted sixty-fourth maxim of war: "Nothing is more important than a central command — under one chief", he did not have in mind the front line of an army alone, but everything in the organization that makes a front line effective.

When Foch took the Central Command, without a military unification of the rear of the Allied army, he directly controlled only the line of communications behind the French army. The great advance of the German armies on March 21, 1918, which had destroyed the British Fifth Army and broken through the Allied line, made necessary the rapid shifting of Allied troops in the different armies to points of weakness in the wavering Allied line.

If French troops were ordered to reinforce the British line, French supplies followed them. If British troops were shifted to the French line, British supplies followed them. Trainloads of military supplies would pass each other, going in opposite directions, — from French supply points to French troops and from British supply points to British troops, — although the creation of a central authority with an appropriate machinery to supply French troops with British supplies when in the British line, and British troops with French supplies when in the French line, would have obviated an enormous amount of lost motion. Again, without this authority and machinery, our Government might continue to use ships to carry essential supplies for our own army, which should be used for bringing combat troops. An enormous surplus of these same supplies might exist in the rear of one of the other armies, which should be transferred to our own army, thus obviating their shipment from America. The purpose of our board, operating under Foch, was to correct such situations.

During the nearly four years of war before our troops became at all active, the British and French armies, under the law of necessity, had steadily been forming pools of essential military supplies behind each army for each army's purpose. For instance, when fighting units were relieved from front line activity for rest, their essential transportation only would follow them. All such camions (trucks) not essential for troops at rest would be placed in camion reserves, for the use of the army in action. Pools of ammunition, also, were gradually created behind the division instead of behind the smaller military units of a division. Armies, when under emergency, demand changes in organization to meet emergencies. When allied armies are amalgamated as one army, under a condition of great emergency, pooled reserves behind an allied army become as important as pooled reserves behind a single army.

One of the early actions of our military board in control of the co-ordination of the supply activities of the advance Allied rear was to create an inter-Allied automobile reserve, to enable the supply of subsistence and ammunition stores for forty French divisions to be assured, at a distance of over fifty kilometers from rail heads, and to assure at the same time the transport of ten complete French divisions with their artillery. We calculated that 24,000 trucks would accomplish this purpose, and had actually built up for Foch a reserve of 11,000 trucks at the time of armistice of November 11, 1918.

The armistice alone prevented a demonstration under Foch of what in modern allied warfare will hereafter take the place of the flying cavalry reserve of old-time warfare. One of the first actions which we took was the issuing of orders for the pooling of the ammunition behind the French and American lines, which was carried out. The discussion of the new questions involved in the science of fighting allied armies as one army, as it developed during the last four months of the Great War, was a novelty even to veterans.

I also discussed before the War College a science likewise evolved only out of conditions of dire necessity — a science which possibly could not be safely taught in any war college unless, perhaps, as a postgraduate course to veteran officers of long service. This involved the principles which must be recognized in the supply operations of an army on its last legs. Unless, over all the subordinate units of an army in such condition, there is created a new machinery for the breaking-down of the normal watertight compartment system of supplies among the army services, complete destruction of the army may result. I can perhaps indicate the nature of my discussion by an illustration.

Supposing a ship at sea finds herself with its fuel entirely depleted and in such an unseaworthy condition that unless her engines can run at their maximum speed she will sink before reaching port. Every lesser portion of the ship, not involved in keeping her afloat and going, then reduces itself in the mind of the captain to terms of possible fuel supply, and every officer, sailor and passenger becomes to him a fuel gatherer, stoker, or engineer. Every regulation, every division of work, every responsibility on the part of subordinate officers, involved in the normal operation of the ship, must immediately yield to a new law of operation imposed by the emergency. The man, for instance, in charge of the dining saloon of the ship, whose life for years has been spent in its care and improvement, becomes suddenly charged with the duty of seeing that its wooden chairs and tables are broken up for fuel, and its paintings torn down to be fed into the flames under the boilers.

The principles which must govern the ship's command in such a situation are subversive of most of the principles established as a result of normal sailing experience. Ships may not often get into this condition, but after two hostile armies in modern warfare start toward each other, a long campaign inevitably brings one or the other to an analogous situation of like desperation.

For a war staff college to instruct its students in the tactics, devices and principles which must be applied by a commander in such circumstances would be teaching to each particular unit of an organization the science of its self-destruction in order to preserve the life of the whole. This possibly would not be conducive to building up the morale of an army, which, so far as its subordinate elements are concerned, must be imbued with the conviction that nothing should ever be allowed to interfere with the normal and proper functioning of the unit.

During the last six months of the war every commander and officer of the Allied armies who had a bird's-eye view of the situation, and was himself in any way related to the activities of the armies as a whole, was an involuntary student of this particular little-studied science.

Every great commander of history has been a past master of it. Napoleon used to say that in planning every battle he made three alternative plans in case of defeat. However, I should regard as of doubtful value a continued course of lessons in army organization in a war staff college based upon the assumption that partial disorganization would ever become an element of eventual victory.

CHAPTER III

DURING my term of office the celebration in which I participated which made the deepest impression upon me was that of the one hundred and fiftieth anniversary of the outbreak of the Revolution. Better than any descriptions of mine are those of James O'Donnell Bennett of the *Chicago Tribune*, under the dates of April 19 and April 21, 1925, and the comment of the *Christian Science Monitor* of April 20, 1925.

(From the *Christian Science Monitor*, Boston, Massachusetts, April 20, 1925.)

Reënactment of those stirring episodes out of which grew American liberty and independence — the ride of Paul Revere and William Dawes, Jr., and the struggle at the Old North Bridge at Concord — to-day was the chief feature of Greater Boston's celebration of the one hundred and fiftieth anniversary of Patriot's Day, a joint commemorative observance in which Charles G. Dawes, Vice President, and Gen. John J. Pershing, U.S.A., retired, are taking leading rôles. The Vice President is the great-great-grandson of the illustrious patriot who rode on the night of April 18, on a mission identical with Revere's.

But dominating the portrayal of early American history, vivid and stirring as it was, was a definite expression of that broad Americanism which seeks peace and harmony for all the peoples of the world. In Faneuil Hall, in the Old North Church, at Lexington and at Concord, leaders of the Nation gave utterance to this thought — the thought that the one hundred and fiftieth celebration of Patriots' Day is not to parade the world's past unharmonies, but to give new recognition to those ideals and qualities of human relationships that led to America itself.

(From James O'Donnell Bennett in the *Chicago Tribune*.)

Boston, April 19, 1925.

Out, far out and bravely shone the lantern lights from the spire of the Old North Church. But the people in the street below saw them dimly for the happy tears that filled their eyes.

Within the building sat notables of the Republic — the Vice President of the United States, the Governors of all of the New England States, two bishops of the old church which was the church by law established in the days of our forefathers to whom the lantern lights carried a message of warning and a call to arms.

One hundred and fifty years ago young Robert Newman, Sexton of Christ Church, which is now known to every school boy as "the Old North Church", hung out the lanterns as a signal to Paul Revere the silversmith, who was waiting on the Charlestown shore, that the British were starting by water to destroy munitions of war which the patriotic colonists had assembled at Concord.

You remember how Revere's instructions to the sexton run in the ballad.

> . . . "If the British march
> By land or sea from the town to-night,
> Hang a lantern aloft in the belfry arch
> Of the North Church tower as a signal light, —
> One, if by land, and two, if by sea;
> And I on the opposite shore will be,
> Ready to ride and spread the alarm
> Through every Middlesex village and farm.

And that is the event they commemorated with song and prayer, and with speeches by Mrs. Nathaniel Thayer of Boston, great-grand-daughter of Paul Revere, and by Vice President Dawes, great-great-grandson of William Dawes, who rode on the night of April 18, 1775, by another road in case Revere were captured or killed by British soldiers.

After the songs and the prayers came the most touching and thrilling moment of all, and that was when young Paul Revere of Boston, great-great-grandson of Paul the silversmith, reverently lifted the lighted lanterns — copies as near as may be of the original lanterns — from the standard on which they hung near the altar and bore them aloft to the belfry arch.

A moment so touching and thrilling that I think no American can quite come into full consciousness of what the Republic means until he has sat through this sacrament of the lanterns annually observed in Christ Church on the night of April 18th.

Trumpet music rang out from the choir loft as young Paul Revere bore his lanterns from their place in front of the altar, and the organ thundered, and all the people in the high-backed pews sang "America", a hymn which the rector had gently pointed out to them was written by the good Doctor Smith who once lived hard by the church.

Half a century ago, when they observed the one hundredth anniversary of the Revere-Dawes ride at Christ Church, Dr. Smith was present and read an anniversary poem.

While the lanterns glimmered before the altar, General Dawes mounted the pulpit stairs and took his place beneath the wide sounding board and made an impassioned plea for development of the national character — the safeguarding of what was good and right in it, the stripping away of what was false and shallow.

With his characteristic vehemence, he hit the pulpit rail a resounding whack and uttered these words: —

"The greatest question before the American people to-day is: 'What of our character?' — for it is this and this alone that counts in the long run."

He pled for sharper self-denial in the nation's life, for cleanliness of mind, for subordination of the individual will to the general good.

"These lanterns," the Vice President said, "which they hung out

AT THE TOMB OF WILLIAM DAWES, IN KING'S
CHAPEL BURYING GROUND, BOSTON, MASS.,
APRIL, 1926

(Front row, right to left) *General Brewster, U. S. A., Vice President
Dawes, Mayor Curley, General Pershing and immediately to the right
of General Pershing, Hon. Beman G. Dawes.*

one hundred and fifty years ago, were beacon lights to a people. To us they still are beacon lights and with them shine the beacon lights of the old New England character. We can profitably take example from it, the more so as we are still a young people and our character as a people still is forming."

He emphasized the significance of the presence in the church of the beloved Mrs. Thayer, saying: "That she is with us to-night, this great-granddaughter of the noble Revere, is one more proof that with the family as with the nation continued prestige, continued usefulness, are due to adherence to high ideals."

He pled for further freedom, declaring that what has destroyed freedom and democracy in the past has been the surrender to a temporary phase of public opinion as distinguished from the solid sober thought of the people.

"Our Constitution," he shouted, and again the pulpit rail caught it hot and heavy, "our Constitution has established the rule of the people as distinguished from the rule of the mob. Guard the Constitution! Guard the courts! They are our beacon lights to-day."

Then came the clashing and clanging of the chimes far above our heads, and the trumpet music and the bearing aloft of the lanterns and the shining out to town and harbor of their light — and I tell you that then the thousands of Italian boys and girls swarming in the churchyard and the streets — for this is now a foreign quarter — were nearly crazy with excitement, for they knew what it was all about — none better. As Mrs. Thayer, who had worked and taught among them, said: "They do not want you to tell them about Paul Revere; they want to tell you."

(From James O'Donnell Bennett in the *Chicago Tribune* of April 21, 1925.)

Vice President Dawes joined with glad New England to-day in celebrating the 150th anniversary of the morning of the nation. This was the great finale of Boston's three-day commemoration of the battles of Lexington and Concord on April 19, 1775.

And such a day! From dawn to sunset the Via Sacra of the Republic — the sacred road that led our forefathers into empire and union — had been thronged with jubilant men and women and happy children.

From the gold-domed State House in Boston to the North Bridge in Concord — 16 miles away — where "the embattled farmers stood and fired the shot heard 'round the world", it has been a day of high excitement and profound emotion. All the way — all this beauteous way of glory — the belfries sang to one another, and the chanting by little children of the nation's anthems had for its accompaniment the roar of cannon and the crash of volley firing.

When you have heard the "Star Spangled Banner" sung on Lexington green to the accompaniment of massed bands and the firing of muskets that were fired on that green 150 years ago, then you have heard something and felt something that will abide with you as long as you live.

Sixteen miles of troops and cavalry and throngs of children; sixteen miles of the rumble of army wagons and the snarling of bugles and the roll of drums; sixteen miles of tablets and unveilings and dedications and presentations and felicitations.

Everywhere flags blossomed and beckoned along the roadside. Everywhere the chimes were jubilating the ancient words of the ritual: "Come let us now praise famous men."

It was a biting day. Lexington green was covered with a carpet of snow — like an altar cloth laid upon that holy place. But the people did not mind; they only stamped in unison and laughed and said that if the Colonials and the Redcoats had met on such a day as this both sides would have shivered themselves into defeat. As a matter of fact, the weather in these parts 150 years ago was unseasonably hot, and the British in their heavy uniforms were wretched with heat and thirst.

The cold did not diminish the enthusiasm of the people to-day any more than did the heat that of their sires on the long-gone day. It is often said that Americans do not know how to make a ceremony joyful. But the people participating in this one do know.

The Vice President, what with the speeches they made him make along the route, the medals which veterans of three wars pinned on him, the salute of 19 guns they fired in his honor, and the avalanches of cheering with which they enveloped him, was the man of the hour.

Just as a church clock in Eliot square struck ten, the World War veteran Sergeant Harold I. Slocum, dressed as a Colonial citizen, leaped on a horse in Eliot square and dashed away on his ride from Boston to Lexington in imitation of William Dawes' ride. Meanwhile, another World War veteran, Master Sergeant Harold L. Philbrick, was riding out of Charlestown toward the north and west over Paul Revere's route to Lexington. Cavalrymen followed both riders. At Brookline, the Vice President saw children enact a little play about the Revolution. What King George got in that play was a-plenty. At Cambridge, the vice-presidential salute of 19 guns was fired by cannoneers just as Charles Dawes crossed the bridge which spans the Charles River at the point where William Dawes crossed it, and at George Washington Square, in front of the Harvard buildings, the Vice President's escort halted while he planted an elm in memory of his ancestor.

At Arlington, now a Boston suburb, but the village of Menotomy at the time William Dawes dashed through it to arouse the Colonials, the womenfolk gave General Dawes doughnuts and coffee, and the menfolks gave him the original receipt for poll taxes which ancestor William paid when he was living at Menotomy.

At Lexington thousands of men and women of the town and of the fighting area for miles around met him, costumed as Colonial citizens and soldiers and as British soldiers in scarlet and white; and the town itself was glowing with flags and streamers and bursting with bands and music.

At Concord, Dawes also viewed miles of parade, comprising infantry, cavalry, artillery, superb emblematic floats and a large detachment of veterans of British wars, led by Maj. Gen. Sir Archibald MacDonald, Knight Commander of the Bath, whom the Governor General of Canada sent to this rebel town of Concord to show it to-day that all is forgiven.

CHAPTER IV

MY brother, Rufus C. Dawes, having undergone a severe operation, is convalescing at a hospital. He is the President of the Board of Trustees, having in hand the proposed second World's Fair at Chicago in 1933, to say nothing of his other business activities, and is worrying about his enforced absence from his office. At the Glen View Golf Club this afternoon occurred an illustration of the attitude of the retired business man who plays golf as to the relative importance of golf and other earthly pursuits. "Why," said such a one to me, "I understand your brother can't play again for at least two weeks! It's too bad, too bad."

Mr. and Mrs. Hoover, on their way to Superior, Wisconsin, plan to spend their time between trains at Chicago at our home and it recalls to me the occasion in December, 1896, when William McKinley, just elected President, spent a night with us at Evanston. I had managed his Illinois preconvention campaign for the nomination. Being a young man and inexperienced in entertaining celebrities, I committed a common error from which, in later years, I have been a frequent sufferer. I had too much for him to do.

In the afternoon I took him for a carriage ride to

show him the town, with the thermometer about ten degrees above zero — which was perhaps the most grievous punishment I inflicted upon him in return for his kindness. But I let my friends know he was to be at the house, and discovered to my consternation that though I had lived in Evanston only two years the whole town was my friend — for that night, at least. The house was crowded all evening, and to cap the climax several hundred Northwestern University students called in a body. The President-elect had come up from a strenuous visit in Chicago "for a quiet little time." Well! He did not get it, and late at night, after he had shaken hands with the Northwestern students who had filed in large numbers through the house and all the other people were gone, I expressed my regret. His reply was "Don't be disturbed. I knew just what kind of a 'quiet time' it would be before I came. It is always so when a President-elect travels."

My friendship for William McKinley is one of the most precious memories of my life. During my four years at Washington as Comptroller of the Currency, during his administration, he treated me as a father would a son. He made of me a constant companion and a trusted confidant.

I would often go over from the Treasury to lunch at the White House with him and his invalid wife, and in the evenings at ten o'clock I frequently walked over from my house at 1337 K Street to the White House and went to the old Cabinet room where I would wait for the President to come upstairs. This he did almost every night to finish up the business of the day with his trusted secretary, George B. Cortelyou, his close friend and mine, as dear to me now after thirty years as he was then. During the Spanish War General Corbin, the Adjutant General, would usually be there with important matters from the War Department.

The President on these occasions was always relaxed. Much of the work was formal and consisted of examining and signing papers covering decisions already made during the day or before. I shall never forget these visits, late at night.

One story the President told then made a lifelong impression on me. He was considering the appointment of a minister to a foreign country. There were two candidates. The President outlined their qualifications, which he said seemed almost exactly similar. He recounted them. Both were able — both of experience — both honest — both competent — both equally entitled to preferment from a political standpoint. Which one of them should he appoint? And then he told us this little story — a story of an incident apparently so unimportant that except for its consequences it never would have been told — an incident so trivial that the ordinary man would have forgotten it. But McKinley was not an ordinary man.

The President said that years before, when he was a member of the House of Representatives, he boarded a streetcar on Pennsylvania Avenue one stormy night and took the last vacant seat in the car next to the rear door. When the car stopped at the next corner, an old and bent washwoman, dripping wet, entered carrying a heavy basket. She walked to the other end of the car and stood in the aisle. No one offered her a seat, tired and forlorn as she looked. One of the candidates whom the President was considering — he did not name him to us — was sitting in the seat next to where she was standing. He was reading a paper which he shifted so as not to seem to see her, and retained his seat. Representative McKinley rose, walked down the aisle, picked up the basket of washing and led the old woman back to his seat, which he gave her. The present candidate did not look from behind his paper. He did not see McKinley or know what had been done.

This was the story. This candidate for a diplomatic place never knew, what we then knew, that this little act of selfishness, or rather this little omission of an act of consideration for others, had deprived him of that which would have crowned the ambition perhaps of a lifetime.

We never can know what determines one's career in life. Indeed, it may be that these little and forgotten deeds, accumulated, are the more important factors — for it is they which must in many cases provide us with the opportunity to do the greater deeds, and we unconscious of it. Why comes this reward in life? Why that disappointment or failure? We cannot know with certainty. This we can know, however, and this story illustrates it — that there is no act of kindliness, however small, which may not help us in life; and there is no act of unkindness, however trivial, which may not hurt us. More than that: The habitual doing of kindness always adds to our happiness, for kindness done is duty performed. Unkindness always breeds an unhappy spirit, for unkindness is duty neglected.

Evanston, July 15, 1928 (Evening).

My wife and I rode down to Chicago in the afternoon and met Mr. and Mrs. Hoover at the train. A large crowd was at the depot. We were taken to Hoover's car, and after his party had posed for twenty or so photographers on the back platform we took Mr. and Mrs. Hoover to our automobile, followed by the usual cavalcade of newspapermen and photographers. We were halted for a final picture just before we started for Evanston, with six motorcycle policemen and a dozen cars of correspondents accompanying us. On our arrival at home there was another crowd, and more photography.

Mr. and Mrs. Tilson and James W. Good, campaign manager for Hoover, rode up with the Hoovers and ourselves.

This evening all is quiet again, but a sense of relief results from the thought that a campaign is not before me. The party left shortly after six P.M., having spent about two and one half hours at our home. Hoover and I finally got into a room by ourselves. He will not make concessions on the prohibition issue; will make a sincere and conciliatory presentation of the agricultural question, and emphasize the desirability of sound governmental administration. He wished me to make a few radio speeches during the latter part of the campaign and said it would be arranged so that they could be delivered at the house. This was after I had expressed a wish not to be requested to make a general speaking campaign.

All in all he feels that the Republican Party will gain steadily in strength as the campaign progresses. Tomorrow he will arrive at Superior, Wisconsin, where he and his wife will visit with President and Mrs. Coolidge for a day or so — then go on to California.

CHAPTER V

Evanston, Illinois, July 19, 1928.

As soon as I had been elected Vice President, I naturally devoted myself to a study of the Rules of the Senate, over which I was to preside. Before that time, in common, I think, with most citizens, I had a general knowledge of the abuses in the Senate perpetrated under the rules, but had shared that general public feeling of indifference which alone stands in the way of their reform.

After presiding over the Senate since March 4, 1925, my convictions as expressed in my inaugural address are stronger than ever. When the rules will be reformed is only a question of time. Granting as they do the power to Senate minorities, and at times to individual Senators, of blocking the wheels of government itself until they are appeased, the time will come when a minority will make an issue vital to the life of government and will stand for it in earnest, as do many parliamentary minorities in Europe at present.

For a majority of Senators, under such circumstances, not to change rules which deny constitutional majority rights would be treasonable. The rules of the Senate would then be changed overnight. But, in the meantime, it is well understood in the Senate that general public sentiment is difficult to arouse upon this question of reform of the rules. Minorities in the Senate thus far have not been determined enough to be altogether regardless of the consequences of so pushing their power under the rules as to precipitate in the public mind a full appreciation of the extent and danger of that power. If the real power of minorities were used as openly as it is surreptitiously, and if minorities would proceed to the extreme of their ability to defeat revenue and appropriation bills, the public would be greatly aroused. It is, therefore, chiefly by the threat of defeat that modifications in legislation are often made in the shape of additional appropriations dictated by selfish interest as distinguished from that of the general public good.

An occasional open exhibition of the extra-constitutional powers of government, habitually exercised quietly under the Senate rules by individual Senators and minorities, is extremely distasteful to the country and more so to the Senate itself. When at the close of a short session, Senator Tillman of South Carolina, by the threat on the floor of the Senate of using his right of unlimited debate, individually gave our Government the alternative of making a $600,000 appropriation for the State of South Carolina or calling another Congress in extra session, the surrender of the Government through the action of both houses of Congress created a public sense of humiliation quite disconcerting to the upholders of the Senate rules.

And yet, from the Chair, I witness continually the quiet but effective exercise of this power, in a manner as truly humiliating to the country and to the Senate as this open act of Senator Tillman.

Sometimes it is not done quietly — as when recently a Senator notified the Senate in open session that they could pass no bills under unanimous consent unless they passed a certain bill for him. He was assured that it would be done the next day, and he then allowed business to proceed. His bill was passed according to the agreement. I saw no comments upon this proceeding in the press.

Evanston, July 20, 1928.

The truth is that the power given under the rules to an individual Senator to obstruct business, even single-handed, is so valuable to him that the Senate will not reform the rules until forced to do so by public sentiment or by the determination of a few public-spirited Senators themselves. This I have always understood. My inaugural address as Vice President was designed, therefore, to arouse public sentiment and define in the public mind the real issues involved in the Senate rules question.

It is one thing to write and deliver an address and another to get the public to read it and think it over. The course I followed to bring my inaugural speech before the Senate to general public attention succeeded. It was simple, consisting of a delivery so emphatic and so jarring upon the atmosphere of the occasion as to compel the general reading of the speech because of the indignation it created on the spot, especially among the Senators. And yet when the public read the speech,

they found it only plain argument and simple statement, not provocative in nature, and addressed wholly
to the reason — not the prejudices or emotions of the
reader.

Ordinarily, of course, the Vice President's inaugural
speech has been a minor incident of the program,
carried out in the Senate in the morning session, just
preceding the inauguration of the newly elected President on the steps of the Capitol outside. For a new
Vice President, elected by the people — and not by the
Senate — to discuss in his inaugural the proper conduct of business in the body over which he is to preside was not customary, but it was difficult to indict
as out of place.

My forcible manner of delivery was resented. Ber-
nard Shaw was right when he said: "No offensive truth
is ever properly presented without causing irritation."

My address was as follows: —

What I say upon entering this office should relate to its administration and the conditions under which it is administered.
Unlike the vast majority of deliberative and legislative bodies, the
Senate does not elect its presiding officer. He is designated for his
duties by the Constitution of the United States.

In the administration of this office, his duty is to be concerned
with methods of effective procedure as distinguished from any
legislative policy of the body over which he presides. It is not for
the Vice President to be personally concerned with the interests
of political parties or with the policies or projects involved in
legislative action, save in that unusual contingency where, under
the Constitution, it becomes necessary for him to cast the deciding
vote in case of a tie. Nor should he, in view of that unusual contingency, assume any attitude towards prospective legislation until

the contingency occurs. Any other course would inevitably lessen the weight of his influence in those impartial and nonpartisan matters with which it is his duty, under the Constitution of the United States, to be concerned.

In my conduct, I trust I may yield to no Senator in fairness, courtesy and kindliness, and in deference to those unwritten laws which always govern any association of gentlemen, whether official or private. It shall be my purpose not to transgress in any way those limits to my official activity determined by the Constitution of the United States and by proper parliamentary procedure.

But the Vice President, in part because he is not elected by the members of this body, nor by a State, but by the people of the United States, and his constitutional and official relations are to the Senate as a whole, should always express himself upon the relation of its methods of transacting public business to the welfare of the nation. For him, therefore, to officially call to the attention of the Senate any collective duty, such as an improvement in the method under which its business is carried on, so far from being an irrelevant and uncalled-for action on his part, is a supreme duty.

In past years, because the members of this body have cherished most commendable feelings of fairness, courtesy and consideration for each other as individuals, certain customs have evolved. These have crystallized into fixed and written rules of procedure for the transaction of public business which, in their present form, place power in the hands of individuals to an extent, at times, subversive of the fundamental principles of free representative government. Whatever may be said about the misuse of this power under the present rules of the Senate, the fact remains that its existence, inimical as it is to the principles of our constitutional government, cannot properly be charged against any party, nor against any individual or group of individuals.

It has evolved as a natural consequence of the mutual confidence of high-minded men, determined that in their official association as members of the Senate full and fair opportunity to be heard on all public questions shall be enjoyed by each and every Senator, irrespective of whether or not they are in the minority, either of opinion or of party.

But however natural has been the evolution of the present rules, however commendable that existing desire on the part of all that the rights of each individual Senator should be observed, the fact remains that under them the rights of the nation and of the American people have been overlooked — and this notwithstanding that their full recognition of the rights of the nation is in no wise inconsistent with the recognition of every essential right of any individual Senator.

What would be the attitude of the American people and of the individual Senators themselves towards a proposed system of rules if this was the first session of the Senate instead of the first session of the Senate of the Sixty-ninth Congress? What individual Senator would then have the audacity to propose the adoption of the present Rule XXII without modification, when it would be pointed out that during the last days of a session the right that is granted every Senator to be heard for one hour after two-thirds of the Senate had agreed to bring a measure to a vote, gave a minority of even one Senator, at times, power to defeat the measure and render impotent the Senate itself? That rule, which, at times, enables Senators to consume in oratory those last precious minutes of a session needed for momentous decisions, places in the hands of one or a minority of Senators a greater power than the veto power exercised under the Constitution by the President of the United States, which is limited in its effectiveness by the necessity of an affirmative two-thirds vote.

Who would dare to contend that, under the spirit of democratic government, the power to kill legislation providing revenues to pay the expenses of government should, during the last few days of a session, ever be in the hands of a minority or perhaps one Senator? Why should they ever be able to compel the President of the United States to call an extra session of Congress to keep in functioning activity the machinery of the government itself? Who would dare oppose any changes in the rules necessary to insure that the business of the United States should always be conducted in the interests of the nation and never be in danger of encountering a situation where one man, or a minority of men, might demand unreasonable concessions, under threat of blocking the business of the Government? Who would dare maintain that, in the last analysis, the right of the Senate itself to act should ever be subordinated to the right of one Senator to make a speech?

The rules can be found, as is the custom in other deliberative and legislative assemblies, to fully protect a Senator in his right to be heard without forfeiting, at any time, the greater right of the Senate to act. The Constitution of the United States gives the Senate and the House of Representatives the right to adopt their own rules for the conduct of business, but this does not excuse customs and rules which, under certain conditions, might put the power of the Senate itself in the hands of individuals to be used in legislative barter. Proper rules will protect the rights of minorities without surrendering the rights of a majority to legislate.

Under the inexorable laws of human nature and human reaction, this system of rules, if unchanged, cannot but lessen the effectiveness, prestige, and dignity of the United States Senate. Were this the first session of the Senate, and its present system of rules, unchanged, should be presented seriously for adoption, the impact of outraged public opinion, reflected in the attitude of the Senators themselves, would crush the proposal like an eggshell.

Reform in the present rules of the Senate is demanded, not only by American public opinion, but, I venture to say, in the individual consciences of a majority of the members of the Senate itself.

As it is the duty on the part of the Presiding Officer of the Senate to call attention to defective methods in the conduct of business by the body over which he presides, so, under their constitutional power, it is the duty of the members of this body to correct them. To evade or ignore an issue between right and wrong methods is in itself a wrong. To the performance of this duty, a duty which is alone in the interest of the nation we have sworn to faithfully serve, I ask the consideration of the Senate, appealing to the conscience and to the patriotism of the individual members.

Having thus directed attention to this issue in my inaugural address in the Senate, I undertook further to arouse and keep alive public sentiment on the question by a speaking tour reaching the different sections of the country during the summer of 1925.

These meetings without doubt, in my mind, demonstrated a marked general sentiment behind the demand for reform of the Senate rules. The audiences were very large, always testing the capacity of the halls in which I spoke. The audiences in a large city would number from six thousand to twelve thousand. I spoke, as I remember, in Indianapolis and Cincinnati; in Manchester, New Hampshire; Newark, New Jersey; Portland, Oregon; Seattle, Washington; Los Angeles, California; Denver, Colorado; Birmingham, Alabama — where Senator Oscar Underwood spoke with me; Lincoln, Nebraska; in New York City, before the annual meeting of the Associated Press; in Chicago, in Boston, and in Atlanta, Georgia.

In the size of the audiences and the reception of the argument nothing seemed lacking. It became evident to me, however, as various Senators appeared with me at my meetings and on my trips, that their attitude before their constituencies, which was sympathetic — often mildly, however — to rules reform, differed radically from their indifferent or hostile attitude in the Senate.

The best hope for the reform is a flagrant abuse of the rules by the Senate. Such an abuse will inflame the public and create a fear of political reprisal on the part of Senators. The effort, by speeches and a campaign such as mine, was effective only in conveying to the public a clear conception of what the issue involved so that when the abuses occurred there might result a quick crystallization of adverse public sentiment insistent upon a reform.

Whether or not this campaign had its effect upon the subsequent conduct of the Senate it is not for me to say. There occurred afterward on several occasions, however, Senate action under the rule providing for checking debate by a two-thirds vote, although the Senate had resorted to this rule but once or twice during the ten years since its adoption, as a result of a popular demand for Senate rules reform backed by President Wilson.

The use of this rule during my term as Vice President was twice brought about by my direct intervention, and through it the bill extending indeterminately the charters of the Federal Reserve Banks and the Farm Relief Bill were passed, in the last short session.

And here let me refer to the chief argument made by the opponents of a majority cloture provision in the United States Senate — the only great parliamentary body in the world not possessing it. It is maintained that the checks and balances of the Constitution are always not a sufficient protection for minorities, or the individual states of the Union, but that this usurped power given by the Senate rules to check majorities in acting under their constitutional rights must at times be exercised for the public good.

That it has been exercised for the public good in one or two instances may be admitted. But is this to be considered a valid argument when it is against our form of government based upon the principle of the rights of the majority, subject only to certain constitutional limitations? Let us see to what catastrophes this doctrine might lead our nation — one of which was avoided in my judgment only by the accident that a two-thirds majority existed in the Senate at the time, which rendered Rule XXII effective in securing a cloture vote. At the last short session of Congress, — December 5, 1926, to March 4, 1927, — the Senate involved itself in the usual jam of business resulting from its abdication of the right to allot its own time in accordance with the relative importance of its business in favor of a right of individual Senators to indulge in unlimited and irrelevant debate.

Involved in this jam with other bills was the McFadden-Pepper Bill, which was a revision of the National Bank Act. It was originally framed in 1924 by the Comptroller of the Currency at that time — my able and experienced brother, Henry M. Dawes. The bill provided for modification of the laws governing the supervision and operation of national banks, and was necessary to preserve their continued functioning in competition with the state banks which operated under charters better suited to modern conditions. The Government did not have the power to compel the state banks to become members of the Federal Reserve System, and such as were members became so on a voluntary basis with the right of withdrawal at will. This left a situation under which the national banks were, in considerable numbers, giving up their charters because their operations under them were so restricted that they could not meet their state bank competitors; and a condition was rapidly developing under which the Government was losing its control over the membership of the Federal Reserve System. The Act, therefore, was necessary for the protection not only of the National Banking System but of the Federal Reserve System, and, what was most important, it carried with it the granting of an indeterminate charter to the Federal Reserve System itself. This bill was first introduced into Congress in 1924.

Two "undercover filibusters" were in progress — one against this bill extending indeterminately the charters of the Federal Reserve Banks, which expired in 1935, and one against the McNary-Haugen Farm Relief Bill. An undercover filibuster is one in which, by extended debate on other bills, the time of the short session is consumed in order to prevent the bill aimed at from being reached on the calendar before adjournment at the date — March 4 — fixed by the Constitution. If the bill is reached on the calendar, the filibuster becomes "open."

Supposing the bill extending the charters of the banks had been defeated by the filibuster, a two-thirds vote applying cloture not being obtainable, the country then would have been confronted with an open and successful filibuster on the bank charter bill in the last session, similar to that waged against the Boulder Dam measure.

When this occurred and Congress had adjourned the country would have realized that the question of the re-charter of the Federal Reserve Banks had become a political question as did that of the re-charter of the Second Bank of the United States during the years preceding 1836. The re-charter of the Second Bank of the United States was attacked. It was the corner-stone of the credit structure of the nation's business at that time. The disastrous financial panic of 1837 followed. The mere possibility that the bank would not be re-chartered started a contraction of credits in prep-aration for such an outcome which led to the panic, and an acute business depression lasting for years.

The credit structure of the United States at this moment, already in a strained and inflated condition, is built upon the Federal Reserve Bank system as a foundation. What might happen to-day if, in addition to the general uneasiness about the credit situation, the country had reason to expect a determined political attack upon the Federal Reserve System, which, with charters expiring by law, could be destroyed by a Sen-ate delay in enabling legislation?

The filibuster organization in the Senate against the McFadden-Pepper bill, which was thwarted only by the two-thirds cloture rule, was composed of the most determined and skillful radicals in the membership of that body. The existence of a majority for cloture on both bills was made possible only by a coalition be-tween the conservatives favoring the bank bill and cer-tain radicals favoring the farm bill. Each faction was willing to accord the other the right to a Senate vote only because each realized that its own bill was lost if it did not. My intervention and initiative as President of the Senate, confronted by conflicting demands from each faction, was necessary to suggest and bring about the joint cloture program — by which the bank bill proponents circulated the cloture petition for the McNary-Haugen bill and the McNary-Haugen bill proponents circulated the cloture petition for the bank bill.

If the two-thirds vote for cloture on both bills had not been available, I believe that this company could not have been saved from a credit panic as well as a prolonged business depression. And yet a majority cloture provision in the rules, which alone would enable a majority of the Senate to function under all circumstances where the Constitution gives them the right to do so, would have prevented the dangerous situation in which this important national enactment was involved. Had it not been for the courageous fight made by Senator Carter Glass, and Senator Pepper, the bank bill would have been lost — but the cloture procedure was essential to their victory.

It is disquieting to realize that at all times every Congressional bill whose enactment is necessary to keep the Government functioning — such as an annual appropriation or revenue bill, among many others — can be indefinitely blocked by a minority, provided only it be not less in number than one third of the Senate. During the last days of a short session this power of obstruction steadily grows in the hands of less than one third of the Senate and finally on the last few days of the short session is in the hands of a few individuals, or of only one. In either the long or the short session any minority of the Senate, provided it be not less than one third of its members, by using against appropriation or revenue bills its right of unlimited debate, can block the business of Government and bring the majority to its knees.

If the underlying principle of our Government is right, then the cloture principle of the Senate Rules is wrong.

In the *Saturday Evening Post* of March 15, 1930, in an article entitled "In the Senate", ex-Senator George Wharton Pepper, of Pennsylvania, writes as follows: —

"In the Banking and Currency Committee my most interesting and important experience centered on the so-called McFadden-Pepper Bill, which was intended to liberalize the charters of national banks, to reconcile conflicting views on branch banking, and to extend the charters of Federal Reserve Banks which were soon to expire by limitation. Simultaneously with its appearance in the Senate, it was introduced in the House of Representatives by Representative Louis T. McFadden, of Pennsylvania, the able and experienced Chairman of the House Committee on Banking and Currency. I presided at many public Senate hearings on this measure when it was in committee, and had charge of it on the Senate floor. The prospect of bringing it to a vote was dimmed by the obstruction of Senator Bob La Follette and others who were supporting the McNary-Haugen Bill, famous for its highly controversial scheme of farm relief. I had just about decided to result to cloture and had a petition to close the debate signed by a sufficient number of Senators, when Vice President Dawes, perceiving the deadlock, sent for representatives of the opposing groups. We met one evening in his room. By the sheer force of his personality, he forced an agreement that both measures should be voted upon. This agreement was carried out. Both bills passed. The McNary-Haugen Bill was vetoed by President Coolidge, while the McFadden-Pepper Bill became law. To General Dawes more than to any other man credit is due for the extension of the Federal Reserve charters."

Evanston, July 22, 1928.

As to the above, Senator Pepper and Senator Glass were the great figures in the passage of the bill through the Senate. It is characteristic of Senator Pepper to speak of his own part so modestly, and of mine in such a kindly way. But while this intervention on my part entailed little effort as compared with the burden Senator Pepper was bearing as sponsor of the bill, I have felt, nevertheless, it was one of my most useful acts as Vice President.

For this reference to it, I am grateful.

The time came, during my term of office, — as it will again in the future, — when a minority became determined enough in its resolve to override the majority in its constitutional rights to risk the general public disapproval caused by a defiance of constitutional procedure and intent. This was when the question of seating Vare, the Senator-elect from Pennsylvania, was under consideration — that is, this question was the one underlying the various parliamentary phases of the contest. The majority, though less than two-thirds, was opposed to seating him. The minority took advantage of the rules, — which regard the right of a Senator to talk indefinitely, whether to the question or not, as superior to the right of the Senate to act, — and it blocked all essential business until the Senate expired on March 4, 1927, by constitutional limitation.

The second deficiency bill was not passed in consequence, and the functioning of government was ham-

pered during the summer, for example, in the operation
of the Federal Courts. The filibusterers were caught
napping one day, or the District of Columbia appropriation bill would have failed also, in which event the
President would have been compelled to call an extra
session of Congress — a humiliating as well as an ex-
pensive necessity.

In closing the session in the midst of the filibuster,
I availed myself of the custom under which the Vice
President makes a brief address, and spoke as fol-
lows: —

"It is customary for the Vice President at the beginning and ending of a session of Congress to address
the Senate upon an appropriate subject. The comments
the Chair has to make on this occasion will be very brief.

"The Chair regards the results of the present legislative session as primarily due to the defective rules of
the Senate under which a minority can prevent a
majority from exercising its constitutional right of
bringing measures to a vote. This is the only great
parliamentary body in the world where such a situation exists.

"On this closing day of the second session of the
Sixty-ninth Congress, the Chair commends to the Senate
the remarks upon the Senate rules which he made on the
first day of the first session of the Congress.

"The hour of twelve o'clock having arrived, the
Senate stands in adjournment sine die."

I may say that I delivered these short remarks with
all the emphasis which gave such offense to the Senate

in my inaugural address. But the atmosphere had changed. The entire country was critical of the conduct of the Senate, and, however critical the Senators may have felt regarding me, they managed to repress public expression of it.

But, as I have already stated, it is only occasionally that a minority gives such a public exhibition of its real power. Instead, recourse is continually had to the threat of the use of the power, which, while it costs the people tens of millions of dollars in additions to appropriation bills and in other modifications of legislation, seldom becomes public.

The gradual weakening of party discipline and power in the country, however, is creating a condition in the Senate tending constantly to increase and encourage the use of the Senate rules as a blackjack in the hands of minorities and individuals, to coerce the majority into legislative concessions dictated by selfish and sectional interest. The nomination of candidates for the Senate at general primaries often makes it possible for Senators, elected through the strength of the public habit of voting for a straight party ticket, to gain their seats by being "regular" at election time, only to turn "insurgent" after taking their seats. Again, the lines between the two parties are constantly becoming weaker as differences among our people tend to become economic in nature instead of chiefly being governmental, or rather constitutional, as in the past.

Economic issues affect different sections of the country in different ways and degrees. Hence the tendency toward the bloc system; for those having similar economic objectives form into groups in the Senate with ties stronger than those of party.

These blocs are numerous enough now in the Senate to constitute a majority when they unite. But a majority composed of a fusion of minorities divided as to economic purposes cannot act constructively for the nation. They can generally unite only in a policy of obstruction or in raids on the Treasury. In the latter procedure, they secure the passage of several appropriations, no one of which alone would pass on its merit as a national benefit. When one bloc seeking an appropriation votes for the appropriation demanded by another bloc solely to get votes for its own, it is the American people who suffer, and selfish interests which profit.

The Senate, because of growth of the bloc system and abuse of its rules, is steadily losing its power to act constructively for the nation; and in proportion as the bloc system grows, abuses will be more frequent under the rules. The rules encourage the formation of blocs, for they provide the way for making them powerful through amalgamation despite the smallness of their respective numbers of members.

CHAPTER VI

Evanston, Illinois, July 22, 1928.

To-DAY Mrs. Dawes and I drove up to John Mc-
Cutcheon's at Lake Forest. He was giving a luncheon
to Miss Earhart, the first woman to take the trip to
England in an airplane. During the past years I have
met, officially and personally, a number of the trans-
oceanic and arctic flyers. Chief among these was Colonel
Lindbergh, who dined with us informally in company
with my cousin Lincoln Ellsworth, of the Amundsen-
Ellsworth expedition to the North Pole and across
Alaska.

Commander Byrd also spent a day with me, coming
to Washington to urge the grant by Congress of a Congressional Medal to Ellsworth, which was made.

The French and German flyers, accompanied by the
Ambassadors of France and Germany, also called upon
me officially at the Capitol, when I presented them to
the Senate — which adjourned for fifteen minutes for
the purpose in each case. Chamberlain called and was
presented in the same way. I talked for some time with
all of them, and as a result noted one common quality
they all possessed — that of modesty. They were, generally, natural in manner — some were more or less
diffident. Lindbergh was an especially pleasing character; this was true also of Byrd and Ellsworth.

Lindbergh described to me at length his trip across the Atlantic. When I told him that I was much impressed by his famous first remark as he landed in the night at Paris, where a great and breathless crowd awaited him, — "I am Charles Lindbergh", — he replied that he had never made it. He said that at first there were no newspapermen who reached his plane, around which the crowd pressed in such a way as to endanger it. His first remark was to ask for officers to protect his plane from damage.

Byrd also gave me an account of his attempted trip to Paris, where he could not land because of the fog, and his return at night to the coast of France where he made a forced landing in the sea.

He went over in detail his plans and preparations for his proposed flight over the Antarctic regions.

Monday afternoon I left with a party of friends for Traverse City, Michigan, where Mr. R. Floyd Clinch entertained us. We went to Traverse City on the *S.S. Manitou* and returned Tuesday night by rail. My occasional golf games in the past, being played in my native habitat, where a Vice President is not a curiosity, have been conducted in comparative quiet and privacy — the latter being further assured by the circumstance that my golf is mediocre and of itself attracts no spectators. But at Traverse City it was different. Our party went through a strenuous program all day. Headed by a fine band, we were driven through a decorated street lined with several thousand people.

While we did play golf for a time in the afternoon, it was in the presence of a large gallery, which certainly did not improve our game. However, all of us had a very fine time, notwithstanding that during the day we dedicated a golf links, visited a canning factory and an insane asylum, planted a tree in the presence of a Legion delegation headed by a drum corps, attended an official luncheon and dinner, visited an old and dear friend, Chandler B. Beach, aged eighty-nine, whose summer home was eighteen miles away from Traverse City, made two speeches, attended a reception by the American Legion, and did various other things as called for by a program carried out on a time schedule.

We reached Chicago Wednesday (yesterday morning).

Evanston, July 28, 1928.

I have just received a letter from my friend Sir Josiah Stamp of England, who with Sir Robert Kindersley represented England on the First Committee of Experts of the Reparation Commission of which I was Chairman. In the course of his letter he says, "I was recently in Berlin and naturally discussed Reparation settlements with Gilbert, Luther, Schacht and other friends of 1924. I am bound to say I am all for going slow on the next step."

He had reference of course to the final settlement of the reparations question, which is being generally discussed as a consequence of Gilbert's suggestion in his report that Germany is entitled to a final fixation of the amount of reparations she is to pay now that the

Experts' Plan has resulted in the stabilization of Germany's currency and economy, and demonstrated within limits her capacity to meet annual payments. On September 1 this year will commence the fifth and final year of the Dawes Plan, and Germany will unquestionably meet the standard payment of 2,500,000,000 marks during the year 1928–1929.

All commentators seem to agree in principle that justice to Germany demands that the total sum of reparations be fixed; and yet I can well understand why Sir Josiah is "all for going slow on the next step." It is probably because of the immense difficulties which are involved in securing the unanimous consent of all the beneficiaries to a settlement, and the disturbance in general economic conditions and public confidence which may result from a prolonged negotiation resulting possibly in a disagreement. No one without experience in negotiations involving unanimous consent agreements among independent sovereignties, during and after the war, can form any adequate idea of the difficulties involved. As I said in my address to the Reparation Commission and as Chairman of the First Committee of Experts at Paris in 1924, the unanimous consent agreement among the Allies, which resulted in the Central Command of their armies in 1918 under Foch, resulted alone from the fact that the alternative was defeat and destruction.

Thus in 1924 there was first secured on our committee, and later at the London conference, a unanimous agreement in the adoption of our plans — for the same reason. All Europe faced ruin as an alternative to agreement. The pressure for agreement was simply over-whelming.

Anyone who participated in these negotiations well understands that it was not confidence in the plan that was the prime factor in its adoption. Many of the great economists of the world openly predicted its failure — and the great majority of them would express only hope rather than expectation of its success.

But there was nothing left to do but agree. For Europe not to agree meant what another general European war at this time would mean — that European civilization might perish. Adopted, the plan at least meant hope. Rejected, it meant certain ruin for all.

At present it is lack of the pressure of a great emergency need for a final settlement of the reparations total which will hinder agreement upon it among the Allies.

The total reparations have already been fixed at an impossible total at Versailles. While all admit their payment in such an amount is impossible, yet, having been agreed to by Germany, they, together with the Experts' Plan, represent a "status quo" which from a superficial standpoint operates adversely to Germany alone.

As a matter of fact anything short of a final settlement constitutes a continuing danger to the economy and peace of the civilized world. This conviction will determine the attitude of the real statesmen of Europe, but they will confront great difficulties in the way of constructive action. Ever opposing them will be the curse of the world — the fomenters of often avoidable war, the nationalistic demagogues who in each country will seek to exploit their pitiful personalities and selfish plans regardless of the common weal. Every effort to arrive at a reasonable settlement will be denounced as a betrayal of the Allied peoples by the Allied demagogues, and of the German people by the German demagogues. This is what delayed any really constructive step toward reparations settlement for six years after the ending of the war and until the formation of our Experts' Committee.

It is the knowledge of what this means that Stamp probably has in his mind, and that leads him to doubt whether the time has yet come to take up the problem seriously. Undoubtedly the time will come. But a failure to agree now, involving all Europe in acrimonious political struggle, should be avoided.

No one in this country, like myself, not closely in touch with political conditions and the trend of public sentiment in Europe can say whether or not the time is ripe for the effort. But I do know that before the statesmen of Europe lies a problem — not so difficult from an economic standpoint, but vastly difficult from a political standpoint because the penalties for neglecting its early solution are not sensed by the masses of the people in the same degree as they were in 1924 when we of the First Committee of Experts undertook our work at Paris.

Evanston, August 1, 1928.

Received a letter from Loesch, the Chairman of the Chicago Crime Commission, asking me in the name of the Commission to undertake the co-ordination of the work of some seven hundred local associations now existing and devoted to constructive civic progress. Loesch and his Crime Commission are in the midst of a crusade against the lawlessness and corruption existing in our city and its government which promises results. The public is at last aroused and the movement, refused support by the City Council, has been financed by popular subscription. It is impossible for me to undertake the work while occupying my present office, but I have a sincere feeling of regret that I cannot help in the fight upon the lawless element there.

Senator James E. Watson of Indiana visited me Monday. As a veteran and successful politician he seemed incredulous at my satisfaction with the prospect of my return to business. One of the sad things to me about life in Washington is the steady procession of men leaving public life at an age too advanced either to hope to return to it or to be usefully active in other endeavors. The Chinese cover the situation in their proverb: "He who rides a tiger cannot dismount." Many of these men lead lives of unhappiness, mourning the loss of past prominence and prestige. In the journal of Gideon Welles, Secretary of the Navy under Lincoln and Johnson, I found him in revolt at the lack of attention he received when he returned to his New England home after the exciting eight years of service at Washington. My own prospective return to Chicago where I have ties of business induces no melancholy reflections of this nature and possibly for this reason.

CHAPTER VII

STARTED last Saturday from Chicago for a visit to this place, where my family and I have gone for the last three summers. My wife, my children Dana and Virginia, Miss Decker their governess, my grown daughter Carolyn and her husband Melvin Ericson, my brother Henry M. Dawes and his wife, compose the party. We are visiting Mrs. A. E. Humphrey, the widow of Colonel A. E. Humphrey who, himself, planned and completed this beautiful fishing camp, than which in my judgment there is no finer in the Country. We are surrounded by great mountains, and the elevation of the camp itself is about eighty-six hundred feet. At the camp is a lake of about sixty acres in extent which Colonel Humphrey formed by building a great dam across a gorge between the mountains. Into this and descending from the snow-capped mountains, through a beautiful mountain valley flows a splendid trout stream. On a ledge of the mountains back of us is another lake of some twelve acres formed by the damming of another mountain stream.

These waters afford trout fishing which I have never seen equaled. The fish are the native Rocky Mountain trout and rainbow trout.

One can have as rough or as smooth going in fishing as he desires. At places the gorge is so steep that a narrow path for pack horses forms the best means of travel. We reached here after a short stop at Colorado Springs yesterday (Monday) morning. Yesterday I took the smooth fishing. My catch was twenty-five trout — all over ten inches in length. Anything under this in length was thrown back. To-day I took the rougher up-stream fishing and stopped with ten over the regulation length. There are certain places where the trout are so plentiful that one moves along so as not to catch his limit too soon, in my case because I want to average only twelve a day.

A National Forest Reserve encloses the Humphrey place on three sides, and there are no public roads over which automobile tourists can reach it. If there were there would be no good fishing. The automobile has brought many changes in American life, adding much to its happiness, but spelling death to American hunting and fishing. The important problem of the conservation of American wild life is receiving more attention, and properly, than ever before — but except in a few states like Pennsylvania it is not receiving enough. When it is estimated that five million hunters and fishermen go out every season, what chance has wild life to survive unless, in addition to strict enforcement of stricter laws limiting bags and catches, there is increased governmental and state activity in establishing game farms and fish hatcheries?

Wagon Wheel Gap, August 8, 1928.

After a good climb, am this minute sitting on top of what we should call a mountain in the East, but what out here is regarded as a moderate-sized mound. And this sentence as I write it suggests a timeworn thought. How completely the reputations of public men depend upon their contemporary environment! The deteriorating parliamentary personnel due in this country to the direct primary is responsible for an overestimation by the public of the qualities of many who, measured by the leaders of the past, are but mediocre after all. It is when strong men compete that great men become greater, and in these days the field of politics on which contenders may struggle does not especially attract strong men.

I doubt whether, outside of two or three men, any lasting reputations are being made in the American Senate to-day. When the issues which divide the people are largely economic rather than constitutional and governmental, and concern the material rather than the moral interests of the nation, posterity will forget the leaders of the period.

It accords fame to those who have contributed to its woe or weal. It is interested in the woe and weal of past generations only as they were the result of the establishment or disregard of some moral principle, or some principle of government, or the discovery of some scientific fact or mechanical principle, which directly affected for better or worse its own life. Therefore, among the men of this generation in America who will be remembered longest, the inventors and scientists will probably outnumber the statesmen. But it is not safe to generalize carelessly. There are great men still among us in public place — many of them. As I have sat as Presiding Officer of the Senate, when much of the time the proceedings do not demand close attention, I have had ample opportunity to study, compare and judge the members. In my judgment, of course, I am fallible and subject to the subconscious natural limitations of human nature, which lead one to regard most favorably those who agree with him in his view of things and whom he personally likes. But I try to overcome these and be as fair as possible. It is especially interesting to me to assume as existing a public emergency calling for leadership in the nation of a high order, and then pass on the qualifications of the men before me to achieve it. Naturally I recognize the difference in the qualities which leadership demands in an executive, as compared with an administrative place in civil, as compared with military, duty — and as a consequence often mentally transfer Senators to other than parliamentary fields in forming my eventual judgments.

In now recalling these judgments of Senators, among others the name of James W. Wadsworth, of New York, recently defeated for re-election, comes to my mind. My high estimate of his qualities has not been influenced by a close friendship. I have never had any intimate associations in work or interests with him. But viewed from every angle, not only as a Senator but as one qualified for constructive leadership in the public interest, — mental or moral — military or civil — in Congress or out, — I regard him as most unusual.

Wagon Wheel Gap, August 9, 1928.

Am up in the mountains again this fine morning. The cool invigorating air and the bright sun bring back something of the joy of youth. A panorama of magnificent views is spread out before and below me. The great Continental Divide is only eighteen miles from where I sit. Such surroundings and circumstances should induce mental perspective and discourage meanness of soul, and hence whatever of the spirit of general criticism there is in my system, this is a good time to get it out. Uncle Joe Cannon used to say of a certain Senator that he was never happy unless he was "damning everything over a foot high or a year old." In these days this remark might still apply to a few Senators. I do not want to seem to criticize criticism. While I always sympathize with the pulling horse instead of with the driver who whips and scolds him, I realize that the whippers and scolders perform a necessary and useful public duty. I do not indulge in personalities, although at times in the past when I was "firing at the flock, the wounded birds that fluttered" might have created a contrary impression. I comment upon a certain type which I regard as unfortunate. A man is not responsible for the temperament with which he is born. If he is born with a natural tendency to grouch he never gets over it. It is not his fault. If he is born ignorant — that is, without the ability properly to interpret facts — he never gets over it. It is not his fault. I have often noted in the Senate that ignorance, when it is a natural gift and not the result of mental indolence, is a rather attractive human quality when associated with courage and sincerity. It creates a sense of their own superiority in the minds of others without creating irritation. It inspires kindly treatment from the world. But we have some individuals who seem to have been cursed at birth with the double heritage of ignorance and grouchiness. Of these only I speak. None of them ever would have arrived in public life had it not been for an extraordinary congenital endowment of nervous energy — the human quality particularly at a premium under the direct primary system. This is the one gift which everybody envies them. Such men, although they are adept and successful publicity seekers, have no great influence; their astonishing amount of misdirected energy cannot make up for their lack of common sense. Their frequent diatribes usually evoke no reply, for, as the Spaniards say: "It is a waste of lather to shave an ass."

Wagon Wheel Gap, August 10, 1928.

Writing out in the mountains again.

Had a wonderful afternoon of fishing yesterday. Caught so many trout that in order to keep down my average to twelve per day I will have to lay off to-day and go light all the rest of the time — to my great regret. Will go along this afternoon and watch the other fishermen. Yesterday I probably exceeded my legal ten-pound limit of fish, and I devastated my moral limit. Roy, the manager for Mrs. Humphrey, and an old-timer here, who accompanied me, when I would suggest that I had caught enough would say that it "might be years before they would rise again so well." We both knew he was lying, but when natural desires are aroused truth is unpopular. In my weakness I yielded to the tempter and the temptation, and after reflecting upon my sins last night, am disciplining myself for the rest of the trip. How few so-called "sportsmen" there are who, when the game or fish are coming well, do not exceed their limit, legal or moral! They will excuse themselves by shooting enough ducks, for instance, to consume in addition to their own the limit of the guide accompanying them. Nevertheless they will earnestly preach before the fireplace in the evening the doctrines of the Izaak Walton League after having thus violated them in spirit during the day.

Their reason tells them, even if their conscience is asleep, that in their own interest the spirit as well as the letter of the law should be observed; yet in the solitude of the forest or waters, when the opportunity comes, they yield to an instinct developed in man through the long ages. They ought to be ashamed of themselves, as I am ashamed of myself to-day. My take yesterday was forty-three trout. My virtuous scores for the three preceding days were Monday twenty-five, Tuesday, ten, Wednesday six. My sinful forty-three yesterday brings the total to eighty-four for four days. Not counting to-day, I have three days more here for fishing. For the eight days I will be entitled to ninety-six. I have the moral right, therefore, to take only twelve more trout, or four a day, except to-day which is a day of penance.

It is perhaps a universal truth that after first yielding to temptation the conscientious sinner will resolve never to fall again. This fleeting period of strong resolves induces in him for a time a false and unjustified sense of virtue. It is then that he becomes the sternest critic of other sinners of his own kind. It is a natural thing, then, for me to add here a few words of scorn for those pitiful excuses of the erring fishermen to which when not under a sense of sin myself I have sometimes listened sympathetically. Take, for instance, the excuse that if assurance exists that somebody can be found to eat all the game or fish brought in the extra kill is justified.

We are surprised this year to find the largest fish in the stream instead of the big lake. The trout seem about equally divided in numbers between the native and the rainbow. The fly I find best is a Coachman, size 8. The other day after a long trip in swift water with black flies and no rises, a change to a grey fly soon brought three good-sized rainbows. As I was wondering at this, the explanation came when two grey sand flies dropped on the water and two trout rose to them instantly.

On this trip, as usual, the biggest fish got away. This occurred when I was casting the other evening in the big lake, with Roy at the oars of my boat. We have found in the big lake that the largest fish lie in the evening about sixty feet from the shore opposite the intake of a small mountain stream. If we cast there and get anything, it is generally a large one. I had tried for a half-hour without success, when I got what seemed to be a weak strike. I hooked the fish and commenced to reel in slowly and somewhat indifferently. Suddenly the pole in my hand was half-submerged by a sudden jerk of a strength which immediately changed my attitude into one of excitement and expectancy. For a time I played the fish, giving him plenty of line. As he quieted down I started to reel him in, with Roy waiting with a long-poled landing net. Suddenly he made a magnificent leap fully two feet out of water, and then we realized both what a beauty he was and also that he was not for us, for he broke the leader and fairly won a victorious freedom. There is a two- or three-pound rainbow trout now in the lake which I shall always remember — and I think he will remember me, for I regret to say he is carrying a hook in his mouth with a leader and two flies.

The importance of the general adoption by fish hatcheries, especially those under State Control, of the nursery pond system is so great that I note here the conversation which I recently had with B. C. Hosselkus of Creede, considered the best and most experienced hatcheryman in this section of the country.

When fry are introduced immediately into the stream, river or lake he estimates that only twenty-five per cent are saved. Colonel Humphrey's estimate, I remember, was only fifteen per cent. After a year in a nursery pond Hosselkus estimates that seventy-five per cent are saved.

A part of this method of handling his hatcheries, he told me, is as follows: The green eggs taken from the trout are put in the prepared hatchery trays with water at fifty degrees temperature, and remain there for twenty-one days, when the eyes show through the transparent shell of the egg. A one degree difference in temperature of the water here makes forty-eight hours difference in the time of eyeing — cold retarding it, warmth accelerating it. After twenty-one days the eyed eggs are put in a tub and the unimpregnated eggs which turn white are removed. The eggs are then replaced in the hatchery trays for hatching, which occurs in twenty days.

They are then in the "fry" state and as soon as they swim they should be transferred to a protected nursery pond for a year. If placed directly in regular trout waters, between the larger fish eating them and being killed against the rocks by swift water like that in the Colorado streams, few will survive. Mr. Hosselkus says that with one year in his nursery ponds, with proper food and fifty-five to fifty-eight degree water, a trout will reach eight inches in length. It is then ready for transfer to regular trout waters.

Wagon Wheel Gap, August 11, 1928.

Writing in the mountains again. Yesterday afternoon went with the fishermen but did not fish. Like the "back seat" automobile driver, however, I was on hand with a surplus supply of unsolicited, unappreciated and unheeded advice. Had a fine time myself, but doubt whether I contributed to the general happiness by my comments. It is not quite so cool to-day as yesterday — although it is always cool here — and, like most mortals when in the deep woods on a clear, still and warm day, I feel coming on a comatose condition of mind and body. Poets might refer to this as a period of quiet and peace for the soul, but as a matter of fact it is an attack of sheer laziness. For the time being, however, I recall sympathetically Cowper's appeal: —

> Oh for a lodge in some vast wilderness,
> Some boundless contiguity of shade,
> Where rumor of oppression and deceit,
> Of unsuccessful or successful war,
> Might never reach me more.

Evening, August 11, 1928.

Started out to fish this afternoon with a four fish limit and a determination to try only for big ones. Wonder of wonders! I succeeded beyond any expectation. After throwing back five fair-sized fish I finally hooked and landed a fifteen-and-three-quarter-inch rainbow weighing a pound — the largest fish anyone has caught on the trip as yet. Caught and kept two more, each over twelve inches in length — making my catch three today — nine to go.

My brother Henry and his wife and Carolyn and Melvin left for home this morning. My immediate family and I will leave Tuesday for Taos on our way to visit Mr. Waite Phillips at Cimarron, New Mexico.

Received to-day an interesting letter from Dwight Morrow chiefly covering personal matters, but I quote what he says about Calles: —

"The work down here in Mexico goes along very well on the whole. The assassination of General Obregón is a great blow to the country, because it throws into the political field the question of succession which, as you know, is the baffling question in countries like Mexico. I have been struck with the poise of President Calles, in whom I think the country is getting more and more confidence. As I told you in Washington, I look upon him as a man of industry, ability and courage. He has had in the past some very radical ideas. The test, however, of a public official is what responsibility does to him. Responsibility has sobered and tempered the ideas of Calles. He is still bitterly criticized by many Americans, but I look upon him as a patriot."

At 5:00 P.M. Denver time we listened over the radio to Secretary Hoover's acceptance speech. It was a remarkable address. No one could hear it without inner tribute to the great ability and versatility of the speaker. It was a masterpiece from a political standpoint. From now on we will hear little of the myth that Herbert Hoover is no politician. I do not think, however, that when elected he will seek as a super-politician to avoid the difficult issues which national emergency brings instead of meeting them "head on" when necessary for the public good. This was Calvin Coolidge's strength. Does Hoover possess it? That is a question which no one can answer now — perhaps not even Hoover himself, for the tests of a President are unique. When his ambitions are concerned, will he be safe as a guardian of the public interest? Will he be willing to "take the gaff" at times, and defy temporary public sentiment even at the risk of loss of power, content to receive his just and high reward only when time crystallizes public sentiment into permanent public judgment?

This and this only is the hallmark of real statesmanship. If Herbert Hoover stands this test, he will be one of the greatest of our Presidents — for no one will have entered the office better equipped by ability and experience to cope with the particular problems which apparently will confront the coming Administration.

What will Hoover do when he bears a sole responsibility in a public crisis involving his own political power and popularity? Will he steer by the compass and the stars, or by the wind? Every other test he has stood in his wonderful and in many respects unrivaled career of accomplishment for the public good. I here record the belief that if elected he will meet this final and greatest test as he has met others of the past and become one of the really great Presidents of the Republic.

Wagon Wheel Gap, August 13, 1928.

Yesterday involved a five-mile horseback ride over the mountain trails to the west fork of Goose Creek in the National Forest Reserve. Roy went with me, but we had but one rod between us. The stream is very rocky, water very swift, and trout very wary in such clear water. Fished most of the time in the middle of the stream with waders — hard work in the strong current. Took four trout on a Royal Coachman fly size 8, and surely earned them. Turned over the rod for a time to Roy and he took three more. So this afternoon when I catch five trout more I have finished. It has been a wonderful trip and I have enjoyed it much more because I have exercised reasonable moderation in my fishing.

Evening.

Caught the last five of my ninety-six trout for the eight days. I took ninety on flies, five on a spinner, and in a moment of weakness one on a grasshopper — the latter being much more difficult to catch than the fish.

Taos, New Mexico, August 15, 1928.

We came yesterday 179 miles by automobile from Wagon Wheel Gap to this most curious and fascinating of all American towns. Mrs. A. E. Humphrey and Mr. and Mrs. Albert Humphrey came with us. We arrived at 6:36 P.M.; and in the evening at the Don Fernando Hotel, where we stopped, some of the Indians from the near-by pueblo gave their native dances.

To-day we have visited some of the artists' studios — for this is the habitat of high art as well as of Spanish-Americans and Indians. Last year when I was here and again to-day I met a number of the artists, who are most interesting and pleasant men.

In the afternoon a committee of Pueblo Indians called and invited our party to a dance to be given at their pueblo. We accepted and will go this evening. They did this for us a year ago and it was a most interesting experience. It was a beautiful moonlight night and the Indians danced near a great fire of logs with the old pueblo in the background. The Governor and Lieutenant Governor of New Mexico were with me and during the dance the Indian Governor of the tribe, who was standing near, walked to a little elevation between the dancers and ourselves and addressed us and them.

He was a dignified, fine-looking Indian with one of those wonderful clear-cut Indian faces bespeaking intelligence, authority and perfect poise.

The firelight with its flickering shadows, the dancing Indians, and the pueblo gave him a background as impressive as the picture he himself made. His speech, which was addressed to both the dancers and me, was interpreted to me as he delivered it by an Indian graduate of the Carlisle School. It was in general a statement of appreciation of the honor which they felt was done them by our visit and an exhortation to the Indians to do their best to entertain us. But the moving part was when he spoke of the Indians' pride in their race and about their old pueblo — of the long ages they had dwelt in it and their affection for it. His ending sentences were: "Here we have always lived. Here we are living. Here we shall always live."

I replied as best I could, expressing my gratitude — but as a speaker fell far short of him in every way.

In the afternoon before the dance I had met the Indian Governor and the leading members of his tribe in the council room of the pueblo, where they asked my interest in certain matters connected with their reservation and pending with the Government.

It seems they elect a new Governor each year. I am told the tribe numbers upwards of five hundred. The people here say that they are very cleanly, peaceful and pleasant neighbors. I will add to these notes after our visit this evening to the pueblo.

Evening.

We have just returned from the Indian dance at the old pueblo. It was as interesting and as impressive as that of a year ago.

After the dance was over, the chief took us to his apartment in the pueblo, where were gathered the elders and counsellors of the tribe, to whom he introduced us. We had a most cordial reception, and met many interesting characters. Quite a number of the Indians spoke English.

Cimarron, New Mexico, August 18, 1928.

On Thursday evening at Taos had a pleasant call from Bronson Cutting, United States Senator from New Mexico, who, with some of his friends, came up from Santa Fe to meet us. Waite Phillips, our host at Cimarron, arrived to take us by automobile to his ranch. We left with him at 11:30 A.M., the Humphreys leaving us to go to Santa Fe. We reached Cimarron in time for lunch. The Phillips home is beautiful, and most interesting in its unusual furnishings, many of them symbolical of this unique part of the country and the art of its original inhabitants. It is on a tract of one hundred and fifty thousand acres, practically all of which is in the same wild state as when it was the habitat of Kit Carson and the first settlers of New Mexico. It is a game preserve and filled with all sorts of wild life. Deer and wild turkey are especially abundant. There is a herd of buffalo which, of course, is carefully guarded, and another of elk. Every effort is being made to keep the country clear of the mountain lions, which are so destructive of the deer. At Phillips' camp, fifteen miles distant, where we go to-morrow — by pack horse the last seven miles — there is an almost untouched trout stream — the Rayado.

We spent the afternoon and evening of Monday quietly with our genial and hospitable host and his charming wife and children. Yesterday morning there arrived our friends from Chicago and the East, most of whom have been my companions on my visits to Colorado and New Mexico for the last three years — J. E. Otis and his son, Joe, Kenneth Roberts, Ben Ames Williams, Charles Francis Coe, and John T. McCutcheon, my dear friend of the long years for whom my boy Dana McCutcheon Dawes is named. Roberts, Williams and Coe are on the *Saturday Evening Post* staff of writers.

Mr. Phillips and I met them at the train and took lunch in their car. Then we went in the afternoon to the place in the near-by mountains where we saw so many wild turkeys last year, and where Kenneth Roberts and John McCutcheon fired not once but a dozen times in the general direction of a wandering turkey, which suffered nothing unless from shell shock and surprise. We saw no other turkey, but on our way back in the automobile we sighted a fine two-year-old buck standing about five hundred yards away. Kenneth got out at Mr. Phillips' suggestion to try for him. He missed him the first time, but followed him into the foothills and finally got him. I may say here that the Phillips ranch, being a game preserve, is operated under license from the State and this proceeding was legal — but I think Kenneth was more depressed than elated over his success.

Rayado Lodge, Phillips Ranch, Cimarron, August 21, 1928.

We reached this place over a pack horse trail Saturday afternoon. Waite Phillips, one of the best hosts this generation has produced, has outdone himself in arranging to have "things doing." The hunters of the party, — Kenneth Roberts, Ben Ames Williams and John McCutcheon, — with the energy and persistence which have characterized their lives, have spent most of the time on horseback on the rough trails or lying in wait for wild turkeys. Ben Williams took first rank with an eighteen- or twenty-pound gobbler, and Kenneth second. Phillips has the most famous of the Government lion hunters of New Mexico on the place at present. This is Ritchie, who has killed nineteen mountain lions in this state since the first of the year. He has his dogs with him trying to locate a lion for our hunters. Earlier in the season he killed two on the place and thinks there are only one or two left. Lions are hunted relentlessly in order to protect the deer. Yesterday evening when Ritchie came into camp he had not located a lion, but he brought a brown bear which he had shot. We have already had buffalo, venison, wild turkey and trout on our bill of fare, and to this we will now add bear meat. I have confined myself to fishing, sticking to a moral limit of ten a day on the average. Spent nine hours on the rocky Agua Fria yesterday riding up on horseback and fishing down the gorge on foot — a wonderful day. Since I then took nineteen trout, despite the fact I took only five Saturday evening I can take only six this afternoon. So I am going to the hard fishing where most of the time is taken up in stumbling and slipping on submerged boulders in swift water and disentangling your line and fly hook from the thick growth of bushes along the stream. Mrs. Dawes and the children are enjoying the horseback riding immensely, and as I write are out on a fifteen-mile ride. We are far removed from tele-

GENERAL DAWES, KENNETH ROBERTS, AND
BEN AMES WILLIAMS

RAYADO LODGE, NEW MEXICO

phones, telegrams, mail and the "madding crowd."
One of the best times of all is the evening reunion when
we gather around the blazing log fire at the lodge house.
At this altitude the nights are cold. The relating of the
experiences of the day are then embellished with the
harmless exaggerations incident to the absence of witnesses to the fact. Afterwards comes a general discussion
and the expression by able men of extreme views on
every subject, successfully designed to create irritation
and "come-backs."

Then we walk through the darkness to our sleeping
quarters and see a wonderful sight. At night in this high
altitude the stars blaze with a light which dwellers on
the plains can never enjoy. Nor, again, can they ever see
a new moon and a golden planet slowly swing up from
behind the black background of a great mountain which
intensifies their brilliancy. Such a vision before us closes
the day.

Schopenhauer once said of a man who rises in the
world that if he is of the right kind his sensations are
those of one ascending in a balloon. "He does not feel
that he is rising, but that the earth is sinking away."
Something like this is true of a mountain climber.

Evanston, Illinois, August 25, 1928.

The last two of the four days we spent at the Rayado
Lodge are memorable to me chiefly for two things. The
first is that I caught a rainbow trout measuring sixteen
and seven eighths inches — one eighth of an inch longer
than the best one at Wagon Wheel Gap. I rode horseback many miles and sloshed around considerably in

swift water and on slippery rocks in pursuit of this trout and his lesser fellows. He was caught in a small pool about halfway down the falls of the Agua Fria Creek. The other was the fact that on the last day I "walked the canyon" of the Rayado. The canyon is about ten miles long, but the first half-mile and the last three miles we negotiated on horseback using two sets of horses. Mr. Phillips' son Eliot, my son Dana, and Mr. Phillips' nephew Lee walked the whole ten miles. The rest of the party, Mr. Phillips, Ben Ames Williams, John McCutcheon, Charles Francis Coe, the guides and myself walked about six and one half miles. This statement conveys but a weak impression of the performance, which involved scrambling, crawling and wading under the term "walking." The trip consumed about eight hours, including a stop for lunch of fried trout, bacon, coffee, bread and butter, consumed on the banks of the rushing mountain stream.

At the end of the canyon trail automobiles were waiting and they carried a tired party fifteen miles farther, to the starting point of four days before — Mr. Phillips' ranch house at Cimarron. After dinner we motored fifty miles to Raton, where we took the *Navajo* on the Atchison Railroad for Chicago, arriving this morning. A fine trip.

(Written of our visit to Cimarron, by Ben Ames Williams)

Past the corner of the freight house at Raton, across the railroad tracks, lay a swimming sea of lovely color, a sweep of tawny prairie and a mesa turquoise-blue. But this way lay the mountains, so

none gave the prairie any least regard. Men will lift up their eyes
unto the hills.

From the siding at Cimarron, remotely ridged with flat-roofed
'dobe houses from whose doorways dark-skinned children peered,
a road flung like a ribbon across the prairie grown uneasy here,
brought us to the ranch house whose contours suggested those of
an ancient mission, as though it had been built devoutly at the
feet of the mountains brooding there, waiting there, inviting there.

Horseback we ascended. The sure beasts tirelessly footed the
long slants and switchbacks of the climb. Once from a jetting
shoulder we saw the prairies deep behind us. A still pool of gold
and opal and blue, they seemed to scale upward to a horizon in-
credibly remote yet still at the very level of our eyes. Then the
trail dipped breakneck to the green Bonito, scaled to a dizzy
height once more, and swooped like a stooping hawk to where the
pearly Agua Fria meets the clear Rayado to tint its waters too.

Yet the heights were still above us. Another day, striving toward
them, we threaded a forest that never knew steel and burst at last
into a pasture pressed against the sky, mile upon mile of it, and
toward its end a herd milling in open round-up while the calves
bawled fearfully even before they felt the fire. We stopped a little
for that business, then up once more, straddling a wooded scarp,
dipping and ascending again into an English countryside of spread-
ing lawns cut by jutting tongues of aspen. The pale boles of the
trees diffused dull gold. The eye could run for a mile or more among
these verdant lawns. They were, said Gene, the pastures where wild
horses dwell.

A fit place, too. Here one might dwell in a friendly equality
with the nearer summits. Here a wild thing might find its solitude.
Across the pleasant lawns our horses plodded, while we peered
through the aspens as new reaches of the pastures opened to our
eyes.

They broke abruptly from a covert at one side. Six mares, bay
or black, raced at full gallop toward the rim rock down which no
less venturesome foot could pursue. Behind, urging them, drove
the great black stallion. Once they were safe away, he checked and

stood, holding us in swift survey. The sun struck him. His mane was like the break of an inky cataract; his tail seemed fit to brush the ground, and his black coat caught and flung toward us the red caress of the sun. He stood thus for an instant memorable, then his hoofs flung sod and he was gone.

Our trail from that spot led downward, toward where the more prosaic prairies lay. There was no more finely thrilling height to climb.

CHAPTER VIII

A DELEGATION of thirteen Japanese students on an excursion trip in this country called at the house to pay their respects this morning. Most of them could speak English and were a very intelligent and fine-looking lot of young men. I showed them a piece of Mayan pottery, dug up from under eight feet of ground in Coclé province, Panama, on which in clay was perched as an ornament one of the Japanese symbolical monkeys with his hands over his eyes. Everyone knows the three Japanese monkeys "Hear No Evil — See No Evil — Speak No Evil", one monkey with his hands over his ears, one with them over his eyes, and one with them over his mouth. When I was at Panama last year President Chiari, knowing of my interest in Central American archæology, presented me with thirty duplicate pieces of pottery from their national collection, of which this piece was one. At the Panama museum all three of the monkeys were frequently represented on the prehistoric pottery. When in Panama I was constantly looking for evidences of a prehistoric European and African connection with the old Central American civilization, and did find in the museum the model of a rather doubtful elephant of which I had a photograph taken. But I was surprised at the more direct evidence of an Asiatic connection afforded by these figures of the three monkeys. Upon my reaching home and employing the Japanese repairer of pottery from the Field Museum to mend one or two pieces of Panama pottery broken in transit, he told me that the symbol of the monkeys originated in China, not Japan. This reminded me that I had been shown at Panama photographs of a Mayan clay image wearing a Chinese conical cap, and another which resembled a Chinese dragon. These latter may have been accidental resemblances, but to me the fact that these Chinese symbolical monkeys — all three — are found in considerable numbers on prehistoric Central American pottery is very good evidence of an Asiatic origin, or at least communication. I have never seen any reference to these symbols in any writings on the old Central American civilization.

Manitoulin Island, Ontario, September 3, 1928.

Mrs. Dawes, the children, my brother Rufus and his wife and son Palmer and myself are here visiting my brother Beman, whose camp is located on Lake Manitou. It is a beautiful place. The fishing is good. We are catching small mouthed bass and pike in reasonable numbers.

My visit recalls our last summer's stay here and our experiences on the way. We stopped at Buffalo, New York, for the dedication of the Peace Bridge. The British and Canadian Governments were represented by the Prince of Wales, Premier Baldwin and Mackenzie King, Premier of Canada, and our Government by Secretary Kellogg, Governor Smith of New York and myself. The ceremony took place on the center of the

OPENING OF THE INTERNATIONAL PEACE BRIDGE
AT BUFFALO, N. Y.

*Vice President Dawes on the American Side of the Bridge greeting the
Prince of Wales on the Canadian Side. At extreme left of the picture
is Mrs. Dawes, who is soon to cut the ribbon, thus opening
the bridge to traffic.*

bridge where the two official groups met. The Prince and I shook hands and exchanged informal greetings over a ribbon stretched across the bridge; Mrs. Dawes then cut the ribbon with a pair of gilt scissors. Both parties next rode to a platform on the American side, where an audience estimated at seventy-five thousand was gathered. When the Prince and I stepped from our car I insisted that he precede me to the platform, as that appealed to me as the proper courtesy to show our guest. When he and I went through formal affairs later in the afternoon, on the Canadian side he insisted that I precede him. I mention this merely because some American papers criticized at length this proceeding on the American side as indicating that our Government was improperly taking a back seat because I did not step ahead. Washington indulges in much discussion of questions of personal precedence, and to such a degree is offense sometimes taken if the precedents are not followed that the State Department undertakes to give advice in the matter, especially in connection with official dinners and other official occasions. I suppose this saves a lot of petty and undignified quarreling. But I do not think the American people care a "whoop" about these things.

The principal addresses were made by the Prince of Wales, Premier Baldwin, Premier King, Secretary Kellogg, Governor Smith and myself. In my address, as the Geneva Naval Disarmament Conference had just ended in a failure to agree, and this was a peace celebration, I commented upon the result.

The speech was referred to by some of the newspaper

correspondents as "undiplomatic"; but it was not so. Common sense is never undiplomatic. Premier Baldwin asked me to sign my reading copy as a souvenir for him, and the Canadian Minister told me afterward that his government had indicated its agreement with its conclusions. The editorial comments on both sides of the boundary line were commendatory, and I think it expressed the common sentiments of the English-speaking peoples. The important portion of the address was, in part, as follows: —

There should not be discouragement at the slow progress of the naval discussions and the adjournment of the Geneva Conference without a solution. That meeting was but an incident in the steady onward march of the principle agreed upon by the great naval powers at the Washington Conference, in accordance with which two great English-speaking peoples pledged themselves to equality in naval strength. It was not a mistake to call the Conference. It has demonstrated again the desire of the peoples represented to eliminate competitive war preparation, and again has revealed and emphasized the common acceptance of the fundamental basis of the Washington Conference.

It has served to educate all of the peoples as to some of the details of the special necessities of each nation, and gives public opinion the opportunity to bear upon those comparatively minor details which are still the subject of debate.

Perhaps before this Conference was held there was not the preliminary careful appraisement by each conferee of the necessities of the other — perhaps the exclusive concentration by each conferee upon the necessities of his own nation resulted in predetermined ultimatums before a comparison of views — perhaps the public announcement of respective programs early in the Conference produced fears of domestic public repercussion if they were reasonably modified, as would be necessary to effect an agreement.

Experts may be slow in performing their difficult duty of interpreting in terms of respective ship programs the principle of equality between the English-speaking nations, but it is unthinkable that Great Britain and the United States, solemnly pledged to the principle of equality, will again place upon their peoples the burden of competitive naval building because temporarily their experts disagree in their practical interpretation of that principle.

If in their respective programs under the principle of equality the United States requires heavy cruisers which Great Britain does not need, and Great Britain requires light cruisers which the United States does not need, there is no excuse for inaugurating a competition under which ships will be built which neither of them need.

The Conference will only result in the stronger demand of the world that the work of interpreting the principle of equality in respective ship programs be continued until a fair agreement is reached.

The British party having learned that we were on our way to Manitoulin Island, invited our party to accompany them as far as Toronto on their boat. This required a motor trip of thirty miles on the Canadian side to the point of embarkation. The Prince, his aide, General Trotter, and I went in the first car and Prince George and Mrs. Dawes in the second. The speed with which we traveled in an open car was disturbing, especially since its occupants did not belong to anti-smoking organizations. If the correspondents could have heard His Royal Highness's comments upon this occasion, they might be justified in pronouncing them emphatic in form but extremely appropriate to the situation.

The fact of the matter is that the Prince is a royal "good fellow", and his unassuming and natural demeanor in the midst of the crowds through which we drove and walked — his ability, tact and kindliness as exemplified in his conversation and actions — explained to me the great hold he has upon the affections of the British people. Wherever he is, he would be the same. And I recall now, with an understanding impossible before meeting him, a touching story of his visit after the war to a British hospital for the severely wounded. A few of those were so terribly disfigured that, in their own desire and to save others the pain which would be caused by the sight of their awful state, — without eyes or nose or mouth, — they were kept in comparative seclusion. The Prince was taken to them. Without words, deeply moved, he paused for a minute and then walked to the cot of the one most disfigured and kissed him. How pitifully weak in comparison words would have been to express as he did then what every British heart felt, not only for those who had endured death, but for those living who were enduring worse than death, that Britain might live.

On the trolley ride which was a feature of our trip to the boat, I had an hour's talk with Stanley Baldwin. I spoke of the great contribution to the Experts' Plan made by the British members — Sir Josiah Stamp and Sir Robert Kindersley — who were selected by him but appointed by Ramsay McDonald, who temporarily succeeded him. He joined in the commendation. He discussed at length the great English strike, and gave an interesting account of how, at the most critical time, he was approached by certain political leaders who pleaded with him, "for God's sake, and for the sake of the country", to yield in his stand. He answered that they were the ones who should yield "for their country's sake." But Baldwin did not yield, and as a result Britain contributed to the world a demonstration of this truth: that a general strike is revolution, and must be dealt with by government as such.

In his preliminary, patient, generous, and conciliatory quest for a peaceful settlement, Baldwin braved the bitter criticism and hostility of the conservatives, and in his final and unyielding stand for the nation's rights, that of the radicals. But of such stuff and such alone are statesmen made.

I have found the task of presiding over the United States Senate for the last three years, while frequently most interesting and exacting, at times rather irksome. This is natural, for most of my life has been spent in executive and administrative positions with specific objectives and well-defined authority and responsibilities. In such positions one becomes accustomed to condensed and clear statements of facts accompanied by arguments based upon them which appeal to reason and common sense rather than to prejudice or emotion. There are many able Senators of business and legal training whose addresses are a delight. Their public life is devoted to constructive service exacting in its demand for hard work and as a rule useful in proportion to it. Conscientious and considerate, with minds bent upon creating conviction upon debatable propositions and projects of immense public importance, they command a respect and influence when speaking greatly disproportionate to the size of their senatorial audience. Indeed the surface indication of a useful speech is often a vacant Senate floor. Some constructive Senators, like Wadsworth and Reed of Pennsylvania, who always speak with thorough preparation on any important subject, are such finished, persuasive and inviting advocates that they can under almost any circumstance hold the attention of the Senate on nonpolitical measures of an economic nature.

It is discouraging to contemplate the abuse of the powers given by the rules in efforts to embarrass an earnest, industrious and able Senator like Warren, who has charge of the presentation of great appropriation bills covering hundreds of millions of dollars in their items. The business of the United States Government is the largest in the world, involving the collection and disbursement annually of about four billion dollars. Since appropriation and revenue bills provide for the vital machinery of government without which it cannot sustain itself, they rank first in their right to the time and attention of the Senate except occasionally when some great national emergency exists. To be considered intelligently they should be considered continuously, unless the necessity for time for further investigation is demonstrated by the discussion, and the postponement of consideration will add to its eventual value. All other great parliamentary bodies control their time, allotting it to subjects in accord with their relative importance to their respective countries. When the great fiscal bills of a Government or any other important measures are under consideration no speaker should be allowed to project himself impudently athwart the purpose of the parliamentary body as a whole and delay its legitimate and necessary work by a speech unlimited in length and totally irrelevant to the subject under consideration. The rights of the body should rank first. They should not be surrendered to gratify either the vanity, the malice or the selfish personal or political purpose of any individual. But they are so surrendered in the Senate.

I suppose there is no Senator in the Chamber who involuntarily has listened to more bombastic and demagogical speeches in waste of the Senate's time than Senator Francis E. Warren, its oldest member and Chairman of the Appropriations Committee. In charge of an appropriation bill whose items he is patiently explaining to the Senate, he cannot flee the chamber when one of the chronic time-wasters addresses the Chair and starts to rant. He must sit it through. If he protests at a waste of time which, especially precious in the short session, means nothing else than one of two things — the failure of the bill and an extra session, or the passage of the bill without proper consideration or explanation — he is treated with scant courtesy and sometimes with truculence and poorly concealed contempt. He has dared to assume that the necessary business of government is more important than Senator So-and-So's irrelevant political diatribe. Horrible! So, being duly rebuked, he sinks back in his chair until the Senate is freed again for business, sometimes from sheer weariness of the speaker, but more often because to continue longer would endanger the publication of the speech in the morning paper.

Senator Warren is one of a group of Senators whose laborious and important work, because it is constructive and useful instead of spectacular, attracts little public attention. Senator Smoot, chairman of the Finance Committee, has won his high position in the Senate and in the country by sheer ability and indefatigable industry. The value to the public of such men cannot be overestimated, but is not generally appreciated as it should be. It is they and their like who perform most of the difficult, disagreeable and necessary work, speaking only when they have something to say and accomplish. They are so accustomed to criticism that it generally fails to arouse any response from them. Standing between public measures and those who would modify them for personal or political motives, they are abused as if they were malefactors and were not actuated by one guiding purpose — the public interest.

These constructive men are not confined to one party. They are the seasoned statesmen and veteran workmen of the body. Some of them are brilliant speakers and have achieved great reputations, but all are indefatigable workers. Some of them speak rarely but always with commanding influence. Senator Glass is one of the foremost of these veterans — honored in the Senate and in the nation. A brilliant debater, he never rises to his feet for an extended address without knowing his facts and his subject. It was his aggressive courage and incessant attention which saved the bill giving indeterminate charters to the Federal Reserve Banks, in my judgment the most important single measure to the business of the country passed in the last decade. His colleague Senator Swanson is also conspicuous in this class. The two give the old State of Virginia a representation and influence in the Senate of which it may well be proud. Swanson is a man of great mental strength and culture, and his speeches are profound and constructive. Such brilliant efforts are no accident. Behind them is unceasing work.

These men belong to what may be called the "working class" in the Senate. In using this term I mean constructive work as distinguished from work with a destructive purpose. The latter, at times, is as necessary to the public good as the former, and quite as exacting. Again, at times every constructive worker has to become destructive. Underbrush often has to be burned away before a house is built. But there are certain men who so like to wield the torch that, while occasionally and usefully burning away underbrush, they are not content until they burn some houses as well. These natural house-burners are represented in the Senate. At times, with great public benefit and acclaim, they will burn a rotten structure. If they would be content with this, as Charles E. Hughes was when he conducted the insurance investigation, all would go well with them in public life. But unfortunately for their highest ambitions they always, in their career, try to set ablaze too many good structures, and a common-sense public never makes a hero out of one whom they come to consider a pyromaniac.

CHAPTER IX

Mayfair Hotel, New York City, September 13, 1928.

My family and I arrived at Chicago last Monday morning after a most delightful visit at Phelps, Wisconsin, with our friends Dr. and Mrs. Frankenthal. The Doctor is a lover of nature and for twenty years has found health and enjoyment among the lakes and woods of Northern Wisconsin. It has been here that he has kept constantly renewed the wonderful vitality which enables him to perform his great and humane work as a surgeon with a skill and wisdom which have made him eminent. I feel that if it were not for his genius our little family circle would not now be as it is and we hold him and his noble wife in affection and deep gratitude.

After two days at the bank I received a letter from my friend General James G. Harbord urging me to keep a promise to visit him, and on the spur of the moment I got ready and took the Century, Wednesday, for New York. The General and my friend Charles Francis Coe met me at the depot.

I have spent a rather hectic day which is not yet finished as the General and I are going this evening to a meeting of the organization of the Radio Corporation of America, of which he is president, to see the first public demonstration of some new wonder in the science of radio transmission. Just what it is I do not know and am sure I shall never understand.

The last time I was here Mr. Sarnoff, vice president of the Radio Corporation, undertook to explain to me the new method of photographing the voice in the production of talking movies. After he was through, and I was left more mystified than ever, I repeated to him a saying of Balfour. The latter, after discussing an abstruse problem in metaphysics, gave Kant's explanation of it and then observed: "It may be remarked here that with the generality of people they much prefer the existence of a problem which they cannot explain, to an explanation of it which they cannot understand."

I first went downtown with Harbord to see some of my old friends in the business section. Had a visit with Tom Lamont and met at his office, for only a few minutes, Zimmerman — who represented the League of Nations in the financial rehabilitation of Austria — a man whose fine work and ability I have much admired. He told me that he had called to see me at Chicago during my absence, and so my last trip was at the expense of what would have been an interesting interview. I went to see my old acquaintances at the Central Union Trust Company, where in the old days my friend James N. Wallace presided.

Everybody, including George Davison the president and Vallely the bank policeman, seemed glad to see me and I felt as if I were a business man again.

New York, September 14, 1928.

My friend Owen D. Young called for me at Harbord's apartments in the morning, which we spent in visiting with each other and making a few calls together on mutual friends downtown. I am deeply attached to him. We talked over the functioning of the Experts' Plan. As it enters successfully its fifth and standard year, we have the right to a certain satisfaction in the comparative collapse of the pessimistic prophesies of the political economists. The latter, in its early years, were most of them apostles of gloom and quite persuasive ones at that. But the years have demonstrated that they were wrong. They failed to forecast the flow of credit to Germany following the rehabilitation of its currency system and the balancing of its budget, which established world confidence in the stability of its economy.

The resulting transfer of credits to Germany has furnished the necessary foreign exchange to cover easily such reparations payments as were not made by deliveries in kind.

The Experts' Plan is playing its part properly. It has demonstrated that Germany can pay and that Germany has the will to pay. But the moral obligation rests upon the Allied Governments to fix a reasonable and definite sum total of reparations. Its fulfillment becomes more important every day.

New York, September 17, 1928.

My vacation spent among the quiet woods and waters of the West emphasizes by contrast the noises, contacts and complexities of this great metropolitan whirlpool. And yet, it has made me feel younger.

For seven of the last eleven years I have been away from Chicago — in the war, in the federal budget work, in reparations work, in the last campaign, and then in my present office. Many of my close friends there have died. I have lost close contact with the oncoming business generation of Chicago individually. Many more people than before may know me, but there are fewer and fewer people whom I feel I know. It is the old friends to whom one clings, and their deaths create something of a feeling of loneliness in the old surroundings. But here on this visit every minute has been spent with old friends in ceaseless activity. There are so many of them left that I have not yet seen them all. My contacts with them, extending in some cases over twenty years, may have been occasional; but they have been continuous.

My luncheon to-day with Henry L. Stoddard, George B. Cortelyou, Gus Hanna and Senator George Moses brought a delightful recalling of the past and an interesting discussion of the present and future. The other night, with a lot of the old friends, — among them Dr. Ward A. Holden, my classmate at Marietta College, Class of 1884, — I went to the Capitol Theater to see Coe's new picture.

I thought of the changes in our lives in the forty-four years during which I have seen Holden only twice. He is one of New York's successful medical specialists, and I a public official. We used to go together to, and occupy the cheapest seats at, the infrequent plays in the old Marietta City Hall nearly a half-century ago.

Here in New York, Mr. Rothafel at the Capitol Theater not only gave us our seats for nothing, but a fine luncheon after the performance as well.

Perhaps the reason I have enjoyed this visit to New York so much is because I came here with no specific objective except to visit Harbord. Specific objectives in life interfere with perspectives.

I have really looked at things this time. I have really visited my friends with no uncompleted undertakings — as in the old business days — gnawing at my subconscious mental vitals. The magnificent sky lines of New York and the beauty of its countrysides — its curious comminglings of nationalities on its streets — its grand and its sordid sides — these I have seen a hundred times, and yet have never really seen them as now.

I begin to understand how much that concentration of mind upon definite ends, which is so necessary to success in new undertakings, interferes with a proper appreciation of one's surroundings. And much of my life has been a series of new undertakings. Made my first trip yesterday to Staten Island, where for some years we have owned the gas company. Ordinarily my thoughts would have been only on its business and its fine prospects. But I came away with other reflections, for I had visited the house where at a ripe and rotten old age Aaron Burr, a Vice President of the United States, ended his disillusioned days in poverty and loneliness. What a tragedy of suffering his life had been.

Over in Trinity Churchyard the day before I had seen on the grave of Alexander Hamilton a fresh wreath of flowers, which seemed symbolical of the continued national appreciation with which his memory is adorned,

while that of Burr who killed him in his prime is ex-
ecrated and his grave forgotten.

Evanston, September 20, 1928.

Arrived home yesterday from New York. My visit,
as has been the case with every visit I have made there
since 1898, was rendered more pleasant by the constant
company of Charles Augustus Hanna, who has been
my faithful friend since 1887 — the year I settled at
Lincoln. Such friends as he make life worth the living.
In his modesty he seeks always to hide his light under
a bushel. His literary work, done in the leisure hours of
his work as chief examiner for the New York Clearing
House, has won him distinction among students of
American history. His book "The Scotch-Irish in Scot-
land, North Ireland and America" is standard authority
here and in Britain. His dedication of it I have always
remembered: "To the forgotten dead of that indom-
itable race whose pioneers in an unbroken chain from
Champlain to Florida formed the advance guard of
civilization in its progress to the Mississippi and first
conquered, subdued, and planted the wilderness between."

Evanston, September 23, 1928.

On my trip to New York I read a current biography
written by one of the new school of historians who endeavor to make "best sellers" by emphasizing at length
and in detail the scandalous episodes in the lives of ancient leaders, merely using their real accomplishments
as a background for them. This afternoon at the house,

while I was rereading Plutarch's "Lives" and Cæsar's "Gallic Wars" to check up on some of the statements in this book, my friend General Enoch Crowder called, bringing with him General Richardson, formerly Commander of the Thirty-ninth Division. The conversation drifted naturally to the subject of qualifications for military leadership. I called attention to one unusual qualification which the Greek and Roman generals were supposed to possess — that of public speaking, the ability to inspire their troops to victory by an address to them when drawn up in line of battle just before an engagement and in sight of the enemy similarly deployed. The addresses they are supposed to have made, though repeated by ancient historians in detail, must be regarded chiefly as what the historian thinks the speakers would have said in the circumstances. Yet to recall the terrible environment in which these addresses were made renders even these historical essays dramatic. In ancient warfare the hostile armies drawn up in battle array often were separated from each other only by the distance an arrow could be shot. The combat was to be chiefly hand-to-hand with the broadsword. Every soldier knew what that meant, and he visualized the coming battle in a manner impossible in modern warfare.

A general steps before his army to commence his exhortation. Every soldier knows that at its completion the order will be given for him to advance — to slaughter or be slaughtered with no quarter given — in a fight with men at whom he is looking. No circumstances can be imagined involving a greater strain upon either a speaker or his hearers. And yet the fact that these addresses were so generally made indicates their effectiveness.

Of all great generals of ancient times I imagine Julius Cæsar best rose to the tragic psychology of such an occasion.

As an orator at Rome he was considered as second to Cicero alone, but Cicero could never have equaled Cæsar at Vesontio. Here it suddenly developed that Ariovistus with a great German army was marching against him, who was commanding only four Roman legions of about fifty-four hundred men each. The statements of the Gauls about the strength of the advancing Germans and their invincibility spread a terrible panic among the Roman officers and all ranks of their little army. Cæsar called a council of war. In the concise and measured account of what he said, given by him in his "Commentaries", he writes as a historian; but no reader of it can fail to sense either its import or effect when he remembers Cæsar's tremendous personality.

Furious at the widespread exhibition of fear and cowardice among both officers and soldiers, he upbraids them in scathing terms — then reasons — then, abruptly, says: "I intend to attack at once, breaking camp at the fourth watch of this next night. I want to know whether honor and duty or cowardice is first in your minds. Run away if you will but I — I and the Tenth Legion, we stay."

And they all stayed.

CHAPTER X

Evanston, Illinois, September 24, 1928.

THE Republican National Committee telephoned asking that I make the first speech Saturday night over the large chain broadcasting which they are inaugurating for the last weeks of the campaign.

I told them that I was working on a speech but was afraid I could not finish it properly by that time and in addition, since I was trying to condense it into a very short common sense proposition, I thought the nearer to the end of the campaign I made it the better it would sound. They evidently communicated with Washington about it, for Mr. Hoover's secretary, telephoning for him, said that it was not necessary to hurry it for Saturday but he hoped I would make two addresses. This I will be glad to do unless they agree with me that one will receive the most attention and have more weight. Took lunch with Roberts and Joslin, Washington correspondents respectively of the *Kansas City Star* and *Boston Evening Transcript,* and my brothers Beman and Henry, and had an enjoyable time.

Roberts and Joslin discussed the bitterness of some of the disappointed candidates for the presidency in both parties with whom they had talked. It was a mournful recital. Nobody is especially diverted by the exhibition of a sore toe. It is neither interesting nor pleasurable to others, and only adds to the ache of the possessor. I wish I could quote Emerson exactly; somewhere he speaks of the lack of acute sorrow even on the part of his friends when a prominent man falls from the pedestal. It is wise for public men to remember this in disappointment and avoid the sacrifice of dignity in a hopeless quest for sympathy.

Evanston, September 30, 1928.

Have finished my campaign address for the radio. It comprises only about 1175 words. The preparation of an address of this length requires more thought and work than one many times longer. My idea is that my address should be delivered late in the campaign, for then is when the confusion of opposing political addresses is at its worst and a short speech is most effective if it appeals to common sense and does not try to cover too many things. In my speaking during the 1924 campaign I hammered constantly at one or two main considerations, not a large number. The average man listening at a radio, if he is not interested in an address, is not under the embarrassment of having to rise in his seat and leave the hall. By turning a little radio knob he can be free. In addition, as an inducement to turn it, he can have his choice of several other speakers, to say nothing of musical programs. Common sense indicates that a political address over the radio to be most effective should be brief and to the point.

The radio waves do not seem to transmit personal magnetism. One evidence of this is the fact that a crowd listening to a speech through a "loud speaker" outside the hall never applauds. While a speaker of eloquence and personal magnetism can arouse the emotions of a crowd in his presence by an appeal direct to the emotions, this apparently cannot be done successfully over the radio. The mental operations of the radio listener incited by the speech may arouse his emotions; but with a crowd, in the presence of a magnetic orator, their emotions dominate their minds and generally completely subjugate them. This latter never happens to a radio audience. The radio therefore assists the reasoning speaker and handicaps the demagogue.[1]

I hope and expect that it will eventually change the present methods of political oratory by demonstrating the greater effectiveness of reason as compared with bunkum, however eloquently delivered.

Evanston, October 4, 1928.

Have been called on frequently by those active in the campaign during the last week. Governor McMullin called on his way to confer with Secretary Hoover and again on his return. To-day I have a telegram from Congressman Tilson, Chairman of the Speakers Bureau of the Republican National Committee, saying that I was wanted for one of the large closing meetings of the campaign at New York City. Answered that I believed my short radio speech would be most effective in its present form over the radio alone, but that I would expand it extemporaneously before the New York meeting, if desired. I have prepared what I believe is an

[1] The evolution in radio oratory of the last few years has somewhat changed my views on this subject. — C. G. D.

effective kind of speech for the radio, and I have been confirmed in that belief by listening over the radio to many of the long speeches of this campaign. To compromise and alter the method of address in order to satisfy a visible audience of a few thousand, when it involves a lessening of effectiveness upon an invisible audience of millions, seems absurd. On Tuesday evening, at the home of my friend Albert Lasker, I had a visit with my probable successor as Vice President — Senator Charles Curtis. He seemed pretty well tired out. He had his hand in a sling and not much of a voice left. Took him out to inspect the Vice President's automobile and to introduce the Government chauffeur, whom I hope he will retain. Last night I listened to him over the radio and was surprised at his vigor and good voice after so short a rest.

He referred in his speech to the vice-presidency as amounting to nothing, which indicated modesty and was said jestingly. But when I find him tired, with a husky voice and bandaged arm, resting after a five thousand-mile trip and preparing to start on ten thousand miles more, I am inclined to think that he places quite a high value on the office.

I think that he will be more careful of his strength hereafter. He is so good-natured and kindly that he yields to the insistent demands for a speech at every train stop and converses between stations with the local politicians who board the train. I found this latter in my campaign of 1924 more wearing than the speaking, and finally made it a rule on a day requiring frequent speeches from the rear platform of the train to stay in my stateroom between stations, leaving a request not to disturb me.

This led to one of the miraculous happenings in the life of my wife. One of the most modest, retiring and quiet of women, she made a rear-end platform speech in my place. We were going on our special train from Chicago to St. Louis, where I was to address one of the large meetings always to be expected in a metropolis. I had made speeches at the four or five towns where the train was stopped for that purpose. We were only a short way from St. Louis when the train stopped to take water. A large crowd was present and demanding a speech. It seems that a local committeeman on the train, learning of the proposed stop, had wired ahead without authority and announced a speech by me.

The committeeman and some others started down the corridor to awaken me in my stateroom when they met my wife on guard and adamant. Like Leonidas at Thermopylae and the boy on the burning deck, she was there to stay.

The scene, I was told, was far from peaceful, for it was the neighborhood where the committeeman lived and he confronted the hard alternative of pacifying either my wife or the neighbors he had called together. The argument became so heated between those who upheld Mrs. Dawes and those who sided with the committeeman that my wife suddenly announced that she would speak to the crowd, and — mirabile dictu — so she did. And this is what I was told she said: —

"My husband has made five speeches to-day and is

going to make one to-night. I won't let them wake him
up to come out. He didn't know the train was to stop
here. Now, you ladies here, you understand, don't you?
You wouldn't do it either, would you?"

"No," they cried with one voice.

The men laughed, and the trouble was over. I knew
nothing of the occurrence until that evening.

Mrs. Dawes, my nephew Henry, and I went into Chicago this evening to the Rufus Dawes Hotel for men
and the Mary Dawes Hotel for women. I never visit
these hotels without happiness. In the fifteen years that
the Rufus Dawes Hotel has been in operation over
1,800,000 guests have been accommodated. Both hotels
are run with closest economy and everything goes to
the guests at cost — that is, the hotels are run so as
to be self-sustaining, not including of course any return
upon the investment save the great one of service rendered.

The menu at the Rufus Dawes Hotel I noted when
there was as follows: Stew ten cents, hash ten, baked
beans ten, sandwich five, soup five, oatmeal five, coffee
and rolls five. We charge twelve cents for a bath, nightgown and bed. For the single rooms to which one floor
is devoted we charge eight cents extra.

No other hotel in the city provides a bed for less than
twenty-five cents.

The I.W.W. lodging near us charges ten cents for
sleeping on the floor. Everything has gone up in cost
since we started. Then we could come out about even
on a five-cent charge for a bath, nightgown and bed.

The hotel is running light at present with about four hundred guests each night.

We found every one of the two hundred and sixty-six rooms of the Mary Dawes Hotel for women occupied, as is usually the case.

The menu in the cafeteria of the women's hotel is more varied than at the men's hotel, but includes a special breakfast for seven cents consisting of oatmeal, coffee, bread and butter. The rooms in the women's hotel run from ten to thirty-five cents a night. I do not believe more is given for the money anywhere. Without return on the investment we run about even, because of outside custom at the cafeteria at lunch time when some dishes like roast beef run as high as thirty cents. While the hotel was originally intended for working girls there are quite a number of elderly women who make it a permanent home. This is because of the intervention of my dear mother for whom the hotel was named and who was present the night it was opened about twelve years ago. Surrounded by the guests, Mother sat in the fine parlor of the hotel like a queen on her throne. Among them were several old ladies who had been told by the manager that permanent lodgings could not be engaged by them since the hotel was designed to accommodate only employed young women. These old ladies pleaded their cases before Mother, and she with tears in her eyes interceded for them with me. Of course this settled it on the spot. But Mother did not stop there. Up to the time of her death she was in correspondence with some of them. As a result, for years at her request I was engaged off and on in succoring the lame, halt and blind of their relatives, generally wayward children, concerning whom they wrote her imploring her assistance.

As we stepped out of the hotel to-night a well-dressed young man was waiting for us. "I am Joe," he said, and then all that first evening came back to me in recollection. "Little Joe" (he was then) was a young hoodlum born in the alley behind the hotel, and he was the leader of an active gang of young ruffians of about twelve years of age. On the opening night these ragamuffins gathered in force and so annoyed the crowds of guests and visitors coming in the front door of the hotel that an attendant started to telephone for the police. Fortunately, I heard him and, stopping him, decided on another course of action. I stepped out into the yelling crowd of youngsters and said I wanted them to come in and have supper with me. Joe, much embarrassed, accepted for all, and I entered the hotel with the lot. Their procession created something of a sensation. Treated like gentlemen, they acted like gentlemen. Without a murmur they submitted themselves to Mrs. Dawes and Miss Decker, who scrubbed their faces and hands for them before they sat down to a table with Mother at one end and myself at the other. They were rather subdued, but my! how they ate — and especially the ice cream. One of the little fellows told me his father had just come home, and when I asked where he had been he said "In jail." This was Joe, and Joe told me then that the boys would "always be nice to the hotel", and he would do any work he could for it any time, "fur nuthin." And so all these years the boys have been "nice to the hotel", and the manager told me that Joe has called constantly ever since that time to ask where he could help. For some time I kept track of him, but had not seen him for years before to-night. He is now a chauffeur — honest, well-behaved and successful. Why don't we realize more the enormous returns which come from little kindnesses? And these returns come oftenest when we need them most — when the sun is setting and the day's work is almost done.

Since the hotels were opened, many instances have occurred of the most beautiful of all charities — that of the poor for the very poor, of the suffering for those who are perishing. On bitter cold winter nights the streets of every great city are a Gethsemane for many of the homeless and half-clad poor — some of them brought to their condition through no fault of their own, but all of them with a right to help if the religion of Christ means anything. On such nights the Rufus Dawes Hotel is filled to overflowing and then is when it does the most good.

Late one winter night when the thermometer stood at ten degrees below zero, and after the hotel had closed, John Hanson, the manager, heard a persistent knocking at the door. Opening it, he found a shivering and thinly clad man and beside him, sitting on a wheeled board which could be propelled by hand, was another man without any legs. The first man explained that his friend the cripple was sure to "go under" during the night unless he got shelter. He said he was all right himself and could stay out.

To pay for a lodging for the cripple he held in his hands two postage stamps, which was all he had, and

OPENING NIGHT OF RUFUS DAWES HOTEL IN 1914

asked John to take them in lieu of the regular charge of five cents. Of course they both were cared for, — that was what the hotel was for, — but if that had been its only service it earned its cost that single night.

That happened years ago. I don't think, in our present prosperous times, such an incident could occur unless through accident. We care for as many guests as ever — but their average condition is immeasurably better than when the hotel started.

I want here to record my gratitude to my brother Henry, who supervised the building of the two hotels here and the one at Boston and long gave them his watchful and able care. To John Hanson, manager of the Rufus Dawes Hotel, and to his sister Mrs. Haines, manager of the Mary Dawes Hotel, their success is also largely due. Both have been with the hotels from the start. John Hanson was a police officer in the West Madison Street district for twenty-five years before taking charge of the Rufus Dawes Hotel, and now has spent forty years in that locality. They all three have helped make the memorials to my dear son and our dear mother what they would have them.

But next to Henry, the one most responsible for the success of the hotels was John Taylor, now deceased, our first manager of these two and another like hotel at Boston a man of wonderful executive ability and inherent tact and kindliness.

Evanston, October 8, 1928.

Agreed with Republican National Committee to speak at Mecca Hall, New York City, the night of October 29, and over the radio alone at Chicago about October 22, which satisfied them. Received a letter from my friend, Major General Charles Jean Marie Payot, who now commands the Thirteenth Corps of the French army at Clermont-Ferrand, which distresses me. It is to the effect that his physical condition is such from diabetes he must ask for retirement. When I reached France in the War, Payot was Assistant Chief of Staff, Fourth Bureau, French Army, under Pétain, in charge of supplies and transportation for the army in the zone of the advance. I first met him at the meeting of the French Cabinet where he had been called as a military expert when, as representing General Pershing, I proposed a French commander for the rear of the entire Allied armies to be directly responsible to Foch. This of course was satisfactory to the French, but at the next meeting of the Cabinet, Payot also being present, with Clemenceau presiding and with the British Army and Government represented, things became acrimonious to say the least, and ended in entire disagreement. Here was where the friendship of Payot and myself started. It was further cemented later when — after the acceptance by the British and French Governments of my alternative proposal to put the control into a board, consisting of one officer from each army with power to issue orders to the General Staffs when in unanimous agreement — I proposed and brought about his selection as the Chairman of the Board. For the last four months of the war we sat as fellow members of the Military Board of Allied Supply. He was known as the most difficult officer in the French Army to get along with. General Gouraud once told me I was the only officer in either the French or American Army who did it, which was difficult for me to understand, for I loved Payot as a brother. His assistance to the American Army, largely stripped of supplies as a result of submarine warfare and the inability of the United States to get sufficient shipping, was simply invaluable. As Chief of Supply Procurement for the A.E.F., I can testify to this as no other man except perhaps General Moseley of our own G 4 General Staff.

His power was so great, his knowledge so comprehensive, his experience during four years of war so vast, that in matters of supply strategy, as General Harbord once said, the officers of the other Allied armies "sat at his feet."

Our friendship was famous among Allied officers, for he could speak no English and I no French, yet we never misunderstood each other. As Payot used to say, "We were two heads under one hat." During the early part of October 1918, when I was at Souilly in the Argonne, Colonel Morrow, Chief of Engineers of the First Army, was in desperate need of gravel to ballast the standard gauge railroad between Aubreville and Varennes, to which latter point the rails were laid. It was vital to get the ballast, for over this road we were to supply with munitions and rations three divisions then in action just beyond Varennes.

The Germans knew the vital need to us of the track and were shelling it.

General Pershing took the matter out of the hands of Pétain's liaison officer and put it in mine. Ten minutes afterward I had General Payot on the telephone at Provins, or rather his interpreter with Payot by his side. This is what I did *not* say: "General Payot, we must have gravel for ballast at Aubreville or we cannot get munitions or rations over the railroad to Varennes, which will be the rail-head for the supply of three divisions now engaged near Varennes. These divisions are already short of rations as are some of the French troops in this section whom we will help. Munitions are desperately needed and can only be brought up over this road. Please get this ballast for us."

The reason I did *not* say this was because General Payot had lived in a crisis of supply in the French Army for four solid years. This was no new situation to him. Had I said it in this way we probably would have got the gravel quickly — but I wanted it surely and immediately. Telephoning a sentence only, to be interpreted at one time, I said: "Tell General Payot I am in deep trouble." (Pause.) "When I have gone to him in trouble he has never failed me." (Pause.) "I come now in deep trouble to him, my dear friend, and I know he will not fail me." (Long pause.) Then I stated the situation, saying General Pershing had placed the matter in my hands, and made my request. The answer telephoned by the interpreter was: "General Payot is starting by automobile immediately for St. Dizier." In a few hours came from St. Dizier by telephone: "There will be eighty cars of gravel at Aubreville to-morrow morning." Within two days Payot had so much gravel on the road that Morrow had difficulty in handling it.

General Payot has visited me once in this country

GENERAL AND MADAME PAYOT ON THEIR LANDING IN THE
UNITED STATES

(Front row, left to right) *Major General R. L. Bullard, General Charles J. M. Payot, General Charles G. Dawes.* (Second Row, left to right) *General George VanHorn Moseley, Madame Payot, Captain Charles DeMarensches.*

since the war and I saw him frequently in 1924 when on reparations work. I am now looking forward to seeing him in France next spring, and shall go thither at the earliest possible moment.

Ambassador Houghton, now representing our nation at St. James's, talked with me by telephone from New York where he is now a candidate for the Senate. He will make a most useful member if elected. When he was our ambassador at Berlin his services to the First Committee of Experts during its stay of three weeks there were invaluable.

His judgment was mature and sound. His intimate acquaintance with leading German statesmen and industrialists and their confidence in him saved us much lost motion — for the Experts' Plan was a diplomatic as well as an economic task, though not generally so regarded. I well remember my last meeting with him at the White House where Mrs. Dawes and I were visiting in the fall of 1924. He had just arrived from Berlin, and President Coolidge invited Secretary Hughes and myself to a conference with him in the evening of a day when Owen Young and I, having talked the matter over with both the President and Hughes, thought the selection of a man to be the New Agent General for Reparations Payments was finally arranged and approved by all the powers provided he could be induced to accept. Young had left for New York.

But Houghton brought a report to the conference which changed our idea of the political aspects of things in Germany and their bearing upon the matter. So I had to take a midnight train to New York, where I persuaded Young to consent to his own nomination to the place. This he was reluctant to give, and finally did so only when I appealed to his sense of duty. He was the man whom we felt sure would be approved under the new circumstances by all the countries interested.

The place was first offered to another[2] as originally intended, but he was unwilling, after Houghton's exposition of the situation and for other reasons, to take it — although all the governments involved agreed to his selection.

So Young became the first Agent General for Reparations under the Experts' Plan, thus adding to his already great services to the cause of peace that of the installation of the machinery under which the Experts' Plan has successfully operated thus far.

While in this important work, he was assisted by my brother, Rufus C. Dawes, and Henry M. Robinson. After its completion he resigned and was succeeded by Parker Gilbert, of whose successful career the world knows.

Evanston, October 16, 1928.

Was much interested in a cable from London by John Steele in this morning's *Chicago Tribune* relative to Parker Gilbert's interview with Stanley Baldwin and Winston Churchill, Chancellor of the Exchequer, in regard to the final settlement of German reparations.

Steele says: "The plan agreed upon provides for the appointment of a new Dawes Commission, as discussed

[2] Dwight W. Morrow.

at the Six-Power Conference at Geneva during the League of Nations meeting. The discussions now concern the personnel of the commission.

"It has been pretty well agreed between the British and French that the leadership of the new commission will be left to the Americans. The American members named tentatively are Owen Young, R. C. Leffingwell and either Rufus Dawes of Chicago or Paul Warburg."

He says further, "There is a strong desire on the part of all the European statesmen that Charles G. Dawes act on the committee, but this is impossible while he is Vice President, and it is hoped that the whole affair will be cleared up before he vacates his office."

This dispatch is probably under Gilbert's authority, and indicates a degree of preliminary agreement among the powers most encouraging for an early settlement. An evidently inspired statement copied recently from French papers — mildly upholding the Ruhr occupation but referring to it as "no longer necessary as a military protection to France" — leads me to believe that Poincaré and Briand are paving the way with the French for an earlier settlement than I had before believed possible.

No better intermediary between the governments in the preliminaries could be found than Parker Gilbert. Besides possessing great ability and tact, he is unostentatious. His brilliant record as Agent General for the past four years is no accident. He has made for himself a secure place in history.

In his visit with us this year at Evanston, he was hopeful as to the prospect of a final settlement, which he had been urging in his report; but was far from certain that it could be accomplished at an early date.

It is difficult for one at a distance to discern a real trend of public sentiment in a foreign country. If public sentiment, however, was not generally favorable to settlement at this time, statesmen would not be arranging one which, to be effective, must be ratified by the Parliament in each of the countries receiving reparations payments and in Germany as well.

On train to New York, October 19, 1928.

Yesterday noon addressed the Society of Spanish War Veterans at lunch. Took along General Lord, the Director of the Budget, who spent most of the day with me.

In the evening, introduced him in a short speech, when he delivered one of his fine addresses at the annual banquet of the Illinois Chamber of Commerce at the Congress Hotel.

Lord is a remarkable man. I take pride in his success, for it was upon my initiative and insistence that President Harding appointed him as my successor as Director of the Bureau of the Budget. The fact that he was an officer of the regular army was urged against him at the time, since it was assumed that the Director of the Budget should be a business man. But after my association with the leading officers of the army for two years in France his officership was to me only an additional recommendation.

After my return from the war, General Lord, then Chief Finance officer of the army, came to Evanston to see me and to explain the new army reorganization bill then before Congress. The bill was intended to embody some of the lessons learned in the war. On this side of the water and in France during the war, army organization passed through a process of evolution. At the end of the war the A.E.F. found itself with a superimposed co-ordinating business control consisting of seventeen departments which centered in my office on the Administrative Staff of General Pershing. Among them was Finance, and General Lord, who had been Chief Finance officer in the War Department at Washington, and I found that, under practically similar conditions of confusion and emergency and without contact, we had evolved similar devices and methods.

Before the Military Affairs Committee of the United States Senate I afterward made an argument for the recognition in the army reorganization bill of some of the general principles which from experience we both have found to be indispensable to army effectiveness.

This all led to contact with General Lord during the year when I was establishing the budget system, when he gave most valuable co-operation and when I came to know his unusual qualifications as my successor. No one is fitted for the position of Director of the Budget who is not possessed of determination and courage along with other essential qualities. His most effective powers come only from the attitude toward him of the President, whose agent he is and in whose name he must speak and act. Six years of unwavering support and confidence from President Coolidge and his own indefatigable industry and brilliant administration have made General Lord a power in government for the public good.

CHAPTER XI

AFTER a walk in Central Park yesterday morning, I plunged into the maelstrom of politics. I had expected to make one speech in New York, but when I retired last night I had made four. The first was one at the Waldorf, where Charley Hilles was giving a lunch to the New York State and City Republican organizations in honor of Secretary Hoover. Besides Mr. Hoover, Senator Moses, Mr. Marshall and I spoke. After lunch, at breakneck speed, was taken to an overcrowded hall where I spoke to the Young Men's Republican Club. General Harbord, T. C. Desmond, Allan Hoover, and Floyd Clinch accompanied me. Then I was taken back to the Waldorf, where I introduced Mr. Hoover to the Service Men's League in a short speech. Finally at night, at a great indoor meeting at the new Madison Square Garden, I spoke with Mr. Hoover at the closing meeting of his campaign. It was an inspiring sight. The twenty-two thousand auditors held small American flags, which in their enthusiasm for Hoover they waved in unison, creating a blaze of color and a bedlam of cheering at the same time. Hoover's speech was a masterpiece. For sustained intellectuality his political speeches have seldom, if ever, been equaled.

I spoke first, and afterward an interesting incident occurred when I was handed, on the stage, a telegram from friends at Marietta, Ohio, "The Bests and the Buells", referring to my speech as heard at Marietta, Ohio, twenty minutes or so before.

This morning I spent downtown in New York and I met no one all that time who had not heard the speeches over the radio or in the audience. Bell boys, red caps, policemen, taxi drivers, bankers and business men, all had heard them and spoke of them. I never before adequately realized the tremendous audience among all classes that the radio creates. On the stage we sat for most of the time in the brilliant focus of several spotlights which were very trying to the eyes, and upon inquiry were informed that the "movietones" were at work.

All day long the party faced cameras, and for a day my experiences in the 1924 campaign were all repeated.

I am led here to say something of the motorcycle police escorts which I have made it a rule for the last four years to decline except when necessary to get through a crowd to keep a speaking engagement.

After several narrow escapes, due to the high speed which the escort generally insists on increasing when street travel and traffic is greatest, I proceeded on the theory that the motorcycles were escorting me — not I the motorcycles — and compelled my chauffeur always to slow down to a reasonable speed.

Of course the escort then regretfully slows down. To the ordinary citizen on the streets these escorts are not only dangerous but extremely annoying. At Los Angeles at one time, in running against traffic at high speed when we had nothing but leisure time on our hands, the sudden stopping by a siren signal of a long line of automobiles compelled one of them to turn out a foot or so in order to avoid a collision with the machine before it. One of our policemen on a motorcycle struck the turning motor, and afterwards spent three months in the hospital, being fortunate to escape with his life.

At Chicago General Pershing, whom I accompanied, was once taken on Michigan Avenue in busy traffic hours from the Railway Exchange Building to the Stockyards in about seven minutes, at the actual risk of his life. Of course a certain amount of motorcycle police escorting is unavoidable, but a large amount of the siren blowing and fast riding, with resulting disorganization of street and pedestrian movement, is useless as well as dangerous. It should be subject to more stringent regulation by city ordinance.

Evanston, October 28, 1928.

On Thursday morning, Field Marshal Viscount Allenby and his wife arrived at the house and were our guests until Friday afternoon when they left for Washington. More pleasant and agreeable visitors we have never had. Allenby is a man of mental culture and wide reading, combining with good judgment and clear thinking the decision and firmness of a great military leader.

On noon Thursday we attended a luncheon given in his honor jointly by the Council on Foreign Relations and the English Speaking Union.

The speeches made by Dr. Breasted, Rabbi Wise,

General Malone and others were brilliant and interesting, but each considerably exceeded his ten-minute
allotment. They did so well that nobody criticized, but
it was an illustration of the fact that no fluent extempore
orator can ever be depended upon to keep within a time
allotment. Allenby's response was interesting and impressive, but it was at the evening dinner of the Commercial Club at the Palmer House that he made his
greatest address — one which will always be remembered by his hearers. It was called forth by the illus-
trated lecture, with moving pictures of actual battle
scenes, of the Palestine Campaign given by Mr. Low-
man immediately preceding the Field Marshal's address. We were then privileged to hear the strategy and
history of the great campaign, discussed at length and
at times in detail by its Commander himself. That which
inevitably differentiates from any other the statements
of one responsible for any great collective movement
of men is its clearer perspective. Then a romantic im-
agination is never allowed to obscure real objectives
and magnify the collateral and incidental happenings
of a campaign.

The speeches of all who spoke with Allenby stressed
historical parallels, dwelling somewhat on biblical
prophecy and its fulfillment.

One would think in listening to them that Jerusalem
was Allenby's sole objective and its capture was his
crowning achievement.

It was very evident from Allenby's masterful un-
folding of his military plans and purposes that from a
military standpoint Jerusalem was just a town on a hill,

only important because of the roads which led to it —
a town which he was very glad it was unnecessary to
destroy. While he made it plain that he was not a
Crusader, he is a man with a heart, a profound student
of the Bible, and an example in Christian living.

The other speeches of the day were uplifting and
some of them most illuminating on other subjects than
this campaign. But in Allenby's address we heard the
Commander himself upon his campaign as it was, and
everything else we heard became unimportant in comparison.

His marked characteristics as a man were all of
them manifested in this address: his modesty, his desire not to appropriate credit belonging to others, his
devotion to the bare and unadorned truth, his high
purpose and his quick and wise decisions.

His simplicity and directness were a joy to me. A
number of reporters gathered at the house to interview
him. They started as usual by asking Allenby what was
his first impression of Chicago — expecting the usual
reply, which would be an apostrophe to its power, its
prosperity, its high buildings, its opera or its stockyards,
as the case might be. Allenby replied "Why! What a
fine clear day it was."

On Friday morning General Malone and Will Boyden
came to the house and we drove to Fort Sheridan,
where Marshal Allenby was received with military honors — the troops passing in review before him, General
Malone, Commanding Sixth Corps Area, Admiral
Craven, Commander of the Great Lakes Training
School, and myself.

REVIEW OF UNITED STATES TROOPS AT FORT SHERIDAN, ILLINOIS,
COLONEL F. B. SHAW, COMMANDING, OCTOBER 25, 1928

(Left to right) (1) Aide, (2) Lady Allenby, (3) Field Marshall Allenby, (4) Vice President Dawes,
(5) Vice Admiral Ziegmaier, Commandant Great Lakes Training School,
(5) Colonel F. B. Shaw, U. S. A.

On Thursday evening when driving home after the banquet both Lord and Lady Allenby thanked me for the following statement, which I made in my speech introducing him at the Commercial Club dinner: "I know that the world justly acclaims your great and victorious Palestine campaign, and that this one of your achievements will have the foremost place in history; but the thought comes to me that your qualities of greatness had their most crucial test when you covered with your cavalry the retreat of the gallant British Army preceding the First Battle of the Marne."

Will Boyden had charge of all arrangements for the Allenbys and they were admirably carried out.

Last night Mrs. Dawes and I attended a dinner given at the Drake Hotel to the French Ambassador, Paul Claudel, at which I presided and introduced him. He was here in connection with the dedication of a monument to his countryman Louis Pasteur, one of the great benefactors of mankind. This monument project was conceived by our own great Dr. Frank Billings, a pioneer in the West in the use of Pasteur's methods, and was carried to success largely by his efforts. The Ambassador is distinguished not only as a diplomat but also in the field of literature. His speech was far from conventional, and in ability and interest was exceptional.

Evanston, October 29, 1928.

The papers announce a total registration in the United States for the coming election of 43,000,000 voters, an increase of nearly 14,000,000 and indicating,

after allowance for stay-at-homes, an increase of 6,500,-
000 in total votes over 1924. In my judgment this
means an overwhelming victory for Hoover and the
Republican party. The gubernatorial election this fall
in Maine, where the Republican candidate for governor
recently polled 143,000 votes, indicates that the increase
in the vote will be largely Republican. Coolidge in 1924
polled in Maine only about the same number of votes,
although a presidential candidate. The Democratic
candidate for governor in the election polled 38,000
votes less than Davis — Coolidge's opponent.

As a result Maine gave the unprecedented Republican majority for governor of around 84,000. I put
these figures down from memory, but they are approxi-
mately correct. In Maine, therefore, the increase in the
normal vote cast this year in the gubernatorial contest
was almost wholly Republican.

I am sorry to say it, but I am afraid that the chief
cause of the increased registration and the coming
landslide is due to the submerged and widely disclaimed
issue arising in the minds of the intolerant because of
Governor Smith's religion. Our Constitution gives every
man the right to worship God in his own way. We have
been heretofore comparatively free in our political contests in this country from this ugly prejudice. Its injection into this election, despite the efforts of leaders
on both sides to prevent it, is to be deeply deplored.

To-day have been talking with my brother Rufus
about the 1933 Chicago Second World's Fair, of whose
board of trustees he is president, and whose plan of procedure has been evolved by him. Rufus' idea should

make the second World's Fair mean to this new generation in its new industrial and social environment what
the Fair of 1893 meant to that generation in its environment.

He maintains that this is the day of collective and co-
ordinated action — of co-operation. He points out that
constructive ideas are no longer concealed by competitors but are freely exchanged among themselves for the
advancement of their industry. As an instance, he cites
the chemical consortium in Germany, where investi-
gators work together for the advancement of chemical
science and share immediately their discoveries, thus
immensely accelerating the progress of the science as
compared with its progress when a new discovery is
kept secret until the discoverer devises his own method
for its utilization. The Fair he proposes will be composed of exhibits of the separate arts, sciences and industries, showing their development from their be-
ginnings, and each as a whole in charge of their exhibits.
In other words, the Fair will not be a conglomeration
of the exhibits of competitors, but the exhibit of the
growth of industries — made, too, by the members of
its different branches in co-operation, and not com-
petitively, along lines laid down by the National Research Council. He points to the fact that the exhibition by the Baltimore and Ohio Railroad at Baltimore
last year, of the development of railroad transportation in this country, attracted an immense attendance.

He points out also that the new Fair will cover not
simply transportation but all industries and arts in a
similar way. Further, he says the industries will un-

doubtedly contribute the bulk of the cost of their own exhibits.

Evanston, November 2, 1928.

The difficulties in the way of the final settlement of reparations are beginning to manifest themselves as the effort to secure governmental agreement upon the plan for a second experts' committee proceeds under the able guidance of Parker Gilbert.

I cannot feel that the Allied governments will keep their hands off this second committee of experts to the extent they did with our first committee.

As it was, they barred a finding by us of anything but a capacity for a present annual payment and the means for balancing the budget and stabilizing German currency.

I note that the French now claim that their experts on the first committee kept in close touch with the Government during our deliberations. This was certainly true, and in the contemporaneous notes of our work, which I kept, are constant references to the contact and influence of the French Government in our work.

Their present position may be that it is practicable to have "independent experts", but it must be remembered the solution to be reached must command unanimous Governmental acceptance and to insure this the experts, excepting those from America, who are not named by our Government, must be largely guided by their governments in their negotiations.

Each of the Allied governments, in effect, has already announced certain attitudes toward the question of reparations which morally must determine that of their own experts.

Britain apparently will accept no settlement under which her debtors shall pay annually a sum less than the annual sum she has to pay the United States as her debt settlement. France apparently will accept no settlement under which Germany shall annually pay her less than the sums she has to pay the United States and Britain on her debts, plus what will cover the cost of rehabilitation in her devastated districts. Belgium probably wants what will cover the amount of the German marks which Germany put in circulation in Belgium during the German occupation, and will so instruct Francqui and Theunis who it is said will represent her. And I may say here of that able Belgian Francqui, to whose genius the recent stabilization of Belgian currency chiefly is due, that "He wants what he wants, when he wants it."

These considerations would suggest to one not in touch with the situation that if the experts' committee reach a conclusion which shall be acceptable to all it will be one whose main features are now pretty well understood by the Allied governments interested.

The final settlement of reparations is a matter of immense importance to the peaceful progress of Europe, especially if it can be concluded with reasonable satisfaction to Germany as well as to her creditors.

Evanston, November 3, 1928.

Took lunch with my friend John McCutcheon at the Club and Stanley Field joined us. The resulting con-

versation covered the progress of the new Zoölogical
Garden which John is sponsoring, and the Field Museum
which Stanley is managing. The expeditions which the
Field Museum is sending out, in combination with other
institutions in archæological and other research, are
adding both to the possessions of the museum and to its
"prestige." John has two worse than "white elephants"
on his hands in the shape of two Indian rhinoceroses
which have recently been captured and are in some out-
landish place across the ocean. Some time ago James
Simpson authorized the purchase for the zoo, at his
expense, of two rhinoceroses of this variety; but they
are very rare and the hunter, having "sold futures" on
them so to speak, fell down on his job, and the matter
was considered closed. Simpson being abroad the question now is "Has the Statute of Limitations intervened
or is the offer still good on the recently found rhinoceroses?" So the hunter is hunting John, and John is hunting Simpson — the rhinoceroses in the mean-time having a prolonged rest.

This is but one of his problems as he has recently
been presented with some elephants for which accommodations are not ready.

Last night a dinner was given to John by members
of his old college fraternity, where many beautiful
tributes were paid him. I was not there, but I wish I
could have tried my hand at telling my own feeling
for this intimate friend and associate of twenty-five
years. Of all the friends I have ever had I think John
has the kindliest ways and the most sympathizing heart.
Everyone knows and praises his commanding talent

and recognizes him as one of the outstanding cartoonists and writers of his time. But his innate modesty and his unfailing and self-sacrificing generosity to all classes of people without claim upon him, evidenced at every possible opportunity, cannot be known to all. If it was I verily believe John would not have a cent left in the world. He gives away an enormous amount of work too, in drawings for charity and for friends who should not ask him — for he is sadly overworked. That one with such a gentle nature should be such a daredevil in taking unnecessary risks has kept me more or less alarmed about him for years. He has had many narrow escapes from death, one particularly when he was flying with Lee Hammond and they were forced down on Lake Michigan during a storm.

At the first International Aviation Meet in 1912 at Chicago I stood with Orville Wright and watched the passenger-carrying race in Grant Park, the planes flying very close to the ground and making short turns around pylons about fifty feet high. Frank Coffin, an aviator, had lunched with John and me and mentioned that he was to fly in this race after lunch. So John, having pleaded for the chance, was flying with Coffin in a Wright machine of the original type. It was from Mr. Wright during the race that I learned that the chances of the machine side-slipping at the turns was such as to give him the gravest anxiety. As for me, after watching the first bank that the machine made, I gave up John for lost. However, from that day to this he has risked his neck in unusual aviation whenever the opportunity offered, and in various other exploits too numerous to mention.

On Pennsylvania Railway en route to Washington,
November 7, 1928.

The election yesterday, with its triumphant victory for Hoover, its breaking of the solid South and its unprecedented number of total votes cast, will long be remembered and discussed in its bearing upon the future of American politics and policies. The issue of prosperity of itself, without the interjection of the submerged religious issue, would probably have won a Republican victory; but the existence of the latter in the minds of the voters makes difficult the proper interpretation of the result as to many other subordinate questions discussed in the campaign. In general it may be said, though to this some may demur, that the larger the vote cast, the more discriminating it is. This was true in Chicago, where the issue of good government and the alliance between crime and politics personified in minor candidacies determined the result in its local bearings. In the country at large the overwhelming influence of the religious issue is clearly manifest both in the North and the South.

I had a striking illustration at home last night of the annihilation of time and distance which has been wrought by the telegraph and the radio. After listening to the election returns over the radio until the result was clearly forecast, I dictated telegrams of congratulation to Hoover and Curtis to my secretary Ross Bartley, who telephoned them to the Western Union office and probably to the Associated Press. Within half an hour I heard them read over the radio from the *New York World* broadcasting station in New York.

(Left to right) *Speaker of the House, Nicholas Longworth, and Vice President Charles Dawes, looking over the ballots of the electoral votes for Hoover at the Capitol.*

HERBERT HOOVER AND CHARLES G. DAWES

Yesterday at home I had a most interesting call from Sir Basil Blackett, who was the representative in Washington during the war of the British Treasury, returning later to London to become second in authority in the British Treasury. Later he resigned to become the financial member of the Council of India — in other words, the Finance Minister of that government. He brought a letter of introduction from Tom Lamont. Our conversation was for the most part on the present reparations situation, upon which we had somewhat similar views, although we agreed that mistakes of opinion increase with distance from the actual field of negotiations. Sir Basil is on his way from India to England and like myself at present has only the long-distance view.

CHAPTER XII

MRS. DAWES and I got off the train this morning. As the hour was early and I wanted a walk, I headed for the Vice President's chambers in the Capitol, where I am now writing. The Senate Chamber and this office were undergoing a housecleaning. I do not mean this in a political sense — that cleaning out occurred Tuesday. Everything was in confusion, rugs and carpets up, and cleaners busy.

I have cleaned out the cleaners and utilize (perhaps that is too strong a word) the time in a few notes before leaving the deserted Capitol to go downtown.

The Vice President's room — come to think of it — is an impressive one. Its chief ornaments are Rembrandt Peale's portrait of Washington — painted in 1795, and said to be his best likeness — and a great chandelier brought up from the White House after some Rooseveltian alterations of that mansion.

During the session of Congress, whenever the Senate is not sitting, large delegations of visitors are piloted through the Capitol corridors and invariably either pass by or through the Vice President's office, depending upon whether or not that official is seated at his desk — his door as a rule being kept open for better ventilation. In case he is there the visitors all stop and peek in — or walk sideways past the door to look in. It was under these circumstances that the late Thomas Marshall called out: "If you don't come in, throw me a peanut."

To those who have heard the guides solemnly describe the historical relics of the Vice President's office the following Capitol legends of the office may seem irreverent, but they are at least worth noting.

Of the Dolly Madison mirror from the White House, which is not large and hangs about eight feet above the floor, it is said that it was hung so in order that the tall Vice President Fairbanks could use it to tie his cravats. The fine mahogany cabinet which occupies the west side of the room is only interesting to the old-timers among the Senate employees, as the alleged depository of the fatal bottle of brandy which Andrew Johnson drank just before he made his inaugural address to the Senate as Vice President, and which after nearly upsetting him quite upset his speech.

Will have to cease now. The movie men are moving en masse into the office, so the telephone announces. They have Charlie Curtis in tow and want our pictures together out on the front steps.

Later.

Spent an hour with Andrew W. Mellon, Secretary of the Treasury, my friendship with whom has dated from my service as Director of the Bureau of the Budget in 1921–1922, with offices in the Treasury Building.

Ever since that time I have held him in affection and respect. He speaks from a vast experience with equipoise and perspective, and with the clearness and decision which always characterize a great administrator — especially in Government finance. He tells me he is seventy-three years of age, but in appearance he seems younger than he did several years ago. His handling of the enormous Treasury transactions of the post-war years without unsettling our national business progress will give him a distinctive place in the history of our governmental finance. I hope and trust that he will remain in office during the Hoover administration. I took lunch with Governor Young of the Federal Reserve, Colonel McIntosh, Comptroller of the Currency, Mr. Pole, a Chief in the Comptroller's office, and Major Lohr.

The five years I spent in the Treasury as Comptroller of the Currency and later in the Budget work make me at home in the old building and among its occupants. The dingy corridors and the fine old structure, dating from Andrew Jackson's time, have more interest to me than any of the public buildings of recent times, however magnificent. My picture, painted by Anders Zorn when I was in the early thirties, hangs on the wall of the Comptroller's office behind his desk. In the old days it seemed to my friends and myself only a fair likeness, but at sixty-three years of age it looks good to me. Of the six Comptrollers of the Currency serving since my term, ending in 1901, five have been my close friends — and one was, as Tom Ochiltree said, "not only my brother, but my personal friend." The five are Ridgely, Murray, Crissinger, my brother Henry, and McIntosh. John Skelton Williams, who served under Wilson, I did not know well.

My wife and I attended in the evening the first state dinner of the season at the White House, where we had a most pleasant time. The President escorted Mrs.

Dawes to dinner, and I escorted Mrs. Coolidge, as custom prescribed at this function. All the Cabinet except Secretary Hoover and Dr. Work were present, and a limited number of guests were at the dinner. After dinner a musicale was given at which several hundred were present. Was much impressed with the piano playing of Madame Yolande Merö. I never heard Chopin's Etude C Major played better.

A double number of military aides in dress uniform lined up in the hall as we passed to the dining room, and the White House seemed unusually brilliant in consequence.

The President was most affable and agreeable and Mrs. Coolidge was charming in her attention to all present. As we gathered in the smoking room after dinner, the conversation among the Cabinet touched occasionally upon the long vacation from such festivities which most of the group were anticipating after March 4.

The President and Mrs. Coolidge evidently are looking forward to the time when they lay down their official cares, and I think this is so with Secretary and Mrs. Kellogg, who, like the Coolidges, will leave public life at the height of accomplishment and public regard — the time all should leave it if they are wise. But I suspect the existence of much suppressed regret among some others, which is natural enough.

On Century train for Chicago, November 13, 1928.

These notes ceased on the afternoon of November 10, last Saturday, when our train pulled into Trenton. We taxied over to Lawrenceville, where we visited for two hours with our son Dana, attending Lawrenceville School and domiciled in "Dawes House", which years ago I helped give to the School in memory of my son, Rufus Fearing Dawes. After this visit we arrived at New York, where we stayed with our friends, Mr. and Mrs. Owen D. Young. During the last two busy days, so much of interest has occurred that I am wondering whether I can cover the visit in these notes so as to leave anything of the impressions I carry away, dominated as they are by one tragic and pathetic remembrance.

Until almost into the morning hours on Saturday Young and I talked together, much of the time, of course, on reparations. And so first upon this subject:

I found Young's diagnosis of the situation the same as the one I have before outlined in these notes, and based upon the same reasoning. If the committee to revise the Experts' Plan is appointed, it will be in effect to conduct a diplomatic negotiation, not altogether an expert research, and under limitations fixed by the governments — which fact now, before the appointment of the committee, practically forecasts its possible major conclusions. These limitations, as I have already noted, seriously jeopardize the possibility of arriving at any results acceptable both to the Allies and to Germany.

The uncertainty of the situation became more manifest when, during my stay, Young received a cable from Gilbert saying that, owing to the French Cabinet situation, the committee would probably not be appointed until January, "even if other possible complications were avoided."

Yesterday, after lunch, Young attended a meeting of the Board of Directors of the New York Federal Reserve Bank, and was authorized to cable Gilbert offering him the position of its governor. When Gilbert visited me recently at Evanston, he emphasized his desire to leave his position as Agent General for Reparations as soon as he had successfully conducted his office through the five years, which is the experimental period of the first Experts' Plan, and which now ends within a year. He is apparently unwilling to leave it without a supreme effort on his part to have the sum total of reparations fixed on a reasonable basis, something to which Germany is entitled and, which, unsettled, is a handicap to the peaceful progress of European economy. Even if his efforts now develop the fact that a present settlement is impracticable, they have been worth while; for it will be generally acknowledged that if his able leadership does not avail, no other will.

But the calling in of experts again may succeed, after all, for the governments may be more amenable than we think.

In a talk with Secretary Hughes at General Vanderbilt's dinner Sunday night, he stressed the differences in the environment of our first committee and that which would surround any new one, and told of his long-distance discussions with Poincaré through Jusserand upon the relation of governments to the proposed work of the first committee of experts, when he urged for it as free a hand as possible.

On Sunday morning Young and I motored to Long Island where we took lunch with the family of the late

Henry P. Davison and about fifty of their close friends and neighbors. Afterwards all proceeded to Mineola and attended the dedication of the Henry Pomeroy Davison memorial building of the Nassau County Chapter of the American Red Cross. At these exercises a fine eulogy of Henry Davison was delivered by Thomas Lamont. In simple language, he outlined the wonderful career of this leader and benefactor of man, which finally flowered brilliantly in the crowning achievement of the financing and directorship of the activities of the American National Red Cross in the Great War, and ended shortly thereafter in sudden death. Tom's peroration was beautiful and touching, inspired as it was by a sense of deep personal bereavement.

On Sunday evening, General and Mrs. Cornelius Vanderbilt gave a dinner at their home at which about fifty guests were present.

On Monday noon General Harbord gave a lunch at India House, and in the evening I addressed a joint meeting of the New York Post Society of Military Engineers and the Metropolitan Section of the American Society of Mechanical Engineers. Major General Ely, Admiral De Steiguer, General Harbord, General Vanderbilt and others joined in the discussion which followed my speech. After the speech, I made a short visit to the Armistice Ball of the British Great War Veterans at the Plaza Hotel, another brilliant affair, and when I was taken to the center of the hall, the dancing stopped and "The Star Spangled Banner" was played by the band. I mention these things to give the contrasting background of a tragic and pathetic incident — one which brought me for the last time to the side of a boyhood friend, and has been unrolling for me ever since the memory of days long past.

On Sunday evening in the midst of all these festivities I received a telegram from my son-in-law at Chicago saying, "BRAD HULBERT DIED YESTERDAY CHARLES BACIGALUPO UNDERTAKER 26 MULBERRY STREET NEW YORK ADVISES BODY IN HIS CARE." At Miss Eell's private school at Marietta, Ohio, which I attended at the age of twelve years — fifty-one years ago — I first knew Bradford Hulbert. I remember him then chiefly as a good-natured boy who was always laughing, and who, with a front seat in school and a book so held that the teacher could not see his face, would twist his countenance into the most absurd grimaces for the benefit of the rest of us on the back seats. Our ways soon parted, but we had become good friends, and the next occasion of our meeting was during the week of my graduation from the Cincinnati Law School in 1886. Tom Dawson (afterwards Minister to Chile and Colombia) had won the hundred-dollar prize for the best essay and was spending a portion of it upon a dinner in a private room at the old Denison Hotel at Cincinnati, to assuage the disappointment of his four competitors, of whom I was one. When we were seated, Brad Hulbert walked in with a napkin over his arm. He was a waiter at the hotel, and was visibly embarrassed. It took me some time to get him at his ease. That was the last time — forty-two years ago — that I talked at length with him. But I have seen him several times since. The first time was on the streets of Chicago, at least twenty years ago, when I recognized him as a dilapidated and disconsolate tramp with ragged clothing. But he had recognized me first and turned away. He would not allow me to catch him. If I walked fast after him, he would walk faster. If I started to trot, he would trot faster. I knew then that pride had not left him, and a man who keeps pride is never wholly lost. It was not until years after that I heard from him. He appealed for help from a New York public hospital, which I gave, writing him that he could call upon me any time. But he did not do so for another space of years. When, several years ago, once more in sickness, he asked for fifty dollars, I sent it, and then continued to send him twenty-five dollars a month thereafter until his death.

When, on Monday morning, I visited the undertaker named in the telegram, he told me that when Brad cashed my checks at his lodging house, he had said that I was his friend, and when he died alone in his room and was taken to the morgue the lodging house keeper told the undertaker to notify me. The last time I saw him was at the City Morgue yesterday morning. Owen Young and I were unrecognized when we went there with the undertaker and while the search was made for his body, which was there with eighty others. Owing to some mistake in his name on the commitment papers, the first body shown me was not his. But on the second steel litter which was drawn on its rollers from its alcove, there, beneath the terrible mask left by long years of poverty and dissipation, I saw the face of my boyhood friend. His wasted body was covered with an old and frayed overcoat. He had died uncared-for in any way.

Besides the Morgue attendant, Mr. Young, and myself, there were present three soldiers in uniform who had been looking for a missing comrade. As I stood uncovered, they took off their caps and one of them said: "Is he your brother?" "No," I replied, "just a friend." But as I walked away, I thought, "Are we not all brothers?"

Some days after this, I received the following letter: —

November 23, 1928.

Hon. Charles G. Dawes,
Washington, D. C.

My dear General Dawes: —

I cannot refrain from expressing to you my appreciation of your continued friendship for Mr. Brad Hulbert (or Hulbert Brad, as the name was inscribed on the tablet of his coffin). He was, for over a year, an attendant upon the services of my church on Oliver Street, Manhattan Borough, New York. I knew him quite well. You were a continuing inspiration to him. In the worst of his sordid surroundings, his spirit clung to you as a drowning man clings to a plank. He cherished gratitude not alone for the monthly remittances you sent, but for your persistent friendship, revealed in your cheery letters. He was sustained, too, by the memory of happy boyhood days spent with you and your brothers. As he would speak of these associations he would melt in an agony of grief.

In my ministry I am constantly dealing with men of culture, who have preserved, even in their outcast condition, an idealism which kept them on higher levels, though to the world they walked in the mire; and every day I think of the progress of modern psychology by which men are taught to understand themselves. All of us, I imagine, are fighting some weakness *in the dark*. We are subconsciously under the control of irritating and perhaps sinful experiences and habits of years gone by. These forces insidiously working in the soul, unknown to us, cramp our efforts, hold us down. Most people fight for freedom of the soul through faith in God and by the exercise of reason and will power, and so live normally to all appearances. But many do not. They yield and become slaves to unseen vicious soul forces. I firmly believe that many Brad Hulberts could be led back to normalcy if they could be brought under the searchings of specialists in mental hygiene. I can but wish, though it be a vain wish, that Mr. Hulbert had had such a treatment and had responded to it. He was so gentle in bearing, so remorseful because of misconduct, and withal a man of such culture! Even in his ruins he revealed the heights from which he fell. But he should have been an asset and not a liability. We can but grieve and confide his soul to the supreme Father of men.

Believe me,

Very truly yours,

WM. N. HUBBELL.

CHAPTER XIII

Evanston, Illinois, November 19, 1928.

WE ARRIVED Chicago Wednesday morning the 14th. One accomplishment in the busy day especially pleased me. About 2:00 P.M. a delegation of Marietta people, headed by George White, called. They came in distress of mind because they had come to Chicago to urge the Executive Committee of the American Association of State Highway Officials to put Marietta, Ohio, on U. S. Route 50, which crosses the country to the south of it. The recent completion of a new bridge across the Ohio at St. Marys makes alternative routes for Highway 50 between Ellensboro, West Virginia, and Athens, Ohio — one through Parkersburg, West Virginia and one through Marietta. The executive committee had declined to give them a hearing, saying that no more alternative routes were to be added to the map. As the Marietta route would be five miles shorter, people might have an interest in passing through the first settlement in the Northwest Territory. The Association was then in session, but was to adjourn sine die at 4:00 P.M. — thus, without quick action, cutting off any hope of getting together the ten members of the Executive Committee who came from all parts of the country.

I asked a leader in the convention who was a member of the Executive Committee to come to my office, and I armed him with a letter asking for a re-assembling of the Executive Committee and a reconsideration of the matter. On the B. & O. train en route to Newark, Ohio, that evening I was greatly surprised not only to meet the Marietta delegation but to hear from them that the Executive Committee had met and changed their minds, due to this leader, whose name unfortunately I do not recall, and my letter with its exposition of the subject. Marietta, therefore, is on the official road map, and I am sure no one is happier than I because of it.

On the train in the evening were my friends Mr. and Mrs. John T. McCutcheon, Mr. and Mrs. Kenesaw Landis, Mr. and Mrs. Charles Atkinson, Charles B. Goodspeed, and Francis Kilkenny. We were bound for the arboretum — one of the finest in the country — on the farm of my brother, Beman G. Dawes, near Newark, Ohio, where John and Mr. Ireland, as two leading cartoonists of the country, were to plant twin trees. Beman has planted in his arboretum at least fifty thousand trees. He is adding to the present and future interest of the place by having leading men of Ohio and the nation plant trees, near each one of which is placed a bronze tablet stating the fact and bearing a brief summary of the career of the planter. General Harbord, Major General Summerall and a number of others, including myself, have already planted trees. Beman will leave the arboretum to the state of Ohio, whose forestry officials are much interested in its development.

Beman and Bertie make ideal hosts, and in all entertained a company of at least fifty at lunch and dinner. My wife was unable to take this trip so soon after our New York trip.

Evanston, November 21, 1928.

At noon, at the Stevens Hotel, at a luncheon of the Chicago Association of Commerce, Rufus C. Dawes, President of the World's Fair trustees, Senator Deneen, Samuel Insull, Chairman of the Finance Committee, and I, who am Vice Chairman, made addresses upon the World's Fair. The seating accommodations of the Hotel were taxed — seventeen hundred seats having been reserved at the tables. The average attendance at these luncheons is about 450, and the large attendance at this one was a source of encouragement to those in charge of the World's Fair enterprise. At every seat was placed a printed statement of the argument for the World's Fair prepared by my brother, Rufus.

It is so condensed in form and so admirable as a presentation that I insert it here: —

THE DOOM OF THE OLD FASHIONED
WORLD'S FAIR HAS BEEN SOUNDED

A single corporation, the Baltimore & Ohio Railroad, presenting the new idea of visualizing for the public the progress of transportation, ran an exhibition in the city of Baltimore last year. In three weeks they drew more people to their doors than attended the vast Sesquicentennial at Philadelphia in three months.

Imagine the attendance at a Chicago World's Fair at which all the industries will be presented in a similar manner. This Chicago Fair will not be competitive. It will not be a monotonous repetition of competing exhibits. Instead, it will portray intelligently, entertainingly, and educationally the modern spirit underlying the progress of each industry, and of agriculture, art, drama and sport. The progress of science will be on display in buildings conceived with all the skill of modern architecture.

Such a World's Fair cannot fail. The appearance of great associations of industry for concerted action provides the agencies to make it certain of success. It will express the new spirit of the world to-day, which is the utilization for the work of man of the knowledge which science has accumulated, and the application of it through collective and co-ordinated effort and action in industry, agriculture and social organization.

Supplanting the old exhibition idea we have, by the natural evolution of a new generation, a new thought of presenting a panoramic picture, beautifully adorned, of what science and industry have achieved for the world, and may yet achieve. All railroads join the exhibition of transportation. All electric companies offer a co-operative and single exhibit of their collective achievement. The exhibit, in fact, of every industry will be collective, and presented educationally by the best minds in its field of activity.

To celebrate the completion of the first century of its life, Chicago has the chance to present such a Fair to the world. It is well said that opportunity comes but once. Chicago, already pledged the support of competent advisers, must in the next few months accept the opportunity accorded it in the World's Fair plans. Other cities, both in America and Europe, recognize the opportunity and soon will deprive Chicago of it unless she acts now.

RUFUS C. DAWES, President,
Chicago World's Fair Centennial Celebration.

Washington, D. C., November 27, 1928.

Came to Washington from New York last evening on the train with Frank W. Stearns, the President's close friend and a man universally liked and respected. He is the embodiment of the cautious and considerate

AT THE WHITE HOUSE, SUMMER OF 1924

General Dawes, Mrs. Coolidge, President Coolidge and Mrs. Dawes. (In Background)
John and Calvin Coolidge, Mr. Frank W. Stearns and Mr. William M. Butler.

gentleman of the old school. He told me of an amusing conversation he had with the President. The latter was standing at his desk one day with a copy of the "Intimate Papers of Colonel House" in his hand. He looked fixedly at Stearns and said: "Mr. Stearns, the Constitution of the United States makes no provision for the position of an unofficial adviser." "Mr. President," said Stearns, "have I ever given you any advice?" "No," said the President, "but I just thought I would tell you."

Washington, November 28, 1928.

Last night the President and Mrs. Coolidge were our guests at dinner at our home. The other guests were Uncle Will Mills, my brother Beman and his wife, Mr. and Mrs. Cornelius N. Bliss, General Pershing, Miss Mary Randolph, Mrs. A. E. Humphrey, Mr. and Mrs. George B. Dryden, and Mr. and Mrs. Ben Ames Williams. All seemed to have a good time. The President and Mrs. Coolidge are evidently happy at coming liberation from an exacting and burdensome life. We had a moving picture after dinner, and as it did not start early, it was midnight when the President and his wife left. We had not expected the President to stay for the picture, but I don't wonder that once it started he "sat it out." It was the film version of "Abie's Irish Rose", sent to us by our friends of the Paramount Company, which will not be released to the public for many months. It will still require much cutting down, but its appeal is irresistible.

To my relief the President told me he would attend the Gridiron dinner December 8. One of the most difficult tasks of a Vice President is to take the place of an absent President as the guest of honor at one of those affairs and make the closing speech. This I did at the last dinner and one other some time ago. No more important or able audience gathers in this country. The outside speakers invited are those with an established national reputation as brilliant and witty after-dinner orators. As a climax or anticlimax (as the case may be) to their efforts comes the speech of the "ex-officio" guest of honor — not there as the result of competitive selection. This individual — be he President or Vice President — is hammered at during the three hours that the dinner consumes in all kinds of pointed and extremely clever skits, enacted between courses by members of the Club, who through years of practice have acquired the skill of professionals. Being the leading newspaper correspondents of the country and well informed, they unerringly pick out the flaws in the guest of honor which he hopes have been forgotten, and throw them in sharp relief before the audience in his presence. It is impossible to ignore altogether some reference to the good-humored "digs" of the evening in the last speech. For three hours, therefore, the guest of honor sits absorbed in thinking of "come-backs" to some of the amusing but quite personal thrusts. He may arrive for a minute at some peace of mind, with an idea that he has thought out what to say, only to have it rendered obsolete by the act during the next course of the dinner. There is no settled status quo during the evening until, after a kindly introduction, usually sung in chorus by the glee club and containing some compliments as a salve for his punctured epidermis, the guest of honor takes the floor.

And this settled status quo somewhat unsettles the guest of honor. If he comes out all right, he earns his year's salary right there. Nevertheless, these dinners are the most enjoyable of the year to him and everybody else.

During the day some of the Senators have talked with me about the coming session. It seems curious to hear them discuss whether this or that Senator will be willing to concede the right-of-way to this or that piece of general legislation as a measure of surpassing public importance. The power given individual Senators over the will of the constitutional majority by the rules allowing unlimited debate exercises a continuing influence upon the Senate never suspected or dreamed of by the public. Some of the Senators are advising Curtis to resign as Senator so as to allow the present Governor of Kansas to appoint his successor from that state and, incidentally, to allow the Republican Senators to select a new floor leader now. The purpose of this is, of course, purely political.

After listening to some of this discussion, I am led to say that he is no friend who upon request transmits as his own the advice of another.

Washington, November 29, 1928.

We attended a dinner last night at the Spanish Embassy given by the Ambassador in honor of the Infante Don Alfonso, the Infanta Doña Beatriz and their son,

Infante Don Alvaro. The dinner was a small one, composed for the most part of foreign ambassadors, and preceded a large reception to which we did not go. My companion at dinner was the Infanta Beatriz, the Infante Don Alfonso taking in Mrs. Dawes. This young lady, the Infanta, seated between Secretary Kellogg and myself, entertained us both in a conversation which evidenced not only her wide knowledge, but her real ability and mental culture. She is a granddaughter of Queen Victoria, and a sister of the Queen of Roumania, but she needs no prop of high relationship to commend her to attention and respect.

After dinner the Infante Don Alfonso sat with Kellogg and myself, and here again we found a person of most unusual interest — one who would command respect for his ability and character in any environment.

Don Alfonso is here in a study of aviation from a military standpoint, and we became so interested in a discussion of the war that we soon drove away Frank Kellogg, the present outstanding Apostle of Peace.

I told him of the intention of my friend Minister Latour of Guatemala to visit Spain this year, a plan which failed through his untimely death. Latour was a student of Mayan archæology and an authority on that subject, especially interesting to him as his country was once the seat of that great civilization.

Latour, born and brought up in Guatemala, was a firm believer in the existence of a codex which would lead to the deciphering of Mayan hieroglyphics, as the Rosetta Stone led to the unlocking of those of Ancient Egypt. The priests who followed Cortez destroyed as pagan all the Mayan manuscripts which they could find in Central America, with the exception of those which they sent to the Church in Spain. Latour's trip to Spain was planned in order to personally examine those manuscripts in the hope of finding a "codex." Don Alfonso expressed the liveliest interest in the subject, and said there was a vast accumulation of Central American documents in the Spanish archives at Seville which had never been fully studied and many of them never even examined. He offered assistance in any movement in this direction which might be inaugurated.

Kellogg tells me that his cables yesterday morning from Houghton, our Ambassador to Great Britain, indicate some concession on the part of the Allied governments to the idea of "free and uninstructed" experts on the committee to revise the reparations plan — which is more encouraging for something of substantial accomplishment as the result of their work.

B. &. O. train en route to Chicago, November 30, 1928.

Enough of the Senators apparently have banded together to ensure an extra session of Congress after March 4. Their expressed desire is to save for Mr. Hoover the doubtful opportunity of framing a farm relief measure "all his own." Under the rules of the Senate it is possible for a minority of Senators in any short session to so delay the passage of appropriation bills that an extra session must be called to keep the wheels of government moving. So whether the majority of the Senators want it or not — or whether the country wants it or not — or whether the President wants it or not — it would seem already settled at this early date that there will be an extra session. Beneath the superficial amiability of the trained politician, there is, of course, always the shrewd trader with his irreducible minimum of demands. To enforce them he has at last one underhanded, but never-failing, resort, made half-way respectable only by long usage — the threat to block the business of the Senate by unlimited debate under its rules. If an extra session is to be avoided, therefore, it will probably be at the cost of an indefinite number of concessions in appropriations and other legislation dictated by selfish and personal purpose and not by the public welfare.

Pennsylvania train en route to Washington, December 2, 1928.

On this trip and at Washington have listened to a considerable amount of election comment, in which the different speakers delicately intimated that their managerial or oratorical participation had much to do with the result. This always comes after an election, and Senator Swanson, when he sat down at lunch with some of his colleagues and myself the other day, made a preliminary announcement that he would remain only if the subject of "Who Killed Cock Robin" was not discussed. Yet it was. The last election was an earthquake.

The ordinary man, just as did the old Romans, holds in contempt the form of argument which the Romans expressed as *"Post hoc ergo propter hoc."* One editorial rebuke to this kind of post-election vanity, administered many years ago, I shall always remember. It was in the form of a fable dedicated to its victim: —

A rooster and his hens were once in the hen house, and it was very dark and very cold. The hens said to the rooster: "It is very dark and very cold. What can you do for us?" The rooster replied: "I will see," and he went out on a fence post and crowed three times lustily, and the sun rose. As he went back to the hen house, the hens said: "What would we have done without you?" And the rooster said: "I do not know."

Moral: It is not absolutely necessary to have feathers in order to be a damn fool.

CHAPTER XIV

Washington, D. C., December 3, 1928.

ARRIVED Washington 9:00 A.M. and went to my office in the Senate office building, where I answered mail until 11:30 A.M., when I went to my office at the Capitol. It being the opening day of a session of Congress, the staff of shorthand reporters of the Senate, headed by Mr. Shuey of fifty years continuous service, called in a body to pay their respects. A great many Senators likewise called — in fact, over thirty of them came in with cordial greetings. It was a pleasant half-hour, for I have formed many friendships here in the last four years, and I enjoyed the reunion.

The galleries were crowded, as is always the case at the opening of a session of Congress, and as I entered the chamber with the Chaplain the appearance of the floor of the Senate was like that at the opening of a college year, with all the students talking and shaking hands in the college assembly room. At twelve o'clock noon, after restoring order with the gavel, and after prayer by the Chaplain, I ascended to the Chair and announced that as this was the day prescribed by the Constitution for the convening of the second session of the Seventieth Congress, the Secretary would call the roll to ascertain whether a quorum of the Senate was present. Eighty Senators answered to the call, and thus the second session of the Seventieth Congress started.

During the short sitting which followed I administered the oath to three Senators-elect, and the Senate passed the customary resolutions to notify the President of the presence of a quorum of each house — "to notify the House of the presence of a quorum of the Senate" and "to fix the hour of daily meeting of the Senate." The Senate then adjourned out of respect to the memory of the late Senator Gooding of Idaho. My friend Vandenberg of Michigan was one of the Senators-elect to be sworn in. I predict for him a career both brilliant and useful.

In the afternoon called at the State Department, where Kellogg gave me the present status of the plan for the Experts' Committee, as reported to him. We went over a cable received by him to-day from Parker Gilbert giving the text of a proposed grant of power to the committee which Gilbert has suggested to the Allied governments. This would ask the Committee to report upon the total amount of reparations based upon Germany's annual capacity to pay, and make suggestions as to a method of funding a portion of the debt and "commercializing" the bonds. They would also make suggestions as to how the present machinery of the first Experts' Plan should so be modified as to be adapted to the new scheme, if agreed upon. Gilbert also said that it might be decided to give the grant in the words of the Geneva decision, which suggested a power to report on reparations in a definitive way without suggestions as to details. This he stated would be satisfactory to him, although he preferred the longer statement.

The *New York Times* Paris cablegram this morning states that Germany and England have agreed that the Reparation Commission shall invite the members of the Committee to act instead of the governments. This would remove another, but minor, obstacle. Kellogg had not been notified of this. Referring, however, to Houghton's cable that concessions probably would be made to the idea of freedom for the experts from government control, which he had mentioned to me at the dinner at the Spanish Embassy last Wednesday, he said that the German Ambassador had called later and told him that both England and France had stated to Germany, as an ultimatum, their minimum requirements from reparations; at the same time they had assented to the "freedom from control" idea. How can the experts be regarded as "free from governmental control" when they are in effect notified in advance that no decision of theirs will stand unless it produces a certain fixed minimum of annual reparations payment?

In my judgment, if this is the situation, the Allied governments will practically decide beforehand just what the Committee shall be allowed to decide later. The alternative is to let the Committee go ahead without control and outline a plan quite sure to be rejected but out of which valuable suggestions may be salvaged and fitted into a new and third plan, which will result from a diplomatic negotiation between those first in authority and responsibility if not in economic competency. This is quite likely to occur, as I see it now.

Washington, December 5, 1928.

One part of the President's fine message yesterday interested me as a former Director of the Budget, an official who is engaged throughout the year in estimating and worrying about the probable difference between Government revenues and expenditures at the end of the fiscal year — in other words, the surplus or deficit on June 30. These estimates vary, of course, from week to week — sometimes in very large amounts, when Congress makes an unexpected appropriation. The estimate of the surplus this fiscal year ending June 30, next, is given in the message as only $37,000,000 or a margin of less than one per cent on expenditures. The President warns against new appropriations in this session for immediate outlay, — that is, for outlay before June 30, — as such action would result in an unbalanced budget.

What especially pleased me in this connection was his statement "I should not feel warranted in approving legislation which would involve us in that financial disgrace."

In his attitude toward the Budget machinery and in his loyalty to the vital and fundamental principles underlying the new Budget system laid down in the executive order of President Harding dated Nov. 8, 1921, which I formulated and used to call the "Magna Charta of the new system of routine governmental business," Coolidge has been a joy to me.

Outsiders, unacquainted with the solidity of a governmental status quo, especially one over a century and a quarter old, can little realize the opposition of the departments to Sections 3, 4, 5, 6, 7, 8, 9, 10 and 11 of that document.

Seven years have now passed since it was promulgated, and the system of control over the spending departments which it created has made it possible for the President to keep down governmental expenses in a period when those of the states, counties and municipalities of our country are all increasing. If any new President relaxes his interest in maintaining its principles and lessens the vigilance shown by President Coolidge in their enforcement, the result will be seen in constantly rising expenses of government.

Had many callers at the office this morning and when not occupying the chair this afternoon. Had a long visit with my friend Senator Robinson of Arkansas. Among other callers were Senators Barkley, Wagner, Goff, Shipstead, Simmons, Bingham, Johnson and Fess. Presided over the Senate most of the active "morning hour" which is often two hours. When the morning business was concluded at 2:00 P.M., I laid before the Senate the Boulder Dam Bill, which was the "unfinished business" from the last session of Congress. Senator Johnson made a motion to substitute the House Boulder Dam bill for the Senate bill, in view of their similarity and for certain parliamentary advantages incident to that course. After a short discussion this was "agreed to", and this leads me to pay a tribute to a modest young man whose name I have never heard mentioned on the floor of the Senate, nor seen in print during the four years I have been here, but who is a power in government — Charles Watkins. A parliamentary battle had been expected upon a point of order against the regularity of this procedure. That this point of order was not made was because, at Senator Johnson's request, Watkins had written a statement of the precedents involved and given his opinion thereon. This statement, shown by Johnson to those interested in the question, led to the acquiescence of all in its soundness and prevented the contest. Watkins probably stayed up all night to prepare it, as it covered some three or four typewritten pages. He is called a "journal clerk", I believe — a place in which he receives only a moderate compensation; yet by indefatigable work almost every minute of the day and most of the night he has made himself the actual parliamentarian of the Senate and its highest authority on the precedents. For over a year he has been compiling in extra time a new volume of "Senate Precedents." Work, work, work is his only lot, and if he is sometimes praised behind his back by Senators, I am afraid few think to do it in his hearing; and sometimes I even hear him criticized when his advice to me precipitates a ruling adverse to a Senator's cause.

Perhaps it would be unfair to me to say that the reason I have never had a point of order sustained against any ruling of mine as President of the Senate is wholly due to Watkins — but unquestionably it is chiefly due to him. Senate precedents are almost always conflicting, and when Charley Watkins gives me a choice of precedents to follow, I sometimes make my own decision. But it is chiefly upon his advice that I act — and when I have done so, on several occasions Senators versed in the rules and precedents have strongly combated his reasoning as expounded by me; but the Senate has never sustained the opposition.

If those Senators whom I have called to the chair during my absence have occasionally been overruled, it is probably because they did not follow Watkins' suggestion, but endeavored to rule so as to further a political motive — something which Senators tell me is occasionally expected in the chair, but which I have never done.

I shall always be grateful to Charles Watkins, whom, with all due respect to the members of the Senate, no man among them equals in knowledge of the Senate Rules and Precedents. And yet Robinson of Arkansas, Curtis of Kansas, Moses of New Hampshire, Norris of Nebraska, Jones of Washington, and Walsh of Montana are authorities of the first rank.

Washington, December 6, 1928.

Occupied the chair in the Senate about three hours in all to-day, during "morning business" and later in the afternoon for a part of the Boulder Dam debate, and during the executive session after the debate closed. Speaker Longworth was one of my callers during the day and I discussed with him the kind of a resolution to be introduced in the House and Senate for the recognition of the Chicago World's Fair, to which I am giving attention. Have just returned from the judicial reception at the White House this evening. At these large White House receptions I have long adopted a course which adds greatly to my enjoyment of them. After marching downstairs and as far as the Blue Room with the official procession, headed by the President and Mrs. Coolidge, I do my full duty in greeting those assembled there, even waiting until the judges, diplomats, or generals and admirals (as the nature of the reception determines), return to the room after they have passed in line to greet the President. Then, generally with Secretary Mellon as a companion, I slip away to the room at the right of the front door where the Secret Service men and my old friend Ike Hoover, major-domo of the White House, generally hold forth. Just beyond its open door in the main hall the Marine Band, which plays all the evening, is stationed. We have, therefore, three advantages of which the other guests are deprived — we can sit down; we can hear the music; and we can smoke.

Here we remain until about ten minutes before the official procession, which we must join, starts upstairs again. We can tell when to start back to it by the final "petering out" of the long procession of guests coming from the East Room through the hall to the Blue Room to shake the weary hands of the Chief Executive and his wife.

But we have another way of telling. Invariably Mrs. Dawes gets worried for fear we shall not get back in time and either comes herself or sends an aide after us.

Secretary Dwight Davis generally shows up for a part of the evening, and always when he is there we are joined by the Spanish Ambassador Padilla, who smokes a pipe.

Discussed with Mellon the financial situation, his last report to Congress, the reparations question, the French debt settlement and various other subjects, and came away with additions to my stock of knowledge, as always from any interview with this able and clear-thinking friend.

Mr. Ike Hoover, whom I have just mentioned, I first knew when as a young man I used to be frequently at the White House in President McKinley's administration, and Hoover was one of the doorkeepers. From that day to this, whenever I have lived in Washington — nine years now in all — I have kept in close touch with him and with the Marine Band, first led by Santlemann and now by Branson.

Washington, December 8, 1928.

Received a telegram that James A. Patten had died suddenly. He had one of the greatest and most generous hearts. The poor whom he has helped, the weak who have benefited from his strength, the thousands whose lives he has made brighter, are the living evidences of the value of this good man's life.

Last night I attended my last Gridiron banquet, as the next one will be given after I have left Washington for good. It was unusually well carried out; the acting, the hits and the music being of the first order.

Had a fine time. The President made a good farewell address, happy in its references to the occurrences of the evening and full of good sense. This time I did not have to speak, but was not left unnoticed. The Vice President of the United States and the Vice President-elect were ordered to stand. Accordingly, Senator Curtis and I, seated near together, rose and remained standing until what they called the "Dawes Decalogue, or the Letter of a Self-made Has-Been to His Successor" was read.

"Just between us Charlie," it began, "you are getting away to a flying start. 'Helen Maria' was my line, but 'Too damn dumb' will get you just as far. Out of the depths of my experience, I commend to you these Ten Commandments: 'Don't steal the first page on Inauguration Day, and you may be invited to sit in the Cabinet.' 'Don't be afraid to criticize the Senate. You know how much it needs it. The public likes it and the Senate thrives on it.' 'Don't commit yourself to another fellow's candidacy for President. He may hold you to it.' 'Don't pretend you understand the equalization fee. Al Smith found there was n't a vote in it — so did I.' 'Don't try to change the Senate Rules.' 'Don't buck the President if you want to stay more than four years.' 'Don't do your sleeping in the day time.' "

The last refers to my absence from the Senate when my vote upon a tie would have confirmed Charles B. Warren for Attorney General, whose nomination on the subsequent vote was not confirmed. This regrettable incident, happening on the second day of my first experience with the Senate, resulted from my inexperience with the explosive nature of that body.

The day's session was nearing its close and as six more speakers had given notice of their intention to address the Senate, both the majority and minority leaders of the Senate told me a vote would not be taken that afternoon. After I left all the speakers but one dropped out and the vote was taken. Later I came to know better the uncertainties of the Senate. There have been only two other tie votes in three years. The Gridiron Club has never had a dinner since that time without reminding me of this event, at one time bringing in an alarm clock four feet high for my benefit. However, I was in no danger of forgetting it.

Washington, December 10, 1928.

My friend Dwight Morrow has just arrived to attend the Pan-American Conference. He looks much better than he did last summer.

Gilbert, who is very anxious to have Dwight serve on the new Committee of Experts on Reparations, has been sending him copies of his correspondence with the Government. Dwight's diagnosis of the matter of the "independence of the experts" is about the same as mine. He cannot accept for good reasons. When the new President of Mexico asked him the other day whether he was going to leave him, Dwight answered, "There are two people who always control the movement of an Ambassador — the head of his own country and the head of the country to which he is accredited — in my case President Coolidge and yourself. I am staying until one or the other tells me to move."

Dwight's great success in Mexico is easily explained. "I trust them", he says.

Washington, December 11, 1928.

The Senate made some progress on the Boulder Dam Bill to-day. The fact is very evident that the reaction from the campaign has created a better feeling among public men. The debates lack acrimony. There is a sincere effort to compromise on differences, and compliments pass between opponents at this session who were at swords' points at the last one.

Presided over Senate for about three hours.

Many callers at office, including a delegation of about thirty master farmers from Kansas, headed by Senator Capper. Senator J. T. Robinson, Charles Francis Coe, George Agnew Chamberlain, Lieutenant Doolittle (the famous aviator) and my fine son, Dana, took lunch with me at my office in the Capitol. Have just returned from dinner at Ogden Mills's house, at which I had an interesting time. Sat between two very intelligent women — Mrs. Mills and Alice Longworth. Both are especially brilliant and entertaining conversationalists, and one who is fortunate enough to be their table companion never has a dull time.

Official rank determines the seating at Washington dinners, and as the Vice President and the Speaker of the House rank about the same, it has given me the pleasure of Mrs. Longworth's company at dinner many times the last four years.

Met at the dinner my old friend of the war, George McFadden of the War Trade Board — the great representative in France of the War Trade Board, a body whose invaluable service to our army in the war was as indispensable as it was unostentatious. It has never received the acclaim for its accomplishments which it so highly merited. It was a board of action, and it alone could always invoke for our army the immediate cooperation of our State Department, which was so helpful in enabling our army to gather supplies in the neutral countries of Spain, Switzerland and Holland.

Talked with Ogden Mills about the reparations situation. He seems to agree as to the alternatives — either a forecasting of the decision of the experts by the governments, which he is inclined to think will involve a reduction in German payments from 2,500,000,000 marks annually to 2,200,000,000 (about $75,000,-000.00 reduction per year) or a report which will at least be accepted as a basis in part for a new agreement negotiated by the Governments themselves. Mills has been a most competent and successful Undersecretary of the Treasury.

Senator Phipps called to ask me to consider taking Mr. Hoover's place on the joint American and Mexican commission for negotiating a division of the waters of the lower Rio Grande. It was a matter of regret to me to tell him that I could not do so, even if it were agreed that I was wanted.

Had a pleasant talk with James A. Reed. Everybody regrets that he is voluntarily leaving public life after eighteen years of brilliant service in the Senate. As an orator he is in a class by himself — a representative of the fearless and able statesmen of the old school.

I have many times been the target of his shafts of wit and satire, but after all it is really something of a distinction to one.

Washington, December 12, 1928.

The Senate made marked progress again to-day in the Boulder Dam legislation. A unanimous consent agreement was secured with some difficulty to limit debate after three o'clock to-morrow to fifteen minutes for each Senator speaking on the bill and its amendments. This, of course, is "reforming the rules" temporarily. It is one of the several devices used to set aside the rules temporarily so as to enable the Senate for a time to transact business as do other important deliberative bodies. It means that the minority has decided to let this bill pass this session — in other words, to let the majority exercise its inherent rights. It allots, by consent of the minority, the time of the Senate as dictated by the public interest, a right which should belong to the Senate at all times.

Presided over the Senate for about three hours, including the executive session.

Among my callers to-day was Ruth McCormick, Congresswoman-at-large (elect) from Illinois. For this able and tactful woman, whom I have known from her childhood — the daughter of my friend Marcus A. Hanna — I predict a brilliant public career. She has the keen mind, good equipoise and business ability of her father, combined with a charming personality and a kindly, generous nature. Her late husband, Senator Medill McCormick, in his will made me a joint trustee with her of the estate of their three children.

Washington, December 14, 1928.

Spent most of the afternoon in the chair of the Senate, which did not adjourn until 6:00 P.M. Just before adjournment the Senate passed the Boulder Dam Bill by a good majority. Senator J. T. Robinson, John Marshall and Charles T. Chapman of Chicago took lunch with me.

Opposition to the Kellogg multilateral treaty is organizing itself to defeat ratification.

General Pershing's aide telephoned that Mrs. Butler, the General's sister, had died, and that he had left for Lincoln, Nebraska, immediately. Mrs. Butler was a noble woman who lived a life of activity, usefulness and generosity. After her husband's death many years ago, she took over the work of editing and publishing the *Lincoln Law Journal,* which he had founded, and she has been engaged in this successful occupation up to the present time.

After the tragic death of the General's wife and three little girls, Mrs. Butler and her sister, Miss May Pershing, took little Warren, the son of the General, into their home, and in their devoted and tender care and training this fine boy — a young man now — has enjoyed what is invaluable in the upbuilding of character, the influence of a Christian home and high example. In the strenuous duties and military campaigns which have kept General Pershing away from home so much of the time, he has had peace of mind about Warren — his best beloved — because of the devotion of these two sisters to Warren's care. Mrs. Butler's death was a great loss.

Washington, December 15, 1928.

A short but interesting session of the Senate was held to-day. Senator Burton of Ohio was sworn in. The Senate took a five-minute recess in order to greet Orville Wright, to whom I presented the Senators passing in line before us on the Senate floor. Mr. Wright, when at my office, spoke of the most tragic event in my life — the death of my boy, Rufus. He said that he was on his way from Dayton to visit me at Chicago in September, 1912, to adjust differences between himself and some aviators relating to the use of the Wright machine at the International Aviation Meet of the next year. When he arrived at Chicago, the meeting had been abandoned because of Rufus' death the day before.

The Senate adjourned about 1:00 P.M., and I had at lunch with me at my office Senator Borah, Dwight Morrow and John Marshall. Dwight went over the Mexican situation and the status of his work as ambassador. Senator Borah told me something of which I had never heard. He said that during the proceedings of the last Republican National Convention he had called me by long-distance telephone at Evanston to ask my consent to place me in nomination before the convention for the vice-presidency. I had left for the city and he was unable to reach me. He felt that if he had done so, I would have been nominated, and he explained why. Now that the event is over, these reasons need not be repeated.

Borah left us after an hour, and Dwight and I visited for about three hours longer.

Dwight is of the opinion that this Government should have its experts for the new Reparation Committee, and after hearing his views I think he is right.

Parker's note to Mellon, submitted to the President by Mellon, inquired as to whether the Government would (1) appoint the experts; (2) allow Government officials to serve; or (3) allow the Reparation Commission itself to directly invite American citizens to serve. The third course is approved by Mellon. The mind of the President is probably still open. Dwight thinks as this Government is interested to the extent of two and one half per cent of reparations, the dignified and proper thing to do is to appoint experts to look after its interests and not to approach the subject as it did the first committee situation, when it adopted the third suggestion in order to avoid responsibility. It should be said here, however, that our Government did not then have the direct interest in the fixing of reparations that it has since the allowance to us of two and one half per cent. of the reparation payments for costs of the American army of occupation. As for Dwight, he will not accept appointment even if the President should agree to it, for he does not propose to leave Mexico while he feels he is useful there.

In regard to leaving Mexico, Dwight realizes that the present is the time when he could do so with an established reputation which, without fault of his own, may be lost through coming events. The coming year, until the President's succession is firmly established, will be a critical time in Mexico. If he left now, and things went wrong in our relations with that country, it would be said that had he been there trouble might have been prevented; if they went right, that it was because of what he has now accomplished. But Dwight is not an opportunist. His creed is to be useful.

Had a conversation the other day with a Senator who gave utterance to this: "The most dangerous man possible in a position of power is a coward."

Washington, December 16, 1928.

Now that the Boulder Dam Bill is out of the way, the Kellogg Peace Treaty and the Naval Bill will soon be considered. As to the passage of the Boulder Dam Bill, though it still must be fought through other obstacles, that project seems assured in time. When the dam is built, there should be on it somewhere a tablet to Senator Hiram Johnson, without whose untiring and able leadership it would have failed. I never saw a man more faithful and effective in a hard fight than Johnson has been in this one.

Through the long days and nights of a filibuster, and at all times during the last two years when the bill was up, he has been at his post of duty every minute. And this should also be said of Senator Ashurst and Senator Hayden of Arizona, likewise faithful, but to the interests of Arizona, which were involved.

Washington, December 20, 1928.

A busy day. In the morning Senator Hale, Chairman of the Naval Officers Committee, Borah, Chairman of the Foreign Affairs Committee, Senators Swanson, Curtis, Watson, Reed of Pennsylvania, and other leading Senators met at my office and endeavored to reach an agreement to be adopted by unanimous consent of the Senate adjusting the contest which has arisen over whether the Peace Treaty or the Naval Bill has the right of way in the Senate. An agreement was made that both were to be the "unfinished business" on January 3; the Naval Bill in "legislative session" and the Treaty in "open executive session." This merely postpones the conflict, but simplifies the parliamentary procedure under which it will be conducted. When the Senate was to be asked to "unanimously agree" I took the chair. Then ensued one of the brisk parliamentary skirmishes often occurring in the Senate, which arose as a part of the contest itself. The rulings which I made were entirely in accordance with the rules of the Senate, but an appeal was taken from one of them. The Senate by a large majority sustained my decision, and a new status quo was established, which then resulted in a peaceful acceptance of the original "unanimous consent agreement" for the January 3 program.

The Senate then passed the Southern Flood Relief bill which was an aftermath of the Puerto Rican hurricane relief bill passed the other day.

Dwight Morrow, Senator Dave Reed, ex-Senator James W. Wadsworth, Senator James Watson, Senator Dale and Assistant Attorney General Marshall were at lunch with me, but I had to leave them for the chair of the Senate, to handle the parliamentary row on the floor.

Dwight Morrow leaves to-morrow and we expected to have the afternoon together, but one can never count on what is going to happen in the Senate. He hastily went over the reparations situation, which is mixed up again over the method of selecting the American Experts.

At 5:30 P.M. — an early hour agreed upon so that the pages would not have to go home first — I gave my annual dinner to the Senate staff in the Senate restaurant. Over a hundred were present, all officially connected with the conduct of the Senate's business — the Senate reporters, the Senate clerks, the Sergeant at Arms, the Secretary, and the members of their organizations, including the pages of the Senate. The dinner centered itself largely around my coming departure, and was conducted upon the general lines of a Gridiron dinner, save that the Gridiron was not allowed to get so hot. Jim Preston, who presides over the Press gallery, also presided here, with his customary ability. The program given during the dinner was largely planned, and the literary parts prepared, by him; it was a decided success.

Mr. Shuey, over eighty years of age, a reporter of the Senate for over fifty years, made a most interesting résumé of his long experience and included a most eloquent and moving talk to me near its close. He then presented me with a beautiful silver inkstand from the Senate staff, modeled after the one on the Vice President's desk in the Senate. The pages, many of them, spoke, and really stirred my emotions by what they said, especially the little McCarthy boy. I responded as best I could. The pages had secured a moving picture film of scenes occurring during my term of office, in which I had taken a part, which was shown and then presented to me. I liked best the picture where I stood on the Capitol steps surrounded by the pages, with my arms around two of them. I shall miss the boys and my dear friends of the Senate staff.

Washington, December 21, 1928.

The Senate was in session for less than an hour to-day. Just before adjournment I received the engrossed bill providing for the erection of the new building for the Supreme Court and bearing the signature of the Speaker of the House of Representatives. I signed it as President of the Senate. Less than fifteen minutes later Chief Justice Taft telephoned, asking whether I had signed the bill and expressing his anxiety to have it signed by President Coolidge before he left Washington for the holidays. This I arranged within an hour, to his considerable satisfaction. Have always felt grateful to Taft, for in 1886 he marked the examination papers of our graduating class in the Cincinnati Law School, and passed nearly the whole class, myself included. He does not know it, but this was one reason he got such quick service to-day. His father, Judge Alphonso Taft, and Horace Taft, his brother and my law school classmate, were law partners of my brother-in-law, Henry N. Morris, the firm name being Taft, Morris and Taft of Cincinnati. I knew the Taft family well in the old days, and while I did not know William H. Taft, I was his great admirer. While I was in law school an unjustified attack on his father, Judge Alphonso Taft, was made in some scurrilous paper of the city. William H.

Taft, then a young man, met the editor, who had been a prize fighter, on Fourth Street one morning, stopped him, told him to get ready, and then gave him a sound thrashing in a great fight in which a plate-glass window was smashed. After that, I included him with his father and brother Horace in my affection and high regard. Horace is now the head of the Taft School and has had a most distinguished career as an educator.

I have never seen in any account of the life of the Chief Justice a record of this particular personal activity, which, owing to the fact that he himself was an expert boxer, was satisfactorily effective. The friendship with the Chief Justice which I have enjoyed during the last four years has been one of the pleasant things in my service here. He is beloved by all who know him.

CHAPTER XV

En route B. & O. for Chicago, December 22, 1928.

THE Senate remained in session only an hour and adjourned for the holidays. At the opening of the session I called attention from the chair to the fact that to-day was the sixtieth anniversary of the day Mr. Shuey joined the staff of Senate reporters. Pleasant references to him were made by Senators, particularly by Senator Heflin, all of which Mr. Shuey, — now eighty-four years of age, — combining pleasure with official duty, duly took down in shorthand.

Before coming to the Senate called on Dr. Abbott of the Smithsonian Institute and gave him authority to conduct at my expense a Smithsonian investigation and study of the Mayan documents in the archives of the Indies in Spain, if the consent of the Spanish authorities is given — thus ensuring a thorough search for a codex which would enable the Mayan hieroglyphics to be deciphered. The great probability is nothing of this kind will be discovered, but other valuable information certainly should be obtained.

The Doctor will consult the archæologists of the Institute, who will pass upon the feasibility of the effort, and if they decide favorably they will select a man to conduct the work.

Took lunch with Senators Warren and Kendrick, both of Wyoming, the former the great sheep raiser, and the latter the great cattle man, of the state. Of different political parties, they are of the same stalwart type of the able, self-made American leader. Veterans in the Senate as they are, they wield a great influence, always directed toward common sense objectives.

After lunch called on Chairman Hawley of the House Ways and Means Committee. Since our World's Fair resolution contains a tariff provision, it will probably be introduced as a House instead of a Senate joint resolution. Hawley promised hearty support and stated he would call a meeting of the Ways and Means Committee to which the resolution will be referred either the first or second Saturday of January as we might find most convenient. His only reservation was his securing of Representative Tilson's approval, concerning which he anticipated no difficulty.

Evanston, Illinois, December 23, 1928.

We arrived home this (Sunday) morning. The morning papers record the progress of the effort to finally fix German reparations — some of the details of which I have been recording in these notes.

The question of Germany's total reparation obligations and their rate and method of payment must be fixed not only as a matter of justice to Germany, but as one of the greatest importance to the peace and progress of Europe and the world. Unquestionably the report of the second Experts' Committee, while it may not be adopted in whole, at least will provide the eventual foundation upon which the governments will construct their final plan of settlement. Even though the prospect may be doubtful of obtaining a settlement by the adoption of the report without modification, as was the case with our former committee, the injection of an experts' report into the situation as it has developed at this time seems imperative.

When wise statesmen plan for governments they reason in the simplest terms of human nature, for their problem is always one involving elemental human nature. To settle properly an international controversy involving each country concerned is both an economic and a political problem, requiring a machinery in which selfish interests and instincts will tend to offset each other. To appoint as negotiators only men of official position having a personal interest in not offending public opinion would tend to bring about unwise decisions, sacrificing economic principles for temporary political peace. To appoint only business men and economists would tend to bring about decisions that, while applying correct economic principles, would disregard existing public sentiment — which, however prejudiced, ignorant or temporary, would be powerful enough to overthrow them.

To appoint in great controversies, as is often done, a mixed committee of politicians and economists, such as the old Reparation Commission, is unwise; for the reason that wise agreement through proper compromise is well-nigh impossible when a conclusion desired by the economists would endanger the politicians, and a conclusion desired by the politicians would stultify the economists.

Upon such a committee the pressure of governments

upon their political and diplomatic representatives is overpowering, and generally disastrous to the proper compromise between economics and politics along lines of an expediency which recognizes the real essentials of both.

Such was the case with the old Reparation Commission, which voluntarily abandoned an effort to settle reparations made hopeless from the first not only by the nature of the work but by its own constitution.

In despair — with economic chaos threatening Europe and with political and social repercussions impending everywhere as the result of the demonstration of the impossibility of a solely political solution of their difficulties — the governments appointed our first Committee of Experts to take over the reparations problem only in so far as it involved means of balancing the German budget, stabilizing German currency and determining the capacity of Germany to make annual reparations payments. These limitations were made necessary by politics; but they had the result of discouraging governmental interference in our work.

Let no one suppose, however, that the report of our Committee was not itself a compromise between economic principles and political necessities. It was exactly that. But it was a compromise whose finding was dominated by economic experts. That it was accepted by the governments was because, in the existing state of public sentiment in Europe, it was dangerous for politicians to oppose its ratification. It was easier, then, for experts to satisfy the politicians, for the politicians had failed to satisfy the public.

Now, in the final effort to fix reparations, the governments adopt the expedient of an experts' committee because only through that device can there be secured the proper balancing of all the economic and political considerations. The economic phases of the question will first be decided by economic experts. Their report, whether satisfactory to all the governments or not, will be known to all the public, and will fortify every conservative statesman subsequently in his constructive efforts for a final settlement. Politicians must then deal with a public sentiment influenced by confidence in the impartiality and competency of the experts. Against the economic findings of this committee there should be little intelligent protest, and in the final settlement only such exceptions will be made to them as are dictated by an overwhelming political consideration impervious alike to reason or pressure.

In saying this I am assuming that this committee will be able to make a unanimous report.

While I was writing this the young people of the Congregational Church gathered in front of the house singing Christmas carols. I went to the door and thanked them. It is a beautiful moonlight night, with the ground covered with snow and the Christmas lights shining in all the neighbors' houses.

And so, with thoughts of peace and efforts for peace, to bed.

Evanston, December 24, 1928.

Received a cable from Parker Gilbert in Berlin conveying the season's greetings, and saying he would meet me in Washington the first week in January. The papers announce this evening that the President has consented to let the Allied powers and Germany invite the Americans to serve on the committee. Selected in this way they will be regarded as practical arbitrators, and this Government will be held more responsible for any decision made than if it had appointed them directly. Am sorry this latter was not done.

Evanston, December 25, 1928.

A beautiful Christmas at home. The house was full all day. Starting with the Christmas tree in the morning and ending with the moving picture party at the house for the Boy Scouts in the evening, the children, the grandchildren and the old people — everybody — enjoyed the happiest day of all the year. Was at Rufus's house for a time in the afternoon, where he had twenty-two of the family at dinner. The children delivered baskets for the poor yesterday and we remembered many, so that our Christmas was not wholly a selfish one. For a time Christmas was an anguish for us, but over sixteen years have passed since we lost Rufus Fearing, and time has enabled us at least to recall the happiness he gave us when he was with us, without the suffering that every thought of him used to bring.

Evanston, December 26, 1928.

This evening Mrs. Dawes and I were at dinner with Mr. and Mrs. George B. Dryden. Besides a number of our old Evanston friends, George Eastman, the great

leader in the photographic industry, the uncle of Mrs.
Dryden, was present. For the first time from a first
authority I came to understand something of the new art
of color photography — a marvelous accomplishment.
Not only did Mr. Eastman describe satisfactorily the
process but we were shown the actual pictures. We are
living in the age of marvels.

Among the Christmas telegrams I received was one
from General Pershing, who is still in Lincoln where he
went to attend the funeral of his sister. John said, "You
cannot know how deeply I cherish our friendship."
What could make one happier than that, after nearly
forty years of association? To have enjoyed from my
young manhood the loyal friendship of John Pershing
has been one of the great things in my life. It opened to
me the greatest of all experiences — association with
him in the Great War, where as never before I came to
know those qualities which under the grueling tests of
continuing and overwhelming emergency made him a
man among all men — one who will live in history. He
came up from the mass in a fiercely competitive life
under the law of the survival of the fittest. The greater
the crises in the way, the clearer and cooler was his head.
During the battle of the Argonne he saw vindicated his
determination to train his soldiers for open instead of
trench warfare; and his firmly maintained resolution to
keep his army under American leadership saved its
highest effectiveness and brought glory to his country.
What a struggle with the military leaders of the Allies
he had! What it cost him in effort! What it cost him in
nervous energy! What it took in sheer force of char-

acter! How impossible it is to visualize these things for one not with him at the time!

It was my blessed opportunity to be with him through it all — to come to know him in his real strength — to see him in the plenitude of actual accomplishment, and then the victory won; to know his innate modesty and common sense. That he held me and holds me in his confidence, esteem and affection is a joy to me that he also cannot know.

Evanston, December 27, 1928.

Frank Lowden took lunch with me to-day and we had a fine visit together for about two hours. We discussed public questions as "elder statesmen" for only a limited time.

When I think of the columns of printer's ink which have been wasted in comment upon our relations, and then recall how close and confidential they have always been, and how free from misunderstanding, I am impressed with the thought that much of what is called political news in our papers is fiction. He will leave for Europe early in January with Mrs. Lowden, his daughter Florence and his son Pullman. He was in splendid health and spirits. In 1920 Frank came very near the Republican nomination for the presidency. He was defeated because of the misdoings of others, and through no fault or error of his own. He commands deservedly the respect of the American public as well as the respect, affection, and confidence of his friends. His career in Congress and as a war governor of Illinois, whose business he placed for the first time on a proper budgeting basis, has marked him as one of our ablest public men. He has neither apologies nor regrets for the past.

Evanston, December 28, 1928.

John McCutcheon was over for lunch. He is preparing another dangerous trip for himself and wife across South America. One part of the trip includes a two-hundred-mile airplane jump over the forest of Central South America with a one-motor machine. To this, Mrs. McCutcheon objects, and I pray she will have her way. I do not criticize the taking of risks in life, — not to do so at times is cowardice, — but to take them without an objective of commensurate importance is another thing. Mrs. McCutcheon, having been in one airplane crash with John on a trip from somewhere in the North of Europe to Paris, does not fancy a forced landing in the South American jungle.

Am reveling in my library again as I used to do before exchanging evenings devoted to the acquisition of knowledge for those at Washington, so often devoted to large dinners.

I am reading that one-time famous work "The History of Civilization in England" by Henry Thomas Buckle. How cheap and contemptible a book like this makes the alleged historical works being sold by the tens of thousands to-day, simply because they detail immoralities. It, and books like it, stand out from the mass of the "best sellers" of to-day like some of the old cathedrals in Europe, surrounded by the slums of modern cities.

In Buckle's masterful summing up of the character of Burke, where he refers to the devastating effects upon

Burke's peace of mind of the death of his only son, he speaks of "that image of desolation under which the noble old man figured his immeasurable grief." Burke said: "I live in an inverted order. They who ought to have succeeded me have gone before me. They who should have been to me as posterity, are in the place of ancestors. The storm has gone over me, and I am like one of those old oaks which the late hurricane has scattered about me. I am stripped of all my honors; I am torn up by the roots, and lie prostrate on the earth."

Evanston, December 29, 1928.

In reading Buckle's book this evening, especially the chapter on Historical Literature in France, I am impressed with the need at the present time for historians with his power of generalization. While inventive genius has within a short period almost revolutionized the conditions under which humanity has lived for ages, man himself has not changed, nor have the laws which inexorably govern his actions, which, as Buckle says, "are guided by their antecedents, are in reality never inconsistent, but however capricious they may appear, only form part of one vast scheme of universal order, of which we in the present state of knowledge can barely see the outline."

One marvels at Buckle's generalizations as to the effects during all past history of climate and cheap food upon social organization, covered in his chapter upon the Influence of Physical Laws. But in this country to-day "cheap food" is not having the effect in lowering the condition of the masses which he demonstrated was inevitable heretofore.

What is the cause of this, and is it temporary or permanent? Simple answers may occur to one, — our magazines are filled with them — but after contact with a book like Buckle's, one realizes that the depths of the social questions of the present are not being sounded as were those of his day.

Buckle, in speaking of Turgot, defines the historical philosopher who is needed now. He must belong "to that extremely small class of men who have looked at history comprehensively . . . who exclude from their scheme the personal details which ordinary historians accumulate, and concentrate their attention upon those large general causes, by the operation of which the destinies of nations are permanently affected."

Evanston, December 31, 1928.

To-night the old year ends and here in the quiet library at home is where I would rather spend it than anywhere else. It certainly was not always thus. But to the restless, the passing of the years brings one great compensation in an ability to enjoy the quiet things of life — books which do not speak until taken in hand and addressed — the peace of a well-ordered house — the recollections of an active past and the pondering over the lessons which experience alone can teach.

I do not feel that I deserve it, but my friend Dwight Morrow has just wired me: "Much love and best wishes for a new year that will be as happy for you and as useful to others as the crowded years that you have already lived." This and the fact that last night I read over my journal for the years 1896 to 1902 make me realize that I really have lived a "crowded life." (Those were the years of my association and friendship with William McKinley.)

It was in 1887 that my grandfather Gates, after having kept a "day book" himself for forty years, started me on one. At first I wrote only a few lines a day, but as the years went on and my contacts became more important I expanded them. What I wrote over thirty years ago about McKinley was written as a son would write, for he treated me as such in all respects, and few knew him as I did. He trusted me fully and my contacts with him were almost daily when he was in the White House. As I reread last night what I wrote then, I feel that if published it might do much to remove the erroneous idea still held by some that there was something weak and pliable in McKinley's character.

The only President in my lifetime able to completely dominate Congress might not seem to need this service from notes written in my young manhood, — and perhaps he does not — but, as one carrying his explicit and unwelcome orders to those said to dominate him, and as one who observed them implicitly obeyed without exception, what I have written contemporaneously is at least authoritative.

And so, sometime — now that I have more leisure — I hope to publish some of these notes about him. The size of the page in my journal bearing the day date determined generally the length of my comments upon any particular matter. They are, therefore, short; for, even if the subject was one I knew would be historical, I only wrote in a smaller handwriting so as to get more on the one page. Such is the force of habit. Only a few times — notably when he died and I was at his bedside — did I enter much into details. And yet from these notes, one can understand that strength was his dominant characteristic — moral strength, with its most becoming adornments, gentleness and patience.

Yes! when I think of it, my life has been crowded; for, when my friendship and work with McKinley lifted me into important associations with men who afterwards became leaders in government, I was only thirty years old. There is hardly anyone left in Washington, now in public life, who started there in official life when I did as Comptroller of the Currency. Can it be that I am getting old?

In the early evening read an article on "Reflections on Farm Relief" by Professor R. G. Tugwell, of Columbia University, in the December *Political Science Quarterly*. At last there is commencing the same kind of economic and fair consideration of this subject by American economists as was given by that "greatest practical economist of the world", as Lloyd George designated him — Sir Josiah C. Stamp, Vice Chairman of the London School of Economics, Chairman of the London Midland and Scottish Railway, and Director of the Bank of England. It was through friendship for me that he wrote his comments on the McNary-Haugen principles — not legislation. No leading economist criticized his statement, but he endured quite a barrage from politicians in this country.

Evanston, January 1, 1929.

Saturday afternoon I called on my friend, Tiffany Blake, who has been ill. He has left the editorial staff of the *Chicago Tribune* temporarily, on this account. He seems better than when I saw him before leaving for Washington the last of November. Among the things I look forward to when I am through at Washington are the sessions which Tiffany Blake, John McCutcheon and I have had regularly at lunch about twice a week for many years.

Tiffany has one of the most interesting and cultured of minds and from his conversations I always take away something worth while of knowledge. His broad reading and retentive memory afford a fine basis for the exercise of his unusual powers of deductive reasoning and his philosophic observations. I am much attached to him, and am anxious about his health. His wife also has a brilliant mind and for years was a trustee of the University of Illinois.

During these holidays at Chicago, I have seen many of the acquaintances of my former active business life. Many of them have progressed, and by this I do not mean simply in wealth. Dollars and cents are no true measure of progress. These men have gone forward in civic usefulness — in philanthropic and public work — in efforts for the good of others. It is among these that I find the happiest of them all.

CHAPTER XVI

Washington, January 3, 1929.

ON our arrival at Washington, went direct to my office in the Senate Office Building and looked over my mail. There was a letter from General Smith, Superintendent of the West Point Military Academy, saying that the Committee on gifts had approved my endowment of a "Pershing Sword" annually for the Captains of Cadets.

Decided to try to get the resolution recognizing the Chicago World's Fair through this session of Congress, and to act directly. Went to the House of Representatives and saw Hawley, Chairman of the Ways and Means Committee, and Representative Tilson, Republican leader. They said that Garner, Democratic leader in the House, was objecting to a clause in my redrafted resolution which I had gone over with the Senate Finance Committee. Made still another draft which at my request Senator Joe Robinson took to Representative Garner; he secured his agreement to it. Then arranged with Hawley to introduce the resolution in the House, which he did, and called a meeting of the Ways and Means Committee for Saturday morning.

Arranged with Senator Deneen to have the Illinois delegation at lunch to-morrow noon, at which we will post them on the argument for the Fair. Then Deneen and I will go before the Ways and Means Committee

Saturday morning, to which the resolution will have been referred, and urge a favorable report, which we hope to get. A special rule will be asked in the House for a vote on the joint resolution.

I find the best way to get action is to act yourself and not depend upon others less interested.

There is a widespread opposition in Congress to world's fairs, based upon the recent failures involving cost to the Government, and the erroneous idea that this new Chicago World's Fair is to be upon their general plan. So that things are not as easy as they might appear to one not on the ground. Accordingly, I have been pretty busy for some time. We do not expect to ask for any appropriations from the Government.

Presided over the Senate most of the afternoon. As there was a crowded gallery to hear the debate over the question of ratifying the Kellogg Peace Treaty, I called Senator Curtis to the chair for a time so that the people could see their next Vice President in the place he will occupy after March 4. Senator Hale, in his quiet and dignified way, made a very able and convincing speech on the Cruiser Bill for about an hour. It left nothing to be said, to my mind. Borah then moved to proceed to the consideration of the multilateral treaty, and his speech favoring it consumed — with the interruptions — the rest of the afternoon. He always brings to my mind the great parliamentary leaders of the past, and when he speaks it seems a far cry to the tactics which are bringing general discredit upon Senate debates. I favor the Treaty but I favor the Cruiser Bill just as strongly under existing circumstances. It is not proposed to build cruisers to achieve naval superiority but to attain naval equality under existing treaties.

The United States, assured of naval supremacy if it kept on building battleships, called the Washington Conference in President Harding's administration, and, by its tremendous sacrifice in agreeing to scrap new battleships, made possible the naval disarmament treaty as to them. Since the naval experts at Geneva were unable to interpret in terms of ships an agreed-upon principle of equality with Great Britain as extending to cruisers, it is now unwise for the United States to stop building cruisers when other nations continue to build them. And I think, also, that if this bill becomes a law and the world sees that the United States is in earnest in demanding real equality with Great Britain, a new naval disarmament conference will arrive at an agreement covering all types of ships.

As to the multilateral peace treaty, it will be a calamity if it is not ratified. Such an outcome would leave the United States in a most humiliating position. Having asked the world to agree to something to which the world agrees, she would have then declined to agree. The talk about the inconsistency of ratifying a peace treaty "outlawing war" and at the same time passing a bill to build warships, may impress some minds. But the logic of international relations is the logic of events. Other nations, having ratified the Treaty, are still building warships. It was our naval strength which enabled us to dictate the Washington pact for naval limitations in capital ships. If we now pass the Treaty without the Cruiser Bill our comparatively greater naval weakness will lessen our influence in the future negotiations for real naval disarmament.

The struggle of the world away from war will be slow and hard and many steps which, when taken, may seem illogical and backward, will, in due time, be recognized as forward steps. The Lord has established the law of progress under which we live. If we only keep struggling for the right, we have done our part and the right will surely come. There will be wars in the future, for human nature will not change. But some may be avoided. What the world needs is greater contact of its peoples with each other — for continued contacts lead to mutual understandings. This Treaty ensures more contacts and in that alone makes for peace.

Washington, January 4, 1929.

At 1 P.M. Deneen and I met the Illinois Congressional Delegation at lunch and both addressed them. We explained the parliamentary situation of the World's Fair joint resolution and went over the arguments for the Fair in case opposition might arise on the floor. Senator Glenn, Representatives Rainey, Britten, Chindblom and Hull, spoke. All agreed to co-operate. All of the delegation who were in the city were present.

Presided over the Senate for a portion of the afternoon. Borah finished his great argument for the multilateral treaty. It was an interesting and elevated debate, conducted with a dignity unusual in Senate proceedings.

Many callers at the office, including the Dean of the Cincinnati Law School, from which I graduated in 1886.

Someone mentioned to me an interesting fact the other day. The presiding officer of the Senate, of the House of Representatives, and of the Supreme Court are to-day all graduates of the Cincinnati Law School, and all perform their duties in the same building, the Capitol. They are Chief Justice Taft, Speaker Longworth and myself.

To-night Mrs. Dawes and I will attend a dinner given by the Chief of Staff of the Army, General Summerall, and his wife. He is one of the best American generals the war evolved. In the war I came to know General Summerall well, and remember particularly one call upon him in his "dug-out" headquarters of the First Division at Cheppy, near Varennes, during the battle of the Argonne. The immortal First Division, A.E.F., was in a desperate fight that day.

Washington, January 8, 1929.

With Senators Deneen and Glenn, of Illinois, at 11:00 A.M., I went to a full meeting of the Ways and Means Committee of the House in the House Office Building in support of the World's Fair resolution. Deneen made a good statement, as did Glenn also. Questions arising, I made an address of about half an hour, answering them, and apparently aided in satisfying the Committee, which promptly went into executive session. When we were through, and by the time I had walked from the Committee room to my office in the Capitol, they telephoned from the Committee that the vote was unanimous in favorably reporting the resolution to the House.

When I reached the office, I found Senators Borah, Reed of Missouri, Robinson of Arkansas, Swanson, Watson, Johnson and Blaine engaged in a conference upon a compromise program for the Kellogg Treaty — always subject to change as these things go. Borah had prepared a report to the Senate from the Foreign Affairs Committee upon which he said the Committee would unanimously agree. This defined their views upon the effect of the Treaty. The report would be designed to reflect the views of the United States as to what the Treaty meant, just as Chamberlain's statement to Parliament reflected the views of the British government on the same subject. Borah did not want the Senate to pass upon the report. Johnson and others desired it to do so, maintaining that the adoption of the report by the Senate was necessary to give it the same status as an official pronunciamento as Sir Austin Chamberlain's statement — which came direct from the British Cabinet to their Parliament.

I was consulted as to whether, if controversy arose upon the floor as to this method of procedure, a point of order would lie against the motion that the Senate adopt the report of the Foreign Affairs Committee. Upon consultation with Watkins, the parliamentarian, and an examination of the precedents, I informed Borah that the point of order, if made, would not be sustained by me, as the Senate, upon numerous occasions, had voted on the question of adopting committee reports other than conference reports which in the case of the latter, is always done.

If the proposed plan of procedure is followed, it will

preclude any possible adoption by the Senate of reservations to the Treaty, as the Borah statement or report is designed by its liberality to remove the objections to the Treaty by some of the leading "irreconcilables." And yet, is not a report so prepared in itself a reservation?

What will come of the matter is, of course, mere conjecture. I expressed my view to Borah as to the main benefits which humanity and the cause of peace would derive from the Treaty — simple views which I felt had not been stressed enough upon the floor, and which justify the policy of this able statesman in making some concessions to ensure its ratification. I write this, however, without having seen the proposed report.

When the war spirit of the people of a nation is aroused, the tremendous force arising from mob psychology is involved. Upon the issues of the war people do not reason so much as they feel — resembling crowds in their mental processes and limited ability to reason. This is why, when their war spirit is suddenly aroused, nations so often act and reason as little children. Against the flood of resentment among its people, caused by a sudden insult to national honor, or assault upon national interest, a government seeking to keep its policy within reason for the proper protection of its people themselves, as well as to avoid war, will be materially assisted by the existence of this treaty. Nations when angry are just as unreasonable as men — if not more so.

Suppose two angry men were facing each other pre-

PRESIDENT COOLIDGE AND GENERAL DAWES AT
PLYMOUTH, VERMONT

paring to fight. But suppose, before a blow was struck, one should say to the other: "You and I have solemnly resolved and promised not only to each other but to everybody else that when we have differences we will endeavor to settle them peacefully and avoid a fight if we can."

To be able to say that might not stop the fight; yet it might stop it. At least it might delay the fight, and delay makes for peace. It is inconceivable in analogous instances which will arise hereafter, where nations are involved, that this Treaty will not sometimes stop a fight among some nations. One instance where it did, would justify the Treaty. The Treaty, if passed, can do no harm at any time; and yet at some time it is certain to do good.

"To talk it over" among men or nations standing before each other and ready to come to blows does not mean legal arguments, profound and lengthy dissertations on historical analogies, or a Senate debate — it means delay for a last "brass tack" talk. When nations are suddenly involved in such circumstances, there is no opportunity for ordinary diplomatic exchanges as a possible preventive of war. With this Treaty in effect, and under these circumstances, it means that there is a better chance than at present for delay in aggressive action, and for that kind of contact between those first in authority (or their direct representatives) — which, with both parties realizing their responsibility to try to reach agreement, results in a more proper discussion and disclosure of basic facts. When this occurs in the world, there is a better chance for peace.

About all I see in this Treaty is a better chance for peace — but that is a great deal.

To sum up: the Treaty speaks for itself. No nation can ever really misunderstand it. It is more than a "noble gesture." The Treaty registers formally an agreed attitude of the world toward the avoidance of war, and its moral force will be general in its bearing and effect.

It secures for the world the reasonable certainty that before a fight starts there will always be a contact between those representing the two sides of the disagreement to talk it over. One without experience might think that would occur anyway. Talk will always occur on the part of both sides — but proper contact is another thing. If one side or the other has taken a position which does not appeal to an impartial mind, that side will avoid close contact in discussion, and issue statements from a distance.

Other things being equal, neither a nation nor a man with a bad case prefers a face-to-face discussion, since debate brings blows to which direct response must be made, and those blows might be more safely parried or ignored at a distance.

In the war, when a conference among the Allies proposing a simple matter of immensely important coordinated action was to be held, the great trouble was to get an independent authority who anticipated some necessary invasion of his prerogatives to attend it, even if he had reluctantly consented to its convening. Conferences were delayed for insufficient reasons, and all

kinds of irrelevant excuses would be given for inability
to attend. The truth was that some selfish interest had
intervened, — the fear of loss of authority or personal
prestige or the like — which would not stand in a face-
to-face discussion between earnest men acting under a
common emergency.

CHAPTER XVII

THIS evening Count Széchényi, the Hungarian Minister, and his wife took dinner with us. Both the Minister and his wife are musical. Széchényi (pronounced Z-Cheney) brought his saw with him, on which he plays by striking it with a padded mallet and flexing it to produce the required notes. Only a natural musician can play it properly. With a piano accompaniment, which I furnish, the saw, as manipulated by the Minister, produces some pleasing effects. Part of the time Dana joined in with his saxophone, and altogether we had a lively time. Széchényi and I reached our climax with the aria from the first act of Puccini's "Butterfly", but our average was found in the old Johann Strauss waltzes, of which we are both very fond. We have several times before had these evenings, and they bring back the memories of the days before my son died when music meant so much to us and engaged so much of our time and interest.

Because Fritz Kreisler played one of my compositions on his programs in his concerts over the country for several years, I have received some publicity as a "violin player." I have never played a violin — my instruments being the flute and piano. While I used to score out in manuscript for the piano considerable music, which was afterwards orchestrated and played by bands and orchestras in Chicago, I never allowed any of it to be published — with the exception of the piece for the violin which I wrote when I was interested in that brilliant artist, Francis Macmillen, in his younger days. Mediocrity seldom rises above its level, but I realize that mine did in that one piece, which has been a steady seller for fifteen years or so, and has been played in every part of the world. As part of it is scored in double stops for the violin, it is quite difficult to play as it is written.

General Sherman, with justifiable profanity, once expressed his detestation of the tune "Marching Through Georgia" to which he was compelled to listen whenever he appeared anywhere. I sympathize with his feelings when I listen with blushes to this piece of mine over and over again, and then realize that I have "brought it on myself." At my request, the Marine Band has ceased to play it at the White House receptions — but when I was in Washington as Director of the Budget, President Harding, sensing my attitude toward it, used to order it played whenever I was present, as a joke on me. If it had not been fairly good music I should have been subjected to unlimited ridicule. As it is, a toastmaster once introduced me: "As both a business man and a musician", adding "it is a regret to me, however, that I find business men referring to him as a musician and musicians referring to him as a business man."

Washington, January 7, 1929.

Parker Gilbert called at my office and we had a long talk over the reparations situation. As early as October, he says, he suggested to our Government that it appoint its members of the Experts Committee in the same manner as other governments. He has conferred with the President and Kellogg and finds no disposition there to obstruct the naming of any Americans as members of the Committee who seem proper — that is, I interpret, who seem proper to Gilbert. Gilbert is waiting for Young's return from Arizona before deciding on the other member.

His talk was most interesting and covered details of vivid interest to me, since it concerned so many of my old colleagues on the first committee. He says Schacht will make a most vigorous effort for Germany — which "goes without saying." He will spend another morning with me on Wednesday before he leaves. He will see Hoover while here.

Borah to-day tells me that the "reservationists" of the Treaty fight now agree that they will not insist upon a vote by the Senate on his committee report to the effect that the Treaty does not interfere with the right of self-defense or provide sanctions or infringe upon the Monroe Doctrine. They ask, however, that after the Treaty has been ratified the Senate take a vote upon a motion to transmit to the nations, along with the ratified treaty, the copy of the committee report. Borah tells me he cannot see any reason why this request should not be granted. It is possible, therefore, that by this arrangement the Treaty debate will be ended in a much shorter time than expected.

This evening Mrs. Dawes and I went to a dinner given by the Ambassador from Great Britain, Sir Esme

Howard, and Lady Isabella Howard. Among the guests were the Ambassadors from Spain, Japan and Cuba, the Minister from Roumania, and many others — about thirty in all. In a talk with Sir Esme Howard he said to me: "It will be a misfortune if the Cruiser Bill is not passed. Its passage, in my judgment, means that a genuine naval disarmament will come."

The trouble with the last disarmament conference on cruisers was the naval experts — not either the United States or Great Britain. As Dwight Morrow once said: "No naval expert ever likes the idea of equality." This remark Sir Esme Howard quoted to me.

Occupied the chair in the Senate but a short time to-day.

Washington, January 8, 1929.

Busy day, yet with little to write about. The time of the Senate was consumed by speeches on the Peace Treaty. Borah says a few are hanging out still, but agreement upon the plan outlined already in these notes may be reached to-morrow, which will shorten the Treaty debate.

President-elect Hoover is at the Mayflower Hotel and many are indulging in a pilgrimage there. Some who have been to see him drop in at my office on their return. They then outline their own remarks rather than his — which would indicate that he allows his visitors to do most of the talking, a course of wisdom. There are, of course, not enough offices to go around. "Many are called, but few are chosen." When an administration of government changes it is a tragic time in Washington for many. Yet in Washington there is a heartless indifference to ambitious and suffering spirits, for Washington is used to changes. When the appointments are finally made all is outwardly pleasant, for the pride of the disappointed sustains them in the effort to conceal their feelings, and the satisfaction of the successful is restrained to be in "good form"; yet, under the placid surface of things, currents of deep feeling are surging.

This evening Mrs. Dawes and I are the guests of Everett Sanders and his wife at dinner at the Mayflower Hotel. Sanders is the Secretary of the President and has made an exceptional record of usefulness, industry and tact in his difficult and important position.

Washington, January 9, 1929.

When I reached the office this morning Parker Gilbert was waiting for me. Young had arrived yesterday, and they had determined the matter of American representation in the new Experts' Committee on Reparations with each other as well as with Coolidge, Kellogg, and Mellon. Young, who has just returned from Arizona, is reluctant to accept appointment because of the poor health of Mrs. Young. He had left for New York after a very short time here, stating to Gilbert that he would not accept appointment unless I would agree to take his place on the Committee in case he should have to return from Europe on account of Mrs. Young. Gilbert wanted my answer so as to telephone Young and close the matter.

It is, of course, impossible for me to make any arrangement of this kind covering the period I am in office, which is until March 4. After that, I told Gilbert, if Young had to leave I would then agree to serve, though I thought that would not only be unfortunate but really unfair to Young. I said this only when Gilbert assured me that this was an ultimatum from Young, and that Young could not be satisfied without it. Gilbert said that it had been under consideration to postpone the conference until after March 4 so that I could serve on the Committee with Young, but that the psychology of the situation in Europe made the delay inadvisable.

Gilbert suggested that I come to Europe upon the adoption of a report by the Committee, prepared, if necessary and if the report deserves it, to support it. The situation to-day is that Young and J. P. Morgan will be the American members, with Thomas Nelson Perkins and possibly M. A. Traylor, of the First National Bank of Chicago, alternate or deputy members.

The selection of the best and most competent men for this specific task is so important as to override any minor considerations which politicians might urge. The Committee will meet in Paris February 4.

Gilbert, after our talk at my office in the Senate Office Building, went downtown, returning to my office in the Capitol at 1 P.M. At lunch to meet him I had Senators Borah, Smoot, Robinson of Arkansas, Swanson, and Dave Reed.

Presided over the Senate for a time. The Treaty debate still progresses. All suggested compromises as to the form of real or implied reservations are temporarily in abeyance. Kellogg strongly protests against any.

Washington, January 10, 1929.

Dull day at the Senate. Presided for a short time.

I went for a time to Senator Smoot's birthday luncheon in the Senate Finance Committee room. It was his sixty-seventh birthday. He is much depressed by the death of his wife, to whom he was devoted, and he made a touching allusion to her to his friends who had gathered there. Secretary Mellon, Senators Curtis, Robinson, Harrison, Reed of Pennsylvania, and a number of others were present, including my friend Henry M. Robinson.

At the reception at the White House this evening, after marching downstairs with the Cabinet behind the President and Mrs. Coolidge and after I had received my wife's permission, I left for my favorite rendezvous in the cloakroom, where, with Secretary Mellon and Parker Gilbert, most of the evening was spent talking reparations. Secretary Kellogg joined us later.

Owen Young arrives from New York late to-night, and to-morrow Gilbert hopes the Committee members of the United States will be finally decided upon. Some questions remain open about the alternates, which we talked over. Young will talk the whole matter over with the President, who still is considering certain phases of the situation. Gilbert is quite optimistic over the prospects of a final settlement of the reparations question through the Committee. All the members of the Committee from other countries have been announced.

Talked with Mellon about the extra session, which should be avoided if possible. I told him what Hoover had said to Mark Woods, for whom he had sent to talk over farm legislation. Mark told him that in his judgment if he (Hoover) would announce that he favors the present amended bill without the equalization fee, so that the agriculturalists would understand that it was an unmistakable Hoover measure, they would cease insisting upon an extra session. According to Mark Woods, Borah, who talked over the matter afterwards with Mark Woods at my office, told him that under such circumstances he (Borah) would not urge the extra session. Hoover, however, explained to Mark that he was in an embarrassing position, which prevented him doing this except at the suggestion of President Coolidge — and that it was something which it would be unseemly for Mr. Hoover to propose to him. I told Mellon that if this was so Hoover had evidently not talked the matter over with Coolidge, and if Mellon would explain the situation to Coolidge, the latter might take the initiative and make the suggestion to Hoover that he would welcome his co-operation in preventing the extra session in this way. Secretary Mellon said he would see Coolidge in the morning and inform the President in the matter. If an extra session can be avoided by the passage of a farm bill this session, it will be a distinct benefit to agriculture to have the law in effect at once; for considerable time will be consumed in setting up its machinery, and delay may mean that this year's crop may not receive whatever benefit may accrue from its operation. That an extra session will be adverse in its effects on general business, I am in no doubt. Every effort should be made to avoid it.

Washington, January 11, 1929.

After seeing the President, Gilbert, Mellon and Kellogg, Owen D. Young called on me at my Capitol office in the morning, and for an hour and a half we talked over the reparations matter. It is now settled and ready to be announced that Young and J. P. Morgan will be the two members, and Thomas Nelson Perkins one of the alternates.

At a dinner given this evening at the German Ambassador's I saw Mellon, who said he had talked, as I suggested, with the President about Hoover's attitude regarding the extra session as well as toward the President — as outlined in these notes the other day. Mellon said the President doubted whether it would result in avoiding the extra session, but that it is agreeable to him to have Hoover express himself on the bill. He authorized Secretary Mellon to convey this to the President-elect, which he will do. He told Mellon that the bill might provide for the appointment of the members of the Farm Board on March 15, so that the agriculturalists would not be justified in a fear of selections by him.

Also talked this afternoon with Borah, who corroborated what Mark Woods had said on his attitude. He wants no mistake, however, about the farm bill being known as a Hoover measure, if passed.

Nothing may come of all this, but every effort "for the interest of all concerned" should be made to avoid an extra session.

The Senate was occupied to-day in the Treaty debate.

Occupied the chair for a time. My old army comrade, John S. Sewell, formerly Colonel of the Seventeenth Engineers and Commander of Base Sect. No. 1, A.E.F., at St. Nazaire, and Warren Fairbanks took lunch with me.

Washington, January 13, 1929.

My wife and my daughter Virginia and I went to the New York Avenue Church in the morning. I remember first attending this church, which we have attended always when living in Washington, when I was a boy of fifteen. It was the week when James A. Garfield was inaugurated President, on March 4, 1881, and my father, then a Member-elect of Congress, from Ohio, took me there to hear Dr. Paxton preach and to point out the President Lincoln pew. The church meetings are now being held temporarily in the Masonic building while the tower of the old church is being restored. Here at Washington the congregation stands and waits until a President or Vice President has left the church, which he does escorted by the minister. As a result, the absence of one of these dignitaries disturbs the regular order and this, — I regret to say, — makes their absence conspicuous and a matter of comment.

Spent most of the day with my books. President Coolidge called me up by telephone to ask me to help get the Treaty (the "Kellogg Anti-War Pact") ratified as soon as possible. This, of course, I have been trying to do, but told him I would "steam up" to-morrow. He mentioned one or two Senators who seemed a little weak on the proposition, to whom I assume he wants me to speak. During the interminable debate on the Treaty,

characterized by ponderous and long-drawn-out arguments — some of which by the very considerate might
be dignified by the term "legal", but most of them even
more confusing than a legal argument, I find myself
more or less in a state of irritation, waiting for a short
and common-sense discussion of the "human nature"
phase of the problem, which never comes.

What Edmund Burke once said applies exactly:
"Politics ought to be adjusted not to human reason-
ings, but to human nature; of which the reason is but
a part and by no means the greatest part." But of this
view I have spoken before.

I have just passed a delightful evening. Ambassador
Ferrara of Cuba and his wife came in for a family dinner and the Ambassador and I have reveled in a discussion of the classics. We touched on no subject involving a date later than 1520 A.D., the end of the
Renaissance, of which he is a great student. He recently
completed a book on Machiavelli which has been published in Spain and France, and will soon be published
in Italy — a work on which he has been engaged for
twenty years. It was Dwight Morrow who first told me
of Ferrara and his great learning, and I have found my
acquaintance and friendship with him both delightful
and educational.

He keeps up with the triumphant advance of archæology in these latter days when discoveries are so numerous and elucidating. He is a student of Cicero, both of
his history and character. To him the reading of history
is not a pastime, but an absorbing work, as it is to anybody who gets full value out of it. The man who can

read history without engaging at the same time in the
deepest thought of which he is capable, is one who
misses its real lessons. Ferrara has a fine perspective
and yet a vast detail of exact information. His grasp of
modern, economic, and political problems is as unusual
as are his other characteristics. Although a Cuban
citizen of many years residence — he fought in their
revolutionary army during the Spanish war — he is a
native of Italy.

Washington, January 19, 1929.

It is now about midnight, but if one is to keep his
notes contemporaneous he must sometimes keep late
hours. I discovered this in the war. As I promised the
President, I put on steam in the Treaty matter. The
first Senator I called in took immediately to my suggestions, which were that the Cruiser Bill and the
Treaty considered together were the declared and
unified policy of the United States — that if they were
read together and agreed upon together by the Senate,
the desire and determination to co-operate for peace
would not only be properly expressed but the Treaty
would be defined as not abrogating our determination
to recognize our rights of self-defense, a part of which
policy includes the Monroe Doctrine; that reservations
detailing specific acts covered by the term "self-defense"
were unnecessary; that any Senator fearing to be called
to account for his action in voting for the Treaty without
reservations or their equivalent (such as the promulga-
tion of a report by the Foreign Affairs Committee or a
similar device) could protect himself by this statement,
to wit: that the concurrent action on the peace Treaty

and the Cruiser Bill emphasized before the country and
the world their true relation as a definition in combination of a unified national policy.

Encouraged by this first reception of the idea, I telephoned the President, who approved heartily the effort
to have it tried out. Telephoned to him three or four
times the progress of affairs. Borah agreed; Robinson
of Arkansas, minority leader, agreed, and afterward
announced in the Senate he was ready for the vote on
the two measures now as preliminary to future develop-
ments of the idea. Moses not only agreed but promised
to endeavor to persuade his two co-partners in adverse
effort — Reed of Missouri and Bingham. I maintained
that some device to avoid the necessity of a "unanimous
consent" in the matter was possible, and endeavored to
get Moses, who is on the "off side" in the Treaty matter
and knows the rules, to suggest the method — perhaps
only a resolution that it is the sense of the Senate that
the Cruiser Bill and the Treaty should be voted upon
as nearly together in time as possible, in order to
promulgate the idea through discussion of the relations
of the two to each other. If promulgated from such a
source, no reservation resolution would be passed. I
do not know whether anything will come of all this;
but I do feel, after spending much of the day in talking
with Senators, that the effort has contributed something
to the feeling that this problem must be settled ami-
cably, constructively, and at once. Bingham, just before
I left the Senate, said he would agree if the Cruiser
Bill were voted on first, to which he said others made
objection. Somehow, whether by this method or not, I

believe the way will be found out of the present impasse.
The President and Kellogg are both much interested in
having the Treaty passed without expressed reservations.

In the chaotic state of affairs, all the above may become unimportant by to-morrow morning; but these
notes will record at least activity and purpose rather
than indolence.

To-night I went to the annual meeting of the Board of
Directors of the American Society of Military Engineers which met with a bad row on its hands. In the
afternoon, at my Capitol office, six or seven determined
directors had outlined their plans as agreed upon by
the majority of the board in outside consultation. Unless there could be a compromise upon the Lohr controversy between the Corps of Engineers of the Army
and the Board of Directors of the Society, it was evident
to me that the future of this great society was jeopard-
ized. Accordingly, at the meeting to-night as President
of the Society I adopted my tactics in wartime conferences, and at the beginning of the meeting precipitated
a fight that was a real one and that brought out the fundamental issues at stake. The result was a stormy time
at first and a complete and amicable settlement before
we were through, with all parting as friends. It is no
use to go into details. "All's well that ends well." But
I came away with the happiness which one has in con-
tributing even a little to the supremacy of common sense
among sensible men. By this I do not mean to imply
that the controversy would not have been settled with-

out me — but I helped. "And so," as Pepys says, "to bed."

Washington, January 15, 1929.

A short time after I had opened the Senate, Borah came to the desk and asked me to leave the chair and meet him in my office. He submitted an addendum to the proposed report of the Foreign Affairs Committee on the Treaty which at one time all had agreed upon as clearing away objections to the ratification of the Treaty without express reservations. This addendum was a statement that this report was not to be considered as a modification of or reservation to the Treaty. This seemed to me eminently satisfactory, and I so stated. The report as modified gave the contenders against, and the contenders for, each an argument to satisfy their constituencies. That was all the situation required, and this explicit statement that the report was not a modification or reservation to the Treaty was expected by Borah to satisfy the President and Kellogg. He was acting on his own responsibility, and there were still some Senators, notably Bayard and Reed of Missouri, who had not acquiesced. Moses and Bingham had done so.

When he went out to consult others, I telephoned the President to ascertain whether this arrangement, which I fully explained, would be satisfactory if completed, for if it was not, it was due Borah to let him know immediately. The President said that he would not want to be publicly quoted but would say to me: "I think you have done all you can." This, of course, signified acquiescence, and I so informed Borah. Borah

NOTES AS VICE PRESIDENT   235

had not then communicated with Kellogg, but when he came to the office again he had done so. He said that at first Kellogg agreed, but later in the conversation seemed doubtful.

While he was sitting by my side, the telephone rang and I was told that Secretary Kellogg desired to speak to me. I told Borah to stay so that he could hear what I said to him. Kellogg asked my views of the arrangement, stating that he was about to go to the White House to see the President, and that as the latter gave weight to my opinions, he wished to convey them to him. He said he wanted to stand behind Borah, who has made such a splendid fight, and did not want Borah to think otherwise. I told him that Borah was acting on his own responsibility and, of course, assumed his acquiescence. I congratulated him on the situation and told him I had already conveyed my views to the President by telephone. The conversation was detailed but consumed only about five minutes. Borah then knew that both the President and Kellogg approved without qualification his course and, like the fine general he is, immediately started on his final conferences with those yet to agree.

All the world knows what happened only a few hours ago as the result of his success. I took the chair when all was agreed upon and presided during the short debate preceding the vote on the Treaty at 4:20 P.M. (a time which was fixed by unanimous consent), and during the vote. The final and short speech which Borah made rose to the heights of the historic orations of our forebears in the Senate years ago when principles of fundamental importance to our nation's life were at stake.

Surely he and Kellogg have a right to be happy tonight, for there is no reward for long, difficult and toilsome effort in the interest of the public good equal to the satisfaction which comes from knowing it has not been in vain.

Borah has won his fight and to him should go credit, both for his masterful leadership and conduct of debate on the floor and for the last addendum which turned the scale. To Senator J. T. Robinson is due the suggestion of attempting to secure agreement by the making of a report to the Senate by the Foreign Relations Committee instead of by making reservations to the Treaty. This must be considered one of the main factors in the accomplishment. He also made one of the most powerful appeals for the Treaty on the floor.

Charles Curtis, the Republican leader, was most effective in constructive aid all the way through. I find so many other names coming to my mind of Senators who should be mentioned — like Thomas J. Walsh, Senator Swanson and Arthur Vandenberg for marked instance — that I am reminded that, where so many have labored for an accomplishment like this, one perhaps unduly emphasizes that activity which came more directly under his personal notice.

This evening I called up Borah and Kellogg and congratulated them. They said some things which made me happy, too.

Washington, January 16, 1929.

Called on Kellogg and found Sir Esme Howard with him. The latter explained the delay in announcing the selection of Young and Morgan on the Experts committee, stating that he had received a cable from his government expressing its satisfaction, but was waiting until the two names had been submitted formally to all the other governments concerned.

. Kellogg is happy over the Treaty outcome but rather worn out by overwork.

Called for a few minutes on Secretary Mellon. He had talked over the extra session matter with Hoover, telling him the President's attitude. It was too late, however, to change the situation, since discussion has arisen among its friends as to the form the farm bill shall take, and, in Hoover's judgment, any differences should be resolved before the bill is presented in Congress. Secretary Mellon said that lack of time was the only obstacle in the way, and that if the matter had been taken up sooner it might have saved the extra session.

In the afternoon received a telephone call from Secretary Sanders saying that the President invited me to the signing of the Peace Pact in the East Room of the White House to-morrow morning at ten o'clock, and asked me to extend from the chair an invitation to the Senators to be present. This I did — a quorum call first being ordered, to secure a full attendance. It was a dull day in the Senate and I presided for but a short time.

Later.

I have received a letter from Major General Harbord written from Augusta, Georgia, January 11. In it he says: —

Some months ago General W. D. Connor (the President of the War Staff College) asked me to make a talk or prepare a paper for delivery this winter or spring at the Army War College on the subject of my work as Chief of Staff for the first year of the American Expeditionary Forces. I have it in its first form and am sending you a copy and shall be much obliged to you if you will go over it and give me your frank criticism and suggestions if any.

And so this evening I have read General Harbord's prospective address of about eight thousand words and will note here some of my impressions.

Nothing has been written of the A.E.F. organization since the war at once so comprehensive and authoritative, entertaining and yet concise — nothing which has better characterized the greatness of General Pershing or the difficulty and magnitude of his accomplishments — nothing which leaves one's mind clearer as to the competency, modesty, and vision of General Harbord.

My only criticism is that, in his loyalty and in his desire to do full justice to others, he leaves an inadequate picture of his own commanding part in much that was done. As time goes on he will loom larger as one of the most brilliant of all the leaders of the A.E.F. both on the battlefield and in its tremendous supply operations. His record is unique, like that of his great commander — each entered and ended the war respectively in the two highest places in an American army. Only General Washington before them enjoyed such a distinction.

Of my own part in the work of the A.E.F. he says: —

It was already foreseen that ocean tonnage would become the most valuable commodity in the world, and that our supply lines from America would have to be supplemented by supplies obtained elsewheres. The Commander-in-Chief visualized an organization which should comb neutral and Allied countries for supplies and relieve the pressure on American and borrowed tonnage. He placed in charge of it Colonel Charles G. Dawes, destined in post-war days to high political honors, and who has deserved them all. His organization secured twelve pounds of needed supplies of all kinds for every eight that crossed the seas from the home country.

CHAPTER XVIII

AT 10 A.M. this morning I went to the White House for the Kellogg Anti-War Pact signing by the President and the Secretary of State. Was taken to the Blue Room, where the Cabinet was gathered. The President joined us and pointed out where the Cabinet was to be seated when we reached the East Room. He asked me to walk into the East Room with him, which I did — the Cabinet following. About forty Senators were present who were stationed behind the table where the Treaty reposed. We took our seats in front of the table, and then there opened the most formidable barrage from the photographers which I have ever experienced — equal, as one newspaper says, to that when a contract between prize fighters is signed. There must have been forty or fifty cameras and several intensely bright Kleig lights which nearly dazzled us. The orders and noises of the photographers completely destroyed whatever of dignity would naturally have attached to the scene. The President was plainly irritated — and no wonder, considering the impertinent suggestions to "Keep perfectly still" — and to Secretary Kellogg, whose hand is somewhat unsteady, and who had trouble with a very long, heavy and highly ornamented metal pen, to "Keep your

SIGNING OF THE KELLOGG PEACE PACT

(Back row, left to right) *Senator J. T. Robinson, Senator William E. Borah, Senator Claude A. Swanson, Senator T. J. Walsh.* (Seated, left to right) *Vice President Dawes, President Coolidge, Secretary of State Frank B. Kellogg.*

hand steady." However, it is important that the public
see the event, and in the photographs of it all will
look serene, for the pictures were taken in the one and
only minute when everything was serene, on the surface
at least.

Whatever of peace and quiet the photographs may
indicate, I am afraid the press accounts of this amusing
event — for that is what it turned out to be — will
not be equally considerate.

I took Senator Schall from the White House to the
Senate Office Building in my automobile when all was
through, and, as he is blind, described in detail what
had occurred. As I led him to his door, in the Senate
Office Building, a terrific barking from his intelligent
but ferocious police dog greeted us from within. As
the Senator opened the door only the chains of the dog
prevented his springing on me. After the Senator had
quieted him, he inquired whether I would like to shake
hands with this untamed and giant wolf. After my polite
declination of the honor, the Senator told this story,
to really appreciate which one must have seen this
so-called dog and heard him bark. The President, who
is interested in dogs, and had heard of the intelligence
of this one, asked Schall to bring him to the White
House. Senator Schall and his wife led the dog before
the President and extended to the President the invitation to shake hands with him. I may say here in
behalf of the President, who bravely acquiesced, that
he had never heard the dog bark. Unfortunately, Schall
in his desire to show the intelligence of the beast, and
at the time the President held his paw, said *"Laut,*

Laut," which is German for "Loud." The dog spoke, in no uncertain tones. "I could not see," said Schall, "but my wife said the President made a long jump."

The Senate considered the Urgent Deficiency Bill much of the day, and until they reached an amendment referring to prohibition all was serene.

The Senate and the prohibition question when brought together act similarly to a union between water and a Seidlitz powder. Having had long experience with this particular Senate reaction I fled the chair, and left an unfortunate Senator in my place. The subject is of course an extremely important one — but its treatment in the Senate debate is so largely determined by its political bearings that relevant discussion of the particular appropriation item which has aroused the debate occupies but a fraction of the time consumed.

Washington, January 18, 1929.

Presided over the legislature session of the Senate but a short time to-day, but occupied the chair for nearly three hours during the executive session. Senator Borah showed me a letter he had received from Elihu Root in which the latter pronounced the addendum to the committee report on the treaty as "satisfactory", and in his judgment effective for its purpose. This he thought would please Kellogg. Kellogg joined me for lunch and an hour's visit at my office, and as Borah had gone to lunch with Hoover, I told Kellogg about Root's letter. The Secretary seemed satisfied with the reception which the Treaty so far has had in foreign countries. He has already heard from Japan. He seems several years younger than a week ago.

Washington, January 19, 1929.

Later in the morning I called on President Coolidge relative to the arrangements for the presentation of gold medals to representatives of the late Roald Amundsen, to Lincoln Ellsworth, and to General Nobile, for their achievement in the Arctic. Had a pleasant visit, and the President and I covered many topics in our conversation, which lasted some time. He mentioned, among other things, that Hoover had spoken of the difficulty of getting certain men of pre-eminent qualifications to consider positions in the Cabinet because of a disinclination to subject themselves to a contest over their confirmation in the Senate.

Few men of conspicuous achievement have escaped unjust attacks and misrepresentations in their careers, and the vilification in the Senate of Secretary Mellon during almost his entire term of eight years as Secretary of the Treasury is fair notice that rectitude of character and a just fame arising from distinguished public service only stimulate that kind of thing. To attack mediocre or obscure men involves no personal publicity. The critic, like Death, "loves a shining mark."

There has been considerable agitation among Senators during the last four years for a change in the rule requiring nominations to be discussed in executive sessions. If that particular rule should be changed, and the nomination of an eminent man to a high position by the President opens him to a trial by the Senate before the country on any charge which may be made against him by an anonymous letter or by irresponsible people, it will have as disastrous an effect upon the standard of personnel in future Cabinets as the direct election of Senators has had upon the personnel of the Senate.

The Senate was in executive session all the afternoon.

The White House offices where I called this morning bore mute evidence of the passing of power. The halls, ordinarily filled with newspapermen, photographers, candidates for office, Senators, Representatives, and visitors to pay respects, were almost empty. My old friends there, some of whom came to their places thirty years ago under the McKinley Administration, like Rudolph Forster and Latta, all had time to leave their work for a chat. The President was not seeing different men every fifteen minutes. He, too, had plenty of time. The crowd was up at the Mayflower, where the President-elect is staying — and there is the chief center of news and interest.

But I could not help but think that, of the two men, the President is the more fortunate — for he has finished his work, a great and successful one, and leaves with public acclaim, while the President-elect must soon take up great and difficult burdens.

Washington, January 20, 1929.

This noon we had at the house an interesting luncheon in honor of Chief Justice and Mrs. Taft. The guests, besides the Tafts, were Secretary Mellon, Secretary of Labor Davis, Senator Joe T. Robinson, Senator Warren, General Pershing, Comptroller Pole, Mrs. Davis, Mrs. Robinson, Mrs. Warren, Mrs. Pole, Mrs. Towne and Miss Carlisle. The party did not break up until 4 P.M. and after lunch the gentlemen had ample opportunity for a discussion in which there was the most general participation, especially when the question of selective immigration was raised. Senator Warren, one of the wheel horses of the Senate, is disturbed over the status of the great appropriation bills, of which seven or eight remain to be disposed of in the few weeks left of the short session. As the Senate has no power to allot its time properly for the transaction of its business, it has been frittered away by unlimited oratory with the result that now, as generally in a short session, there is a legislative jam which will result in bills being passed by the hundred under "unanimous consent" and without adequate consideration or discussion. The advocates of the Cruiser Bill are becoming alarmed and all are considering the application of the rule providing cloture by a two-thirds vote. It is amusing to note the attitude toward cloture. So jealous are the Senators of the prerogatives given individuals through the power of obstruction made possible by the absence of the majority cloture rule obtaining in all other important parliamentary bodies that they are reluctant to make use of even this kind of cloture. The idea of giving precedence to the right of the majority to perform their duties over the "sacred right of free speech" seems more or less obnoxious. This "sacred right of free speech" in the Senate often translates itself in practice into the right of any individual to indulge for as long a time as he desires in oratory, relevant or irrelevant to the subject under consideration. This, of course, is no true definition of the right of free speech. When the Senators vote by two thirds to limit debate under the present cloture rule they do subjugate this ridiculous privilege to the higher duty they owe the Government under the Constitution.

The invoking of the present two-thirds cloture rule practically negatives the arguments against majority cloture, and this may account for the reluctance to use it. Such public demonstrations of the viciousness of the present rules are not welcomed, but they have to be made. There have been many able Senators, like Oscar W. Underwood, Charles S. Thomas, Atlee Pomerene and others who, in the past, have urged the reformation of the Senate rules and pointed out the outrages upon the public interest which they, in their present form, have made possible.

No one in the Senate, however, has yet undertaken to reform the rules by the threat to use them against the proper conduct of business until they are reformed — in other words, to use them as a bludgeon to force a reform instead of to force through some personal or sectional legislation, generally to the public disadvantage.

Such a Senator needs only to have the qualities of steadfastness in a good cause which his colleagues constantly show in a bad one. He could announce at the beginning that he seeks to block no revenue or appropriation bills in the short session — an underhanded proceeding which has been resorted to so often in the past under the present rules. He might announce, however, that thereafter while he was in the Senate no bill should ever be passed or set for a vote "by unanimous consent" except those involving an unquestioned public necessity.

He could then confidently expect from his colleagues an early proposition involving concessions as to rules reform. The proper reform of the rules can be effected by one man, — to say nothing of a small minority, — but he must be a Senator on the floor and not afraid.

I have seen a Senator unblushingly exact a legislative concession in the open Senate by announcing on an evening devoted to "unobjected bills" that no bill would be passed that night without the fatal "I object" from him, unless the Senate passed his bill. An agreement was made on the spot to pass his bill the next day, which was done.

Washington, January 21, 1929.

The Senate resumed its secret session at noon with the nomination of Roy West as Secretary of the Interior under consideration and confirmed him at 2:30 P.M.

The House of Representatives passed the Chicago World's Fair resolution with an explanatory amendment which was first brought to me for approval. No objection was made to the resolution thus amended and it was passed by the House under unanimous consent. The resolution now comes to the Senate.

The afternoon in the Senate, after executive session, was consumed by a speech on an amendment to the Urgent Deficiency Bill, regarded by everybody as made to use up time so as to prevent the passage of the Cruiser Bill this session — in other words, what is called an indirect filibuster seems going on. The Senate of the United States, with seven or eight major appropriation bills yet to be passed and business of all kinds piling up, seems approaching one of those humiliating concessions to the necessity of cloture. "We are only waiting," said one Senator favoring the bill to me, "until the Senate gets mad enough at this nonsensical performance, and then we will present a two-thirds cloture petition." The Senator, on this particular afternoon when I left, was solemnly declaiming.

The present travesty on common sense and proper parliamentary procedure is possible only because the public is not constantly face to face with it, and does not understand the secretly negotiated trades on personal and sectional legislation which it makes possible.

An evening paper says about the situation in the Senate: —

Some of the staunchest supporters of national defense are opposed in principle to limiting debate by cloture, but these Senators frankly admit that no individual views of Senators on matters of procedure can compare in importance to the requirements of the nation to have insurance of adequate naval defense. Thus, if it is necessary, these Senators will vote for cloture despite their personal dislike for this method of breaking down organized delay.

Again, of the audience of the filibustering speaker, it says: —

At one period Senator Phipps represented the Republican membership (on the floor) while Senators Ashurst and Sheppard represented the Democratic membership.

What a precious privilege it is — this power of obstruction so necessary to "organized delay"! Irrespective of the Naval Bill, what other parliamentary body in the world confronting a jam of legislative business — eight major appropriation bills and other legislation of national importance like the Reapportionment Bill — would lie down supinely, to be run over by an individual member or a small minority, when the national interest was thus at state? Why again must it be only a measure of national defense whose peril finally arouses the conscience of the Senate to its duty?

CHAPTER XIX

IN the morning met Parker Gilbert at the Treasury Department. He is back from Louisville and en route for Europe. Went over the reparations situation, which is not changed in any regard during the last week except apparently for the better.

Saw Governor Young, of the Federal Reserve Board, at the Treasury, who most intelligently discussed the unsatisfactory credit situation in this country, and the policy which, in his judgment, the Federal Reserve Board should adopt in relation thereto. Saw Comptroller Pole, who is leaving for Spokane where he has a $14,000,000 bank on his official hands. He, too, is justly disturbed by conditions which seem to be growing more serious than ever in regard to the inflation of speculative credits. It is a very difficult thing to successfully encourage, at the same time, tight money conditions on the stock market and easy money conditions for legitimate business. The Federal Reserve Board is finding that out. Money flows to any safe point of highest interest rates — nothing can stop it. Until the American people "turn over in bed" and general deflation sets in, credit conditions will grow worse, no matter what the

Federal Reserve Board does. I am apprehensive as to an approaching general contraction of credits. Expanded credits, when they are general, can never be liquidated in an orderly manner. They collapse. History proves this.

The Senate spent the day on prohibition and the Urgent Deficiency Bill — the filibustering tactics seeming for the minute to lag. Joseph Tumulty, Gene Buck, the composer and playwright, John Marshall, Assistant Attorney General, and my old friends Walter H. Wilson, Major Wade Dyar and W. J. Cram, took lunch with me at the Capitol. Tumulty and Buck were especially entertaining and interesting. Senator Pat Harrison was with us for a time.

Later.

The Joint Resolution recognizing the Chicago World's Fair, having been passed by the House, was returned to the Senate and referred to the Finance Committee. As I am piloting this legislation through, I proceeded to smooth the seas as far as possible, and locate the rocks of possible objections in a body which operates chiefly by "unanimous consent."

Senator Smoot, chairman of the Finance Committee, is ready to call a meeting this week. In the meantime I have secured the co-operation of my friend Senator Copeland, after he had satisfied himself that New York did not desire to give a world's fair in 1932, even if it had time to organize one. No man in the Senate is more alert or loyal to the interests of his state than Copeland,

and fortune was with us in the lack of a New York opposition. He promised co-operation, and with Copeland that always means loyal, earnest and real help. Everybody I have seen promises help. In this entirely unselfish movement there is no real reason for opposition, but one can never tell from what source some objection may spring, and an individual or a minority may assert its power over a large majority. Smoot asked me to suggest a report for the Committee's consideration if they favored the bill, which I have done.

Washington, January 23, 1929.

Did not occupy the chair of the Senate for the greater portion of to-day's session. Had a number of interesting visitors at the office. Senator Bruce, of Maryland, of whom I am very fond, and hold in high respect, called as he usually does almost every other day — always with a cheerful word of greeting and with something worth while to say. He is a gentleman of the old school. His classical knowledge and his ability to draw upon it in debate for purposes of illustration or quotation are remarkable. His courage and high principles are acknowledged by all. He is a forceful speaker, but the unusual beauty of his English and his care always to use the exact word which will best express an idea, tend to make his delivery slow. I think no one in the Senate has a more cultured mind. He gives himself wholly to a cause when he is once enlisted, and sometimes loses patience with his opponents — but there is no man in the Senate quicker to forget and forgive the sharp words often spoken in heated debate.

He is a hater of hypocrisy and demagoguery and one of the few conservatives of the Senate who is an aggressive fighter, a hard hitter and "quick on the trigger." Men like him do not long survive the direct primary in these days, but as long as they do, no one is left in any doubt as to where they stand upon important and controversial issues.

To-day I received a letter from Dr. Abbott, of the Smithsonian Institution, accepting my offer to finance a search by the Institution of the sources of Aztec and Mayan literature in Spain. He enclosed in his letter a report on the subject by Dr. J. P. Harrington, of the Bureau of American Ethnology.

Washington, January 24, 1929.

To-day is the fortieth anniversary of our wedding. It is hard to believe that so much time has elapsed since my wife and I started housekeeping in the little six-room cottage at 1400 D Street, Lincoln, Nebraska. The phrase in the wedding service: "With all my worldly goods I thee endow" was a hollow mockery in my case, for after the ceremony at Cincinnati the railroad fare to Lincoln consumed the bulk of my "worldly goods." But it was a glorious time in life — when we figured we could live on eighty dollars a month and I found at the end of the first year that I had earned enough to spend one hundred dollars a month on our living and had four hundred dollars left over for furniture. And then, after a time, came little Rufus Fearing and then little Carolyn, and life was wholly complete.

I recall to-day Governor Oglesby's cry: "My God, to live again those days, when for me half the world was good, and the other half unknown." Such was the world for us then. But to-day it is still a happy world for us. Though the tragic loss of our boy Rufus well-nigh overcame us, kindly time enables us now to speak of him and the happiness he gave us. Our fine son and daughter, Dana and Virginia, are with us all the time, and Carolyn and her children live close by.

I brought home to my wife some flowers, which pleased her all the more because, I regret to say, I generally forget the anniversary until she reminds me of it. But this time I did not.

In the morning in the East Room of the White House I attended a meeting of the United States Commission for the celebration of the two-hundredth anniversary of the birth of George Washington, of which I am ex officio a member. The Commission is composed of members named by the President, the Vice President, and the Speaker of the House.

After presiding for a time the President called me to the chair.

The Commission decided upon the river route for the Mount Vernon Highway from the Arlington Memorial Bridge.

About fourteen of the members of the Commission were present at the meeting.

Presided over the Senate during an interesting portion of the debate on the Cruiser Bill this afternoon.

As the time approaches for my leaving office, many

Senators call and say pleasant things to me. For the Senators individually I cherish a high regard, but collectively, as agents of Government in an organization for business — well! "that is something else again." One of them this afternoon, after telling me how much the Senators thought of me, said, "But the Senate got very tired of you at the beginning of your service." My reply was, "I should hate to think that the Senate was as tired of me at the beginning of my service as I am of the Senate at its end." This of course was a joke, but I had unlimited and irrelevant debate in mind.

Later.

Have just returned from my last attendance at a White House reception, which was for the Army and Navy. Mrs. Dawes, Miss Decker, my little daughter Virginia, and my niece Nancy Hoyt were with me. For the last two it was their first attendance. This started me counting the number of White House receptions I had attended, and was I surprised to find it forty-five — twenty in the McKinley Administration, five in the Harding Administration, and twenty in the present Administration! My delight at all these occasions has been the United States Marine Band. To-night for the last time Secretary Mellon and I "sneaked away" — if I may accurately describe our movement — into the little cloakroom where Tobacco is king and Good Cheer his chamberlain. Secretary Kellogg joined us for a time. These evenings with Secretary Mellon and with the band, near enough to be heard without having our conversation interrupted by it, are among the pleasantest I have spent in Washington. Saw many old army friends in the fifteen minutes I spent in the jam in the Blue Room, among them General Frank McCoy, just back from Nicaragua with his wife to whom he was married since the War. He has made a brilliant record on the field, on the staff, and on all his varied and important details for special duty.

Washington, January 25, 1929.

At the opening of the Senate to-day Senator Heflin announced the death of Oscar W. Underwood, late Senator from Alabama, and the Senate paid him the tribute of immediate adjournment although at his death he was not a member of this body. The entire country will feel the loss of this upright and able man — a leader of his party, first in the House and then in the Senate, and at all times one of the men of conspicuous courage in the nation, in dealing with public and political issues.

My intimate acquaintance with him began after I had made my speech against the Senate rules at my inauguration, when he immediately thereafter introduced a resolution in the Senate for a change by majority cloture providing at the same time ample opportunity for all to be heard. For its passage he fought steadily in the public press and on the floor of the Senate until his retirement from the Senate two years ago. He was a man of delightful personality — radiating good cheer and kindliness.

He was an outstanding Senator, and would have been in any senate of the past — not as an obstructionist

or a filler of the record and waster of the time of the
Senate, for which only impudence and determination
are required, but as a statesman of ability who viewed
his duties from a national and not a personal standpoint, and thereby commanded universal respect.

At 10:30 A.M. I appeared with Senators Deneen and
Glenn before a formal meeting of the Senate Finance
Committee with Senator Smoot in the Chair, called to
consider the Chicago World's Fair resolution. All the
Committee received me kindly and when I took my
seat after explaining the resolution voted unanimously,
without discussion, a favorable report. Senator Smoot
explained that I had already written for him a report
for the Committee which he would have presented
to the Senate. This statement caused amusement, but
no surprise. As a matter of fact, I was in the hands of
good friends and the only thing I had to contend with
was when one of them wanted to add to the resolution
a provision for an appropriation which I did not ask.

In the afternoon, the Senate not being in session, I
visited the House of Representatives — a parliamentary
body with rules under which its business can be properly
conducted.

I sat on the rear bench by the door, but Tilson and
Garrett, majority and minority leaders of the House,
joined me. With them and the others who came I had
a most enjoyable visit, especially with that fine representative of the best traditions of Southern statesmanship — Finis Garrett, the minority leader, now about
to retire from the House.

Later.

Have just returned from a dinner given by the French Ambassador — a large affair. The new French military attaché, General Casanave, was a delight to me, being an intimate friend of General Payot, head of the Fourth Bureau of the General Staff of the French Army during the latter part of the World War. We got to laughing together so heartily that we attracted attention. He spoke English as poorly as I spoke French. When either finished speaking he would pause for the other to stop laughing at the way he did it. It was like a conversation in wartime between Payot and myself, to which Harbord in his book refers as a "Gallicized Weber and Field's debate." Casanave was a brave soldier of the line. He regards Payot as one of the greatest of French generals. That statement alone would endear him to me.

Pennsylvania train en route to Atlantic City, January 26, 1929.

This morning while I was in the chair, to my joy and satisfaction the Senate, under unanimous consent, passed the joint resolution recognizing properly the second Chicago World's Fair. It now goes to the President for his signature. The opinion is so widespread, as well as so well founded, that the day of the old-fashioned world's fair is over that I feared opposition to this resolution by those who did not understand that this new fair project is based not only upon a new plan but upon new and radically different principles. My brother Rufus, who suggested the plan, has quietly and effectively organized the effort behind it for a year and with great executive ability has prevented the internal

friction and the premature publicity, based upon prospects instead of upon accomplished forward steps, which
usually handicap voluntary movements of this kind.

From now on his difficulties will be lessened and the
recruits to his cause, already numerous, should constantly increase. For nearly sixty days I have given attention to the resolution, and its final passage is a great
relief to me. My friend, Senator Joe Robinson, the
minority leader, was on guard in the Senate this morning and his well-worded and brief statement, after Senator Deneen had asked for unanimous consent to the
passage of the resolution, discouraged any possible
objection to a measure wholly meritorious.

Pennsylvania Railroad, en route Atlantic City
to Washington, January 27, 1929.

Yesterday when Uncle Will Mills and Wade Dyar
were with me at the Capitol office, John C. Allen, a
member of Congress from Illinois and a friend for forty
years, called. I told him that Uncle Will, who was now
seventy-seven years of age, was the first man to loan
me money when, as a young man at Lincoln, I started
to branch out from the law. Then John Allen reminded
me that he had loaned me $3,000 at eight per cent.
in 1894, at Lincoln, Nebraska, declining the collateral
I offered as something which would reflect doubt in
his mind as to the wisdom of his action. This had assisted me in my first gas purchase of the LaCrosse Gas
Light Company of Wisconsin.

Allen, who, in the old days, was State Auditor of
Nebraska, said it was he who interested Senator Man-

derson in John Pershing, resulting in his detail as Military Instructor to the University of Nebraska in 1890. Jim Pershing, John's brother, had asked him to write in John's behalf to Manderson, then United States Senator from Nebraska. John Allen said he now has the letter of thanks which General Pershing then wrote him, signed "John J. Pershing, 2nd Lieut. 6th Cavalry." While not responsible for General Pershing's military career, John Allen was thus responsible for mine, for when Pershing came to Lincoln our friendship began, and this later made it possible for me to get a military commission, at fifty-two years of age, in the World War.

John Allen was elected Secretary of State of Nebraska when he was twenty-nine years of age, and moved to Illinois after leaving that office about the time I did.

My uncle, W. W. Mills, is a remarkable man. For forty-two years he has been the President of the First National Bank of Marietta, Ohio, of which the founder, in 1863 — my grandfather Gates — has been the only other President. He has devoted his life largely to philanthropic work.

Washington, January 28, 1929.

Presided over the Senate during the "morning hour" and for a part of the afternoon during the debate on the Cruiser Bill.

I have just returned this evening from the semi-annual meeting at Continental Hall of the business organization of the Government, which was addressed by the President and the Director of the Budget, General Lord. It was an imposing gathering and an inspir-

BRITISH AMBASSADOR SIR ESME HOWARD AND
VICE PRESIDENT DAWES

*Presenting trophy of the city of Daytona, Florida, to Captain Malcolm Campbell
for speed record.*

ing occasion. The Army Band was present and played a short program while the audience was gathering. It comprised the Budget and co-ordinating officers, the bureau chiefs, the heads of the independent establishments of government and the members of the Cabinet. The hall, seating about 1200, was crowded. The general arrangement was (and ever has been since) the same as we had at the second of these meetings, held in the same place, February 3, 1922. The President, the Director of the Budget, the Vice President and the Cabinet were seated at the front of the platform and the members of the co-ordinating boards and chief co-ordinator separately, so as to visualize their special relation to the general body. The rest of the audience took the regular seats in the body of the house.

At the first meeting, June 29, 1921, in the smaller audience hall in the Interior Department, we had not then established the co-ordinating boards or drawn the executive orders creating the organization ever since maintained practically without change. Therefore only President Harding, the Director of the Budget (myself), and the Cabinet were segregated from the main body of Bureau Chiefs.

The speeches of President Coolidge and General Lord this evening consisted chiefly of the summarizing of the fine achievements during the last eight years of what is referred to as the Budget System, in operation under Harding for about two years and a half and about five years and a half under Coolidge. In general I approved the speeches made to-night of the budget work of these two distinguished men.

The high terms in which they praised each other were deserved. None could have administered the Budget Bureau as it was organized better than they — perhaps none as well. They praised not each other alone but, in general terms, the body of the business organization and the department and bureau chiefs who are now co-operating in a smoothly working machine, with a mutual confidence in each other and loyalty to the co-ordinating control over them, a control exercised by the Director of the Budget, acting as agent of the Chief Executive.

But I certainly felt that they might have at least mentioned President Harding — under whom the budget was organized, the machinery for its functioning created, the new and revolutionary principles governing it not only established but codified, and the greater part of its financial results obtained. Under him was brought about, with great difficulty, a central co-ordinating executive control, after decentralized and independent departmental functioning for one hundred and thirty years of government.

When, disillusioned, betrayed and broken, he passed away, he left to President Coolidge and to General Lord — whom he had appointed — a task of administration, not creation. But *his* task had been both.

Later.

I have been going over my old official budget statements. In his speech President Coolidge said: "The expenditures for that fiscal year (1921) exclusive of the debt reduction, were about $5,000,000,000." I find the exact figure was $5,115,927,688.30.

Again President Coolidge says: "Expenditures diminished until 1927 when, exclusive of the amount applied to debt reductions, they reached a point below the $3,000,000,000. This was $2,000,000,000 below 1921."

So it was — the exact figure of these expenditures being $2,974,029,674.62.

But I regret that President Harding's name was forgotten when of this $2,000,000,000 reduction about eighty-five per cent of it — to wit, $1,743,319,789.46 — occurred in 1922, the first year of the two fiscal years of the budget under Harding. The figures involved are: —

Expenditures, exclusive of debt reduction in fiscal year 1921 were $5,115,927,689.30.

Expenditures, exclusive of debt reduction in fiscal year 1922 were $3,372,607,899.84.

Reduction in Harding's first year $1,743,319,789.46 as above.

This also should be said, and it is often overlooked.

It is difficult to appraise what reduction in these expenses were attributable to the change in operating methods inaugurated at this time, and what therefore was actually accomplished in economy as distinguished from the postponement of expenditures to a succeeding year, to say nothing of the natural liquidation in war expenditures then still in progress.

Gross figures of governmental expenditure solely should never be used to demonstrate budget efficiency and economy as they were this evening, but rather the smaller amount subject to executive control in the operation of the routine business of government. In 1922, we did not claim credit for a $1,743,319,789.46 reduction, but we did claim that by the new budget control we had saved in that year $250,134,835.03, and this latter sum we itemized in detail and reported to Congress in response to a resolution requesting it.

Washington, January 29, 1929.

This is the birthday of William McKinley, a great leader, a great and good man, and the last President with such qualities of patience, tact, and commanding strength combined as enabled him to enlist Congress in an uninterrupted support of all his domestic and international policies.

The dreary debate on the Cruiser Bill continued throughout the day in the Senate, the membership on the floor for most of the time being reduced to a half-dozen Senators or less. I occupied the chair for but a short time, coming in, however, to preside when unanimous consent was obtained ensuring a vote on the bill next week.

Senator Curtis, Republican floor leader, by his unparalleled patience, activity, and good nature finally secured the consent of the last man for the agreement limiting debate after a certain time, thus ensuring the passage of the bill this session.

To what humiliating methods is leadership condemned by the Senate rules — to beg from individuals the right for the Senate to act, to listen to childish personal reasons for refusing to acquiesce in permitting what is the duty of the Senate not only to do, but to do when its majority wills — not simply when its minorities permit. Count Széchényi, — have difficulty in spelling his name, — Senator Capper and Wade Dyar took lunch with me at the Capitol. The office was filled much of the afternoon with callers — most of them Senators fleeing from "unlimited debate."

Washington, January 30, 1929.

The Senate was occupied during the day in the Cruiser Bill debate and temporarily on the Agricultural Appropriation bill. Senator David Reed made a powerful speech on the Cruiser Bill.

Spent quite a time at the office in the afternoon with Senator Borah, who is commencing a study of the reparations question and wanted such information and comment as I had to offer. Enjoyed this discussion. Borah's mind is so alert and his comprehension so quick that few explanatory digressions from any trend of thought or argument presented to him are necessary.

Washington, February 2, 1929.

While I did not hear it yesterday, I have to-day read the summary of Senator Burton's speech on the Cruiser Bill. It is a most dignified and courageous utterance. I do not happen to agree with him in his conclusions, as I believe that the passage of the Cruiser Bill, with the time limitation, is not only a step in proper national policy, if universal naval disarmament is not agreed upon, but an essential step to bring about a real naval disarmament agreement in the near future. This view I have before expressed. But this speech is rare for the genuine courage required to make it. It resembles the early speeches of Briand favoring a reasonable attitude of France towards a reparation settlement, which led to his retirement from public office — only to return later when public sentiment formed by ensuing events changed in his favor.

No demagogue has a readier audience than a nationalistic demagogue. No statesman is more easily misrepresented to the public by the demagogue than he who stands always for justice in the international relations of his own country. The latter is never certain of his standing except with posterity. If he lifts his voice in behalf of a just moderation in any authoritative statement of national policy, a moderation which not only properly befits national dignity but inspires international respect, he is denounced as lacking in patriotism. Nothing seems to satisfy a public sentiment inflamed over an international question like extravagant statement couched in offensive terms to the other nation or nations involved.

The demagogue well knows this, and accordingly attacks the statesman who declines to indulge in it as if temperance in expression and fairness in argument were the distinguishing marks of a traitor.

This kind of demagoguery in Europe, for six years following the signing of the Versailles Treaty, dominated public sentiment and determined the national policies of the Allies. As a result, not alone Germany but all Europe steadily marched toward complete economic disaster, which was finally averted only when "Common Sense was crowned king" and our first Committee of Experts was convened.

I honor a man like Senator Burton. He does not need

to interpolate in his speeches allusions to his own courage, as is the habit of demagogues. Courage always speaks for itself. To claim it for one's self is rather the evidence of the innate coward.

In a great cause, where the aroused passions of the masses deaden their intellect, public opinion is never successfully braved and courted at the same time. Nor do the brave fight and fawn at the same time.

Washington, February 4, 1929.

Was in the chair much of to-day's session of the Senate, the debate being limited under unanimous consent to thirty minutes on the Cruiser Bill and each amendment until 4 P.M., and then to ten minutes. It is at such times that the Senate appears at its best. Upon an important bill like this the ablest Senators are heard, and the time is not entirely monopolized by those chiefly noted for garrulity.

The best speakers, of course, are never of the continuous variety. Nor do they permit themselves to lose public interest and respect in constantly seeking public attention by exploiting minor matters or those involving personalities. Their appearances do not lose their dignity by their frequency. Upon occasions of limited debate on an important bill the galleries are crowded. Coming as they do after weeks of unlimited debate the long-time speakers are generally run down and visitors hear speeches which are short and to the point with a minimum of digression. One wearied with the continuous performance of a few familiar speakers habitually interjecting long addresses upon subjects irrelevant to the one before the Senate finds himself agreeably surprised in a limited debate at the number of able Senators, ordinarily quiet, who are heard upon such an occasion. As a prominent newspaper correspondent said to me to-day, "Such occasions show what the Senate can and should be." And thus it always would be in public were its time alloted fairly and in accordance with the importance of pending business instead of being consumed by those interminably seeking publicity or promoting personal purpose by obstruction at the cost of its time.

Senator J. T. Robinson made one of his short and forcible statements on the bill, with that discriminating emphasis on essentials so needful after an "unlimited" debate of weeks, to clarify the dazed and befuddled mind of the average man who has endeavored to follow it. A test vote was had on an amendment which determines that the time clause in the Cruiser Bill shall be retained. The vote was 54 to 28.

This evening we attended a large dinner given at the Mayflower Hotel by ex-Senator Rice Means and his wife. There in the smoking room Senator Watson entertained Justice Stone, Senators Dale, Oddie, Robinson, and myself in his inimitable way. We think so often of Watson as a companionable friend that we are apt to forget how generally constructive is his work in the Senate. His very proficiency in politics prevents a public realization of his more important accomplishments, for it commands the most attention. As the next Republican leader in the Senate the real influence upon the work of the Senate which he has always had will probably be more apparent.

Washington, February 5, 1929.

Occupied the chair of the Senate much of the day, which ended at the passing — by a vote of 68 to 12 — of the Cruiser Bill with the time limit clause retained. The debate, with its ten-minute time limit on the bill and each amendment, was animated, constructive and elucidating — strange terms if applied to the ordinary Senate debate.

In this debate there was dragged into the open one of those humiliating secret agreements made possible by the rules, under which a small minority able to block the Cruiser Bill had brought its sponsors, representing the majority of the Senate, to their knees. Dragged into the open, it was so contemptible that the Senate spewed it out. Yet it was only one of many similar agreements during the last four years.

But this time it failed, and it failed because unexpectedly the real purpose of a proposed modification was exposed by its own proponents, and a humiliation the like of which the Senate continually suffers in secret was not to be borne in public.

When a chaplain in the Navy holds religious services a flag bearing a cross is flown above the American flag, a custom of the long years. That flag is not a Catholic emblem and has never been. It has always flown over both Protestant and Catholics whenever religious services are held in the Navy.

At the last session of Congress, and in the campaign

of 1928, those endeavoring to stir up religious strife in the country referred to this flag as a Catholic emblem in order to arouse anti-Catholic sentiment.

To-day it developed that an amendment forbidding the Navy at religious services to fly this flag above the American flag had been agreed upon by the Navy Department, the Senator in charge of the bill, and, evidently, by other members of the Senate. It was about to be adopted when its author launched into an attack upon the Catholic Church. The cat was out of the bag. It was immediately evident that in order to avoid obstructive tactics against it, those in charge of the bill were, in effect, condoning and even encouraging an attack upon the Catholic Church which all knew was unjust and unfounded.

Fortunately, by unanimous consent, the ten-minute limit on debate was in force. That and that only saved trouble when the Senate by a vote defeated the amendment with only ten Senators voting for it. It was then too late to filibuster, since the time limit was on, and the Cruiser Bill was passed without this humiliating amendment.

I wish the Senators who uphold "publicity" as a cure for all things would turn their attention for a time from the affairs of others to their own, and expose and denounce the secret agreements modifying legislation which are habitually made under the Senate rules and are possible only because of those agreements. That kind of publicity would result in the reform of the rules. Unfortunately, accidents of publicity like those of to-day happen only occasionally.

Washington, February 6, 1929.

I forgot to write yesterday that the President signed the World's Fair resolution, thus making it a law.

To-day was devoted by the Senate chiefly to work on the Army Bill. Had a pleasant call at my office from Elihu Root, my acquaintance with whom dates from his entrance into the McKinley Administration. We talked over old times, especially about President Mc-Kinley. Mr. Root spoke of McKinley's qualities of leadership, which he greatly admired, and said that the talk about his being influenced unduly by others resulted from McKinley's generosity and kindly ways.

"He would call me to his office," said Root, "and show me some plan of action of which he had made written notes. In the course of a week he would have discussed it with a dozen Senators and House members. It would remain entirely unchanged but each of those consulted would leave with the idea that he, rather than the President, had suggested it."

Mr. Root is now eighty-four years of age. He says he has no ailments wherever except a case of "Anno Domini." He is about to go to Europe on his work in connection with the World Court. We talked over Army organization, for Elihu Root as Secretary of War was the father of the American General Staff. He recalled our friend the late Major General William H. Carter and his contributions to the creation of the General Staff legislation.

He expressed interest in the Military Board of Allied Supply, and I presented him with the three-volume report of that body. Wade Dyar and my cousin William

R. Dawes, now President of the Mississippi Valley Association, took lunch with me. We are greatly enjoying a visit at home from our daughter Carolyn.

Washington, February 9, 1929.

To-day is the date and Paris the place of the first meeting of the new Experts' Committee which will undertake the great task of final settlement of the amount of German reparations. Of the new committee of ten, five were members of the first Experts' Committee which met in Paris in January 1924. This afternoon I received the following cable from them and from Doctor Schacht, who is the member from Germany and President of the Reichsbank: "All the old friends, Young, Parelli, Francqui, Parmentier, Stamp, Schacht, send affectionate greetings and their first thoughts on reunion were of their old leader, the General."

In answer I cabled Young as follows: "Please extend my affectionate regards to my old associates of the First Committee of Experts and Doctor Schacht and an expression of my confidence in the successful outcome of their new effort for world betterment."

Washington, February 12, 1929.

Lincoln's Birthday. In the morning Senator Keyes brought to my office a volume containing the manuscript facsimile of the Gettysburg addresses of Edward Everett and Abraham Lincoln. Lincoln wrote out his address in a hand almost as distinctive as is the speech itself. Keyes says there are four copies of this address in Lincoln's handwriting.

In February, 1897, thirty-two years ago, I was at dinner at the house of John Hay in Washington at a time when, as a member of the Executive Committee of the Republican National Committee, together with General Horace Porter and Marcus A. Hanna, I was helping to make the arrangements for McKinley's inauguration, soon to take place. I distinctly remember the statement of Mr. Hay, who was Lincoln's secretary, that Lincoln first wrote out the speech on the back of an old envelope as he was on the train traveling to Gettysburg. Whether Hay then had this copy I do not remember, but I do recollect seeing at his home the copy of the second inaugural address of Lincoln in Lincoln's handwriting. It was not until I heard an extempore address which Governor Richard J. Oglesby, Lincoln's personal friend, delivered on Lincoln's birthday in 1896 at a banquet of the Marquette Club in Chicago, that I felt I had a conception of Lincoln's real stature in life.

In almost all the descriptions of Lincoln's character which I had heard and read, emphasis had been put on his kindness, his generosity to rivals, his gentleness of spirit and his sadness of disposition. Without knowing what, I felt that something was lacking in the picture — something which would stamp him as the great and strong and natural leader of men that he was — one always first. Oglesby in his speech provided it.

He reached his oratorical climax by describing the humble surroundings of Lincoln's early life — the log cabin, with its chinks filled with mud, without flooring, the beds consisting of boards resting on pins driven into the log walls and covered first with straw and then with a coverlet. "In their barrenness and poverty," said he, "one was reminded of the scenes of Bethlehem."

And then, after a pause, he added: "But at this time and at all times, under these circumstances and under all circumstances, Abraham Lincoln recognized no superior on the face of the earth."

That was what unknowingly I had been waiting to hear. Then I understood Abraham Lincoln.

In the Senate to-day Senator Smoot paid a beautiful tribute to the dead President. The day was a very full and busy one. It was rendered memorable to me by the remembrance of my friends engaged in the reparations work in Paris. This is best told by the beginning of the Paris cable to the *New York Times,* published this morning: —

(Special Cable to the *New York Times,* by Edwin L. James.)

PARIS, February 11 — The economic and financial experts of seven nations, gathered in Paris to prepare a final settlement of German reparation payments to the former Allies and also to indicate a way to a final settlement of all international indebtedness left by the world war, held their first meeting this afternoon in the Hotel George V.

The first act of the fourteen distinguished gentlemen was to nominate formally as Chairman Owen D. Young, the first American delegate, who played such a prominent part in the elaboration four years ago of the Dawes Plan, to complete which will be an important part of the work of the present Committee.

This tribute paid to him, the second act of the committee taken on the initiative of Governor Émile Moreau, of the bank of France, and seconded by Doctor Hjalmar Schacht, head of the Reichsbank, was to send the following telegram to Vice President Dawes, who acted as chairman for the first Experts' Committee: —

"The second Committee of Experts at the inception of its first meeting in Paris addresses to General Dawes the homage of its respect and the expression of its hope of accomplishing work as useful as that which was realized under the chairmanship of General Dawes in 1924."

CHAPTER XX

To-DAY the Electoral Vote for the next President and Vice President of the United States was counted before a joint session of the Senate and House of Representatives; and as the presiding officer of the joint session, at its conclusion I made this statement from the chair: —

"The Vice President. The announcement of the state of the vote by the Vice President just made, is, under the Constitution and laws of the United States, deemed a sufficient declaration of the persons elected President and Vice President of the United States, each for the term beginning on the fourth day of March, 1929, and will be entered, together with a list of the votes so cast and ascertained, on the journals of the Senate and the House of Representatives.

"Gentlemen of the joint session, the purpose of this meeting having been accomplished, the joint session is now dissolved and the Senators will return to the Senate Chamber."

Much formality was observed at the joint session. In the Senate at 12:55 P.M. I requested from the chair that the Senate assemble and march to the House of Representatives. I attach the order of the march as circulated by the Sergeant at Arms throughout the Senate: —

The Secretary with the Sergeant at Arms.

Two pages carrying the boxes containing the electoral votes.

The Republican Assistant Sergeant at Arms with the Democratic Assistant Sergeant at Arms.

The Vice President with the President Pro Tempore, Mr. Moses.

The Assistant Majority Leader, Mr. Watson, with the Minority Leader, Mr. Robinson.

The Tellers: Senators Shortridge and King.

The senior Republican Senator, Mr. Warren, with the senior Democratic Senator, Mr. Simmons.

The remainder of the Senate according to seniority as far as practicable.

When we reached the House of Representatives that body arose and stood while the Senators were entering, and as I ascended to the chair. Speaker Longworth, of the House, was seated at my side. After calling the session to order and announcing its purpose, I handed the keys to the two mahogany boxes, in which the electoral votes by States were deposited, to the tellers, who unlocked them. These boxes were on the Speaker's stand before me. I took from the boxes the envelopes, one by one, containing the votes, and as I handed them to the tellers they announced the vote of each state. After the votes by States were announced separately the tellers handed me a written report of the vote and I announced the result — for President, Herbert Hoover 444 votes; Alfred E. Smith 87 votes; for Vice President, Charles Curtis 444 votes; Joseph T. Robinson 87 votes. I then made the closing statement with which I commenced this note.

The entire time consumed by the proceedings was only about thirty-five minutes. There was a large attendance of the members of the Senate and House, filling the most of the floor of the House, and the galleries were crowded. While, following precedent, I had requested the joint session and the galleries to refrain from applause, I was kept busy with the gavel during the announcement of the votes by States — some announcements like those of the vote of Massachusetts and Virginia being vociferously received.

After we reached the Senate a report from the floor was made of the vote in the joint session by Senator Shortridge whom, together with Senator King, I had appointed as tellers. No surprise was evidenced or felt by anybody during all those announcements of things accomplished and known for three and a half months, but it was surprising to note with what intentness and interest the statement of them was received.

This evening at the house, Colonel Latrobe and Captain Brown of the *Mayflower* — the President's aides — called to notify us of the program at the White House for the morning of the inauguration. We were asked to be there at eleven o'clock.

Washington, February 14, 1929.

At 10:00 A.M. attended a meeting of the Regents of the Smithsonian Institution. Chief Justice Taft, the Chancellor of the Institution, presided. Those present included Senator Smoot, Senator J. T. Robinson, Senator Swanson, Congressman Moore, F. A. Delano and Mr. Laughlin. Charles E. Hughes and Dwight W. Morrow and Professor Merriam, of the Carnegie Institute, were among those absent. As usual, the meeting was full of interest — especially the report covering the exploring work being done by the Institution in Haiti and some other of the Caribbean Islands. Everybody connected with the work of the Institution is an enthusiast, and they are to be envied, for no set of men lead lives of greater interest than those engaged in research work to increase the knowledge of mankind.

The Institution sadly needs additional space. Precious specimens, constituting the overflow of the exhibits, are packed away in every corner and closet, and more are constantly coming in. Recently it was necessary to decline the gift of the exhibit of the progress of railroad transportation made by the Baltimore and Ohio Railway at Baltimore — the "Iron Horse" exhibition, visited by a million people in the space of three weeks. There was no place to put it. Why more men of wealth do not follow the example of Mr. Freer by remembering the Institution in their wills is strange. Here is a Board of Trustees recognized by the national Government, and composed of the most eminent and competent men, supported by a staff of trained scientists, continuing the high standard which is guaranteed by the charter of the organization. Those who choose it as their agent in their bequest of art or of money for the public purpose of the Institution are assured of perpetual remembrance, as are the names of those whose memory they may wish to associate with their benefactions. In addition, they are assured indefinitely

of a competent and honest administration of any trust
they may create.

There is now the inevitable jam of legislative business in the Senate at the end of the session, due to the
waste of the time of the Senate under the rules. As a
consequence, hundreds of bills will be passed "by unanimous consent" without proper consideration in the
next two weeks.

Presided over a lively discussion for a time.

Senator Vandenberg is commencing to show his teeth
in a righteous cause — the passage of the Reapportionment Bill. He is a coming man, in my judgment.

Washington, February 15, 1929.

The Senate's time was chiefly consumed to-day by a
debate entirely irrelevant to the bill before the Senate
for consideration — upon the question of whether certain Cabinet officers who admittedly had done their
duty should not be publicly censured for not having
done it sooner. This question of doubtful importance
was not settled, and the resolution embodying it finally
went to the calendar.

Some people delight to fiddle while time burns.

Occupied the chair during the morning hour, during
the executive session, and during a limited portion of
the debate.

Colonel Latrobe called on me at the office in regard
to inauguration day procedure and I told him that I
had learned the Senate would be in session on that
day at an early hour, thus requiring my presence in

the chair at the time the Presidential party was coming to the Capitol, and preventing me from joining it.

He then requested that Mrs. Dawes be at the White House to accompany Mrs. Gann. This I said she would be very glad to do.

This afternoon I received a letter from Secretary Kellogg transmitting the greetings of the Second Committee of Experts on Reparations Settlement, which had been cabled to the State Department through our Embassy at Paris.

Washington, February 16, 1929.

The Senate to-day occupied itself largely with a debate on prohibition, which was the subject before it for consideration, and on the Catholic Church, which was not. Having heard these subjects discussed by the Senators for four years, more or less, and being somewhat familiar with the oratorical treatment accorded them by the individual Senators, I decided to allow some of them to take their own medicine for the most of the day by occupying the chair in my place. Returned, however, for the masterful speech of James A. Reed.

At my Capitol office most of the day. A number of friends called — among them Justice Stone of the Supreme Court.

During the afternoon, a committee of six members of the Gridiron Club, headed by Mr. Groves — who has at times impersonated me in the skits of the Club — called to invite me to a closed dinner of the Club, to be given in my honor. We fixed the date for March 2. What Groves said I much appreciated, as well as this attention from the most brilliant organization of Washington. It will involve a speech, of course, but that thought, while it naturally arouses apprehension, does not lessen my happiness in their remembrance.

Another call which I received, from Doctor Rowe, the Director of the Pan American Union, was much appreciated. He informed me that next week I would be asked by a representative of the President of the Dominican Republic to select and head a commission to establish a system for the executive control of expenditures in that country similar to the one which we established here coincident with the organization of the Budget Bureau. This should not take over five or six weeks, and while I will still have to have considerable information before I can make a decision as to undertaking the work, it is an attractive idea to me.

No work appeals so much to me as constructive work of this nature, especially in a branch of it where I have had the benefit of experience.

This evening we attended a dinner given us by Trubee Davison and his wife. This son of my dear friend, Harry Davison, reminds me of his father in every way — in his appearance, voice, geniality, humor, and high competency. He is making a name for himself as Assistant Secretary of War in charge of Aviation — which would have delighted his father could he have lived to know of it. Harry was wrapped up in his two fine boys, Trubee and Harry. He lived in an agony of anxiety during their brilliant and dangerous service as aviators in the war, in which Trubee was so badly injured. But he lived long enough afterward to be sure that their lives in peace would be as honorable and distinguished as they had been in war.

Washington, February 17, 1929.

My wife, my daughter Virginia and I attended church in the morning and then took lunch with ex-Senator Charles S. Thomas, his wife and daughter. In the evening, Senator and Mrs. Vandenberg took supper and spent the evening with us.

Vandenberg is one of the coming men in the Senate — as I have said before in these notes. A man of strong convictions and unusual aggressiveness, he has ability, patience and judgment. He is also unafraid. Naturally a man of gentlemanly instincts as well as perception, he is confronted by the problem which troubles all newcomers to the Senate.

Shall one resort to the common method of forcing recognition in committee appointments or in getting anything else one wants there, by using the existing Senatorial powers of obstruction — under the rules — against the legislative plans or ambitions of others unless they are granted? It is hard for one to get anywhere quickly in the Senate unless he follows this course — but one naturally shrinks from it. Vandenberg, however, has the courage to do it when fighting for a bill purely in the public interest — like the Reapportionment Bill, which he has now forced the steering committee to place on the preferred list of subjects for consideration. Men less sensitive than he, who have come recently into the Senate, already have found ample space in the newspapers through obstructive tactics and are securing that unusual amount of kindly personal consideration in the Senate accorded to an unreasonableness which, displayed under the same circumstances in a private association, would more than likely result in ostracism.

The present Senate rules encourage and reward in public business the exercise of the selfish instincts of human nature as distinguished from those higher and unselfish qualities which are universally held admirable in other relationships.

Then again, those rules not requiring relevancy in debate, nor allowing a majority of less than two thirds to close debate as in other great deliberative bodies, put at all times the public reputation and dignity of the United States Senate at the mercy of any audacious publicity-seeker in its membership.

Washington, February 18, 1929.

Very busy day. Presided over the Senate during a great debate upon prohibition by Senator Borah and Senator Reed, of Missouri. It was worthy of the Senate of the old days. The galleries were crowded and the Senate floor well occupied while these Senators were speaking.

Spent the morning before the session of the Senate with Arthur Leonard, a business associate of Chicago, going over important personal business matters.

In these days of a strained credit situation in the country, the wise business man is making preparations for a possible credit contraction of serious proportions. This will come at any time when there occurs any lack of general confidence, perhaps before.

Men may talk of the new business conditions which make the old danger signals obsolete, but there is one unchangeable element in the situation, and that is human nature. All human nature is subject to the law of reaction. With human nature in mind, one senses a coming reaction. When men have moved in a mass in one direction for a long time, under the influence of optimism, they always move in the opposite direction when pessimistic. When the latter movement comes, credit sharply contracts and business slows down.

My old friend, ex-Senator Atlee Pomerene, called and introduced his associate in the Government's oil prosecutions, Mr. Roberts. They have been very successful in this important work. Atlee and I were classmates and members of a "Quiz Club" of seven in the Cincinnati Law School, and we have kept up our friendship for over forty years.

He served two terms in the Senate of the United States, from Ohio, with great distinction, and I am glad to say has the same opinion of the Senate rules as I have. This he expressed in the Senate in a speech strongly condemning the rules, a speech made at the end of twelve years of observation of their effects on legislation and the Senate.

Later.

We have just returned from a dinner given us by the Minister from Finland, Mr. Aström. With the exception of Justice Sanford, Senator Goff and ourselves, all the guests were diplomats — the Ambassadors from Germany and Cuba, and the Ministers from Holland, Austria, and Norway.

These last days here are pretty strenuous for my wife who, in addition to her outside duties, is preparing to move our household back to Evanston; but she is equal to them. This afternoon, Mrs. Coolidge had her official family at tea at the White House — to wit, the wife of the Vice President and the wives of the Cabinet officers — probably their last gathering. I do not suppose any wife of any President ever made more friends in Washington than Mrs. Coolidge. Her departure from official life causes general and sincere regret. Mrs. Dawes is very much attached to her.

Washington, February 20, 1929.

Presided over the Senate for a portion of the day.

I have already made, perhaps, too many references to the rules in these notes.

But the situation near the end of a short session is pitiable. Appropriation bills are pressing and in danger of not passing. Other bills are in a jam. Yet most of the day was devoted to irrelevant and time-consuming speeches made for ulterior purposes. Senators on the floor were claiming a filibuster was in progress against the Navy Appropriation Bill and charging bad faith.

To get rid of the jam, "unanimous consent" requests were now and then made, but all were objected to by a few individuals.

These tactics, let it be said, do not result in the passage of less legislation! They are designed to se-

cure modification and trades in legislation by individuals who must be satisfied before the hundreds of
bills are passed by "unanimous consent" and without
proper consideration in the last few days of the session. Senator Blease, for instance, is preventing the
passage of the bill providing for an additional federal judge in lower New York to relieve an enormous
congestion in the work of the Federal Court there,
and other bills designed to relieve crowded federal
dockets elsewhere. He will continue to block them
unless he gets an additional federal judge in South
Carolina. He makes no secret of this and has the courage to avow his true purposes. This is but an open
sample of much that is going on under cover. The acknowledged leaders of the Senate, — constructive men,
— interested in expediting the passage of bills necessary for the proper conduct of government, are running
here and there begging individuals to grant the majority of the Senate the power to act.

The most determined obstructionists are fawned
upon, cajoled, flattered — anything to get their acquiescence that the Senate may do its constitutional duty
— but so far in vain. It is a shameful spectacle — and
yet so common that it passes here as a matter of course.

At some future day in a short session I hope that
in the interest of partial reform at least a courageous
senator will rise and announce a resolution changing
the rules so as to provide, at least in the short session,
majority cloture on revenue and appropriation bills
alone. He will then announce that during that session
he will object to all proposals to pass bills by "unani-

mous consent" and will allow only revenue and appropriation bills necessary to the life of the Government to escape whatever obstructive tactics he and his friends may devise under the unchanged rules — this opposition to cease if his resolution changing the rules is passed.

If he succeeds, at least revenue and appropriation bills cannot be used in the short sessions by the filibusterers to force their private and sectional measures through secretly, as Senator Tillman once courageously did publicly to the tune of a $600,000 appropriation for South Carolina.

If passed, this partial reform would make it impossible for individuals in the Senate at times to bring Congress and even the President to their knees by compelling the calling of an extra session of Congress as an alternative to yielding to their demands.

Washington, February 21, 1929.

As most of the day in the Senate was consumed by the filibusters I presided but a short time. The filibuster on the Navy Bill broke down under the threat of a night session and of the invoking of the two-thirds cloture rule. The number of opponents of the bill was small.

It was, however, the knowledge that a two-thirds majority would vote for cloture that was effective. A majority of the Senate less than two thirds would have been impotent. The leaders now say that Senator Blease may have his South Carolina judge, and notwithstanding the adverse report of the Judiciary Committee which has considered his bill it will pass by "unanimous consent."

Late this afternoon bills were passed by the dozen under "unanimous consent." Hundreds more will be passed in this way in the next few days. It is the only way the Senate can get through its business. The bills, of course, cannot receive proper consideration by the Senate, for its time has been used up by the unlimited and irrelevant speechmakers during the past three months. What a way to legislate!

My old friends keep coming to see me, and it occurs to me to paraphrase Balthasar Gracian and say: "It is the friends who greet one at exit, not entrance, who are important."

Washington, February 22, 1929.

According to custom, on the birthday of Washington, his Farewell Address was read at the opening of the day's session of the Senate by James A. Reed, Senator from Missouri.

The impressive way in which this wonderful address was read by Reed could not but have left his audience with increased admiration of its greatness and soundness. Historians tell us that the larger part of the address was written by Alexander Hamilton. This statement in no wise lessens respect for Washington, but increases respect for the versatility and genius of the brilliant young man whose constructive work laid the foundations of American finance. Without this immortal address, posterity never would have had a full appreciation of the true stature of the Father of his Country.

Presided over the Senate for much of the day, and devoted the rest of it to work in my office on the Dominican problem. Got General Smither on the telephone at Lawrenceville, Illinois, and secured his acceptance of a place in the commission. Called Colonel Roop by telephone at Chicago and likewise secured his agreement to serve, provided only that it did not interfere with his marriage in March. Decided to take as secretary of the Commission my faithful and able secretary, E. Ross Bartley, who has rendered me such invaluable assistance during the last four years.

Sumner Welles called, bringing with him the memorandum of the situation in Santo Domingo and its government which I had requested him to formulate. This proved to be an illuminating and concise document demonstrating high capacity, thorough knowledge and common sense on the part of Welles. Sumner Welles was formerly Chief of the Latin-American Division of the Department of State of the United States and later American Commissioner to the Dominican Republic, which in his history he has named "Naboth's Vineyard." His high reputation for ability, of which I have frequently heard, is fully sustained by my contacts with him the last few days.

Washington, February 23, 1929.

I had a complete surprise this afternoon when Henry M. Robinson, a close friend of Mr. Hoover, and representing him, called at the Capitol to ask whether I would accept, if tendered, the appointment of Ambassador to the Court of St. James's. Robinson spoke of the opportunity for usefulness in connection with international disarmament matters and the new diplomatic status which all hope has been created by the Kellogg Treaty. When one reaches my age in life and but a few years, at most, are available for allotment of its remaining activities, he should not make hasty decisions. Yet the most important decisions I have heretofore made have been of that variety.

However, this thing involves such a radical recasting of plans already made, that I will let my subconscious mind work over it until Wednesday, anyway.

My important decisions were all immediate: to go from Marietta to the Cincinnati Law School; to go from Marietta to Lincoln, and from Lincoln to Chicago; to go to the war, and to take up the Budget work under Harding.

Of course the tender may never be made. Politics are always uncertain.

Washington, Feb. 24, 1929.

Yesterday in the Senate there was a public surrender by that body to an individual Senator using the obstructive power under the rules.

I attach the account of it in this morning's *Washington Post*.

Senator Blease, of South Carolina, demonstrated to the Senate yesterday that when a member of Congress wants something for his State badly enough he sometimes runs a pretty fair chance of getting it.

The South Carolina Democrat took advantage of every parliamentary rule available to Senators to prevent the passage of six important judgeship bills until the Senate was willing to include his own state in the list.

His stubborn opposition, evidenced through the greater part of the session to the passage of any judgeship bills unless one for an additional Federal judge in South Carolina also was approved, finally forced the Senate to meet his demands yesterday and thereupon he immediately withdrew his protest; the whole lot was passed.

Some time ago the Senate judiciary committee approved bills for additional judgeships in various parts of the country but reported adversely on Senator Blease's bill for another judge in South Carolina.

Every argument was used on the Senator to let the others pass but he was unmoved. To-day at the request of Senator Robinson, of Arkansas, the Democratic leader, the Senate agreed to let Blease's bill through and in less than five minutes all of the other pending bills were approved.

In addition to the South Carolina judgeship, the measures approved included a Federal judge for the middle district of Pennsylvania, one additional for South Dakota, three additional for the southern district of New York, one additional for the ninth judicial circuit, one additional for the eastern district of New York and also a bill dividing the eighth judicial circuit and creating a tenth circuit.

The Pennsylvania and eastern New York bills went to the House. The others were sent to President Coolidge.

The last week of the session commences to-morrow and the work of passing bills in the open Senate by "unanimous consent" and without proper consideration will go merrily on. Twenty-two bills and two joint resolutions were thus passed in one evening last week, when "unobjected bills" were considered. Ten minutes to a bill is much more than the average time the Senate gives to a measure in passing it at one of these sessions. And yet because of the fundamental defect in procedure under the rules, by which the Senate cannot control its own time, this method of passing bills is the only one under which the Senate can function. At one of these sessions, when the calendar is called "for unobjected bills", at which most of the bills are passed, the Senate is no longer a "deliberative body" as a matter of course.

This afternoon Senator Burton of Ohio and his niece, the Spanish Ambassador, Mr. Pidilla, his wife, and the Netherlands Minister, Mr. Van Royen, and his wife called on us at the house. Showed Pidilla the report of the Smithsonian Institution upon the proposed search in Spain of Mayan and Aztec literature. He offers letters of introduction to the representative of the Institution who will go to Spain.

Washington, February 25, 1929.

Occupied the chair of the Senate but a short time to-day, for a multiplicity of matters kept me at the office. There are many trained and eager substitutes who are ready to perform my public work here, especially when the galleries, as at present, are full, but none are available for my personal duties.

Am considering, of course, the possibility of a tender of the Ambassadorship to Great Britain, but must keep my promise to President Vasquez of the Dominican Republic, whatever may be its effect.

Robinson's statement that Houghton wishes to retire in March and other reasons of which I know nothing may make it necessary to appoint a new man at once to take his place. In this event I will have to forgo the appointment or break my promise, upon the keeping of which the Dominican Government is setting great store. This I will state to Hoover when I see him Wednesday.

Spent some time considering some very intelligent memoranda of Sumner Welles on the Dominican situation.

Later.

Was interrupted here by a call from my friend of war days in France, the Grand Duke Alexander of Russia, the brother-in-law of the late Czar. He called at the house this morning after I had left for the Senate, and his day — not yet finished — has been consumed by a lunch, a lecture, a dinner and some function later to-night arranged by the "society" people who have him in tow. He leaves early in the morning. He is a cultured gentleman who has sounded the gamut of life's joys and anguish. Seventeen of his near relatives have been killed by the Bolsheviks. When at Paris five years ago he discussed with Young and myself the question of coming to America to lecture, and to-night he said he had come to report. Eleven years ago, during the war, when I first met him in France, he had just escaped from Russia and was in the depths. To-day he is happy again. One of his boys, he tells me, is clerking at Marshall Field's in Chicago, and one is employed in a brokerage house in New York. His lecture tour has been a success.

Washington, February 26, 1929.

The Senate this afternoon is debating in unlimited fashion the location for a market site in Washington, over which there is a conflict of local interests — frittering away time over a place to sell spinach, as one Senator said, with other bills of great importance in the existing legislative jam.

Bills can pass now only by "unanimous consent", except possibly the one under consideration at present on the market site and the few still in conference between the two houses of Congress.

Having received this morning from Henry M. Robinson a letter written yesterday in which he said he was leaving Washington 'but would try to get in touch with me from Chicago on Wednesday afternoon by telephone with the idea of receiving a favorable reply.' I realized that I could not answer Robinson without going over the Dominican matter with Hoover. Accordingly my secretary, Bartley, telephoned for an appointment, which brought an invitation to lunch. This included Mrs. Dawes, who went with me to meet Mr. and Mrs. Hoover but left immediately as she was to preside over a luncheon of the Senators' wives at which Mrs. Coolidge was to be present. I had a frank talk with the President-elect, telling him of my promise to go to Santo Domingo which I would have to keep and adding that if it was not inconsistent with fulfillment of the promise and if it should transpire that he wished me to go to England, I should be glad to accept. He replied that he hoped to be able to appoint me after seeing Stimson, who will arrive in about a month, and that the Dominican visit could be made in any event.

Having from long experience come to realize the vicissitudes of the political status quo, I told him to feel no embarrassment on my account if circumstances led him to select someone else. He talked for a considerable time about our relations with Great Britain, and somewhat in detail in regard to the naval disarmament negotiation. He mentioned the difficulty he was having in inducing men of large affairs and of unusual administrative and executive qualifications to accept appointment to the Cabinet — saying that three recently had declined to be considered in view of the treatment accorded nominations by the Senate, treatment which amounts to a trial before the public on ex parte evidence and upon any charge an enemy chooses to make. He evidently has had much trouble in getting together a cabinet of the high standard of personnel which he desires.

Our conversation and lunch, at which we were joined by Mrs. Hoover, occupied almost an hour and a half.

Washington, February 23, 1929.

Had a talk with Senator Borah whom I am keeping informed as to Santo Domingo purposes. He is chairman of the Foreign Relations Committee and I want them to understand in advance the nature of our work. Trouble is not unknown in this republic, and in case we encounter any I prefer to have our case understood in advance.

Washington, February 27, 1929.
At the Capitol — Evening.

Am spending the evening alternately in my office and in the chair of the Senate while that body, tangled in the web of its rules, flounders helplessly. Arthur Vandenberg, deprived of the vote on the Reapportionment Bill by a minority filibuster, in a masterful and eloquent speech upon the Reapportionment Bill, incidentally paid his respects to the Senate rules which enable individuals to prevent Congress from carrying out a constitutional mandate expressed in its first article. But "what is the Constitution among friends" of the Senate rules and their obstructive powers? The Senate is a paradise on earth for the congenital troublemaker.

Have had a most busy day.

Sumner Welles took lunch with me and we talked over procedure in the Dominican matter. I cabled ex-Senator James W. Wadsworth at Honolulu inviting him to become a member of the Commission.

Decided on March 25 as the date we would start for Santo Domingo.

Collected and studied some Budget Bureau material covering its administration after my departure from its directorship. Cabled Seidemann of the Institute of Government Research, now working as an expert in Puerto Rico, asking him to serve on the Commission.

Was interrupted here by the one ring of the bell in my office, signifying that a vote of the Senate was in progress. I went into the Chamber across the hall expecting to take the chair, but was informed that the vote was upon an "appeal from the decision of the Chair" — then occupied by a Senator, who had ruled that an amendment to an appropriation bill which provided $48,000 for a summer White House was out of order. The vote by two to one overruled the Senator's decision.

When I took the chair in his place, — as I would have done earlier except that his ruling was the issue, — he whispered to me that he had ruled the amendment out of order because Hoover had expressed himself to him as against the idea of a summer White House. This illustrates what happens to the Chair when he is moved in his rulings by any other purpose than to faithfully interpret in them the parliamentary laws involved.

Midnight.

Have been in the chair listening to the filibustering speeches droned out by the obstructionists. A humiliating spectacle is presented by this powerful body, helpless of relief from an absurd situation except by the sheer wearing out of the physical strength of those determined that the majority of the Senate should be denied its rights. It is a travesty on common sense and an outrage upon American institutions.

Am now going to sleep on the sofa in my office beneath Peale's portrait of George Washington, who was an exponent of direct action — a sleep which will be subject to interruption, but affording relief from the sight of grown men acting like spoiled children.

1:35 A.M. February 28, 1929.

My fitful slumber has been disturbed during the last hour and a half by the quorum calls announced each time by two rings of the bell in my office. Curiosity as to what was going on led me to arise at the last bell and re-enter the chamber of the "greatest deliberative body on earth."

The Senators were resting uneasily — but, thank Heaven, quietly — in their seats, having sent out the Sergeant at Arms to arrest Senators who have not answered the roll call — a quorum not being present among the disgusted deserters.

When these recalcitrants are brought in they will listen to a continuance of driveling and irrelevant talk. It may be said that under these circumstances in every other "great deliberative body" on earth a majority would immediately vote to close the debate and take a vote.

Will now go back to the Senate lobby and listen to the possible profanity of the arrested Senators as they are brought in. This is to me one of the few pleasant incidents of such proceedings.

2:15 A.M.

Have returned from the Senate Chamber to write a few more lines. As I sat with Senators Deneen and Glenn of Illinois in the almost deserted Senate Chamber a Senator came to us with this statement: "We think we can get them (the four or five filibustering Senators) to agree to a vote at some time to-morrow if we will agree to recess until eleven o'clock to-morrow. What do you think of it?"

My reply was "Lie down, of course. It is much more important to let them have their own way than annoy them by even suggesting that the Senate majority has any rights. And be sure and speak pleasantly to them and slap them on their backs in a friendly way. Then they won't feel resentment that they are asked to make a concession."

The Senator walked away.

I will now return to the Senate.

Later: 2:30 A.M.

When I reached there, the Senators were standing in the middle of the Chamber gathered around the chief filibusterer, who was laying down the conditions upon which the business of the Senate could proceed to-morrow.

All demands as to the allotment of time to-morrow on the pending bill were finally granted by "unanimous consent", and the Senate recessed at 2:45 A.M. until 11 A.M. to-day.

Later at home, 3:15 A.M.

Against a background of forty years of correct parliamentary procedure, instead of that which has existed for that time in this body, the performances in the Senate this week would have justly aroused national sentiment, but they will cause only passing comment — such are the effects of habit upon public psychology.

> Vice is a monster of so frightful mien
> As to be hated needs but to be seen;
> Yet seen too oft, familiar with her face,
> We first endure, then pity, then embrace.

And so to bed.

Occupied the chair of the Senate for only a short portion of the day session. Called Senator Bingham to the chair for the call of the calendar of unobjected bills. This occupied about three hours. My estimate is that about one hundred and seventy bills were passed by "unanimous consent." I will insert the exact figures later.

In other words, the so-called deliberative body passed bills at the rate of about one per minute for three hours. In the general confusion at the end of the calling of the calendar Senator David Reed sharply protested against efforts to pass bills which had never even been referred to a Committee and by an objection blocked one of this nature. The sort of thing occurring this afternoon is what creates multiplicity of laws, and it is the rules which create the situation.

(From an article by Charles G. Dawes in the *Saturday Evening Post* of November 28, 1925, on "Reform of the Senate Rules.")

That the right of obstruction by minorities in the Senate, made possible by the rules, not only impresses personal interests upon public legislation but contributes to multiplicity of laws is unmistakable. The figures prove that any body which at times must grant concessions to individual members in order to secure the right to act as a whole will pass more laws in proportion than a body not under that handicap, as well as modify the bills passed in many instances in a way not in the public interest.

In the last five Congresses the Senate bills and resolutions passed by the Senate, with ninety-six members, exceeded by 182 the House bills and resolutions passed by the House, with 435 members. The exact figures are 3113 for the Senate and 2931 for the House.

But more significant than this, as evidence of the inevitable exactions of selfish human nature when given a chance, and the effect in forcing favorable reports on bills in Committee, referred to by Senator Thomas, is the fact that the Senate, without majority cloture, passed these 3113 bills and resolutions out of a total of 29,332 introduced, while the House, with majority cloture, passed its smaller number of 2931 out of a total of 82,632 introduced.

During the last five Congresses, therefore, the Senate passed 10.5 per cent of the bills and resolutions introduced in the Senate, while the House of Representatives passed only 3.5 per cent of the bills and resolutions introduced in the House. In other words, of bills and resolutions introduced, the Senate, without effective cloture, passed in proportion three times as many as did the House of Representatives, with cloture.

As further proof, if any is necessary, that filibustering contributes to multiplicity of laws, it may be stated that it has caused the President to call, during the last eight sessions of Congress, seven extra sessions. No one can contend that more laws were not passed in the twenty-three sessions actually held than if only the sixteen regular sessions had been held. As a matter of fact, in these extra sessions a total of 386 laws and 99 public resolutions were passed. Again, as a result of filibustering, not only more laws are passed but the laws which are passed often do not receive due consideration.

Later: February 28, 1929.

One hundred and eighty-four bills and four resolutions were passed by the Senate. The session began at 11 A.M. and ended at 7:30 P.M.

Almost all were passed after 4 P.M., when the calendar was taken up, and within a period of three and one half hours. This is at the rate of nearly one bill a minute. A very deliberative body, indeed!

At Capitol, March 1st, 1929.

Busy day. Office filled with visitors, many of them here for the inauguration. Went through a "movietone" performance with Senator Curtis. The Senators are calling to chat and say good-bye. Was in the chair occasionally, but what seems to be a one-man filibuster is in progress. One Senator, now speaking, has been speaking for three hours on the radio bill, completely tying up the Senate, confronted as it was with most important business which must remain neglected until the rights of "free speech" are fully recognized.

Sumner Welles called with a copy of the cable from President Vasquez, including the form of the invitation which will be sent to me from Santo Domingo probably to-morrow.

Gave President Vasquez the following names for the Commission thus far decided upon by me: Harbord, Welles, Smither, Roop, Seidemann, T. W. Robinson, Wadsworth, and E. Ross Bartley as secretary. An inclusion in President Vasquez' invitation of "municipal" governments in addition to the Dominican Government will make it necessary to add another member or two.

Later: 7:30 P.M.

The Senate has been forced to take an unusual and distasteful (to it) step in an endeavor to invoke a two-thirds cloture vote on the Radio Commission Bill. Under Rule XXII, a two-thirds majority may hinder obstructive debate and have the question, "Is it the sense of the Senate that the debate shall be brought to a close?" put to the Senate one hour after the convening of the Senate on the day after one intervening calendar day. This effort has now been inaugurated by the filing of a notice with the Chair signed by sixteen Senators as provided by the rule.

The presiding officer and two Senators, besides the speaking Senator and the Senator employees, are the only people on the Senate floor. Only two and a fraction days of the session remain. A great mass of unfinished and important business is before the Senate. The rights of a great government are being set aside, in order that one man now entering his fourth hour of speaking may continue as long as he desires.

Any majority less than two thirds is absolutely shut out of its rights to end this intolerable situation, and even a two-thirds majority may not do so for two days, plus the time that ninety-six Senators may take to speak, in addition to the two days — each of them having the right to consume one hour.

Later: 8:20 P.M.

A second filibustering Senator has relieved the first one, who is said to be out recuperating so as to be able to come back and start another speech. In the meantime, the representatives of the majority empowered by the Constitution to end such nonsense sit limply and helplessly in their seats, gossiping with each other as to when these one or two individuals will allow them to transact the Government's business.

The galleries are full. A travesty upon good government in the Senate is regarded as an amusement rivaling a picture show. I wonder what the dignified forebears of the present Senate would think could they look down upon this body to-night, stripped of all dignity save its material surroundings?

Later: 9:30 P.M.

The Senate surrendered (as usual in such cases in the short session) to the two filibustering Senators. The concession in legislation, for which they consented to cease talking, was a shortening of two months and sixteen days in the extension of the time of the powers of the Federal Radio Commission, fixing it until December 31, 1929, instead of March 16, as originally provided by the bill under consideration.

Later: 10:00 P.M.

The Senate recessed until 11:00 A.M. to-morrow. During the calendar day of March 1, 1929, the Senate passed forty-three bills and one resolution. The session began at 11:00 A.M. and ended at 10:41 P.M., or eleven hours and forty-one minutes. Thirty-seven of these bills were passed in the forty minutes preceding the close of the day's session. Very deliberate.

CHAPTER XXI

Washington, March 3, 1929.

YESTERDAY I had no time to make any notes, the day was so crowded with a diversity of experiences. Whenever I was not in the chair, my office was crowded with friends to say good-by.

But the day was made memorable to me by the collective farewell of the Senate to me in the afternoon and that of the Gridiron Club in the evening.

In the Senate, after a quorum call to which eighty-eight Senators responded, — an unusually large number, — on motion a recess of thirty minutes was taken, all remaining in their seats. Then Senator Robinson, for the Democrats, and Senator Moses, for the Republicans, paid me tributes for my services in the chair, presenting a silver tray on behalf of the individual members of the Senate.

I am not unduly depressed by censure, as Balfour says, and hope I am not unduly elated by praise — but these two speeches and the approval with which they were greeted completely upset me emotionally. Realizing that I should be unable to reply personally, I had the presence of mind to write a few words of grateful acknowledgment and hand them to John Crockett, the reading clerk, to read.

VICE PRESIDENT DAWES AND MEMBERS OF THE SENATE STAFF

The trumpetlike tones of John's voice, to which we are so accustomed, had vanished when he read it, much to my disappointment. It was not until after the session when he came to me that I realized that old John was shedding tears when he read it.

I insert the *Congressional Record* verbatim report of the proceedings:—

Calling of the Roll

Mr. Moses. Mr. President, I suggest the absence of a quorum.

The Vice President. The Secretary will call the roll.

The Vice President. Eighty-eight Senators having answered to their names, a quorum is present.

(Recess)

Mr. Watson (at 2 o'clock and 37 minutes P.M.). I move that the Senate take a recess for a period not exceeding thirty minutes.

The Vice President. The motion was agreed and a recess was taken.

(Presentation of Silver Tray to the Vice President)

Mr. Robinson, of Arkansas. Mr. President, the Senate has paused during a very busy session to pay respect to its Presiding Officer, who is about to retire.

The functions of a presiding officer in any legislative assembly are in some respects quasi-judicial. This is substantially true of the duties of the President of the Senate of the United States. He is frequently called upon to construe the rules of this body in cases where sharp conflicts arise respecting their true application.

Every Senator knows the difficulty in harmonizing Senate precedents, many of them having been made by majority vote of the Senate in legislative emergencies in times of excitement.

Mr. President, during the four years that you have served as

Vice President, no instance is recalled in which your decision has been reversed on appeal by vote of the Senate. In this respect the record is without parallel. Remembering that on numerous occasions during these four years this Chamber has been the scene of fierce debates, participated in by skilled parliamentarians, it is surprising that you, being without judicial experience, have avoided successful challenge for error in decision.

It must be pleasing to you in this hour to be assured, by one with some degree of responsibility, by the Senators opposed to the political organization with which you have been affiliated, that only unlimited confidence in your impartiality has made such a triumph, such a record, possible.

No mere intelligence, however great, if influenced by partisan or personal favoritism, could produce such conclusive evidence of the respect and good will of the Democrats and Republicans with whom you have worked during the last four years.

Fairness and promptness have marked your conduct. Firmness and justice have characterized your decisions. This declaration is believed to express the conviction of every Senator.

To the tribute respecting the high standard of your official conduct, another should be added — a tribute which cannot fail to inspire in your own breast sentiments of pride and gratification. You enjoy the friendship, the affectionate esteem, of all with whom you have been associated here — Members, Officials, and Employees of the Senate.

Clarity of thought, generosity of disposition, and decisiveness are indeed a fortunate combination of traits which have endeared you to us all.

Success in the realm of business had already crowned your efforts before you were elected Vice President of the United States. Following the World War, in which you served with distinction and courage, the Dawes Commission, of which you were permanent Chairman, performed a service of distinct and permanent value to the world and particularly to the nations of Europe.

As a present proof and a future reminder of the sentiments so imperfectly expressed in these remarks the members of the Senate, every one of them has cheerfully contributed to a gift which is both useful and beautiful.

We present to you a silver tray, selected with especial thought of Mrs. Dawes, whose charm and modesty have won the love of every one in official life in Washington, as well as of thousands in other spheres. (Applause.)

Mr. Moses. Mr. President, the period of parting which is inseparable from public life, comes here to us again, and with it brings a feeling of sadness which we do not attempt to disguise.

There is to be sure, some sense of satisfaction as we reflect upon the friendships engendered by association here, upon the tasks in which we have been permitted to share, and upon the accomplishments which we have produced for the good of our country. These reflections of satisfaction, sir, will rest in our minds as we think of you, as we shall often in the days when you have gone from us in this chamber.

We are not willing that the matter should rest in memory alone. We wish you to have from us a symbol of the affection and esteem with which we regard you and shall continue to regard you. We ask you, therefore, to take with you this gift, the glad offering of all the members of the Senate. Let it be to you a reminder of those associations which the thoughts of the years, we trust, may make more tender and strong, and with it we ask you to take our warmest and constant wishes of length of years, infinity of happiness and renewed opportunities for public service such as you have always rendered, and in which the fine and endearing qualities which have so cemented our friendships here shall be a signal element in all the years which remain to you. (Applause.)

The Chief Clerk, Mr. John C. Crockett, read the response of the Vice President, as follows:

Senators, I had intended to reply personally, but I find that I cannot trust myself to do it.

My dear friends, you have done a very generous and kindly act. You have done me a great honor, I thank you from the bottom of my heart.

The Senate was called to order by the Vice President at 2 o'clock and 50 minutes P.M.

Mr. Fess. Mr. President, I move that the proceedings during the period of the recess be made a part of our record.

The motion was agreed to.

Senator Borah, over the radio last night, in a chain broadcast, paid me the honor of a tribute which will ever be to my children a family heritage. This I insert: —

There is a feature of the inauguration which is of peculiar interest to some of us. It brings about many changes which we record with regret. In a few fleeting hours the Seventieth Congress will pass into history. Our proceedings here for weal or for woe will soon take their place among the records which are closed and laid away. Like all things human, the story has its disappointments as well as its triumphs — that strange mingling of failures and success which makes up life. But therein is found the weakness as well as the strength of a democracy. We tolerate its weaknesses that we may enjoy its glory.

Associations here bite deep into the channel of our lives — contacts are formed and leave impressions which end only with the grave. It may seem to the outside world, judging by surface indications, that the burdens and the care and the associations here pass with the work of the day. We who are participants know different. Responsibility carries to every waking hour both its conscious and unconscious admonitions and spurs all to their highest endeavors. No man worthy of this trust can be indifferent to the things which are expected of him. The ending of a Congress means much, therefore, to those who are members.

Over the Senate of this Congress and the preceding Congress there has presided one of the most distinguished of living Americans — a man high in the confidence and esteem of his countrymen long before he became the presiding officer of this body. Of his career and his distinction generally there is no occasion perhaps at this time to speak. But of him as a presiding officer, there is occasion to speak. His uniform courtesy, a stranger to favoritism or to partisanship, his keen interest in the great problems before us, his acknowledged and exceptional ability — these are the things which have won the respect of and endeared him to every member of the Senate. It may well be understood what an inspiration is found in the standing and high character of such a presiding officer. Not one of us but will cherish in memory our association with one who has brought to this position a life already rich in experience and great achievements.

We take leave of him with a deep affection and with a sense of gratitude which will go with us through the rest of our lives. We want him to rest assured, and we want the country to know, that he carries away with him the best wishes of all with whom he has been associated, for his continued health and happiness and for many years of increased usefulness and service to his country.

In the evening another kindness was accorded me in a dinner given by the full Gridiron Club at which the only outsiders were my secretary Ross Bartley, and myself.

It was conducted much along the same lines as a public affair of the club, until at the end my old friend of thirty-one years, Harry Hall, now a prominent publisher of Pittsburgh, stood before me and delivered a speech of friendship on behalf of the club, closing by presenting me with a large gridiron engraved as the gift of the club. I replied to this speech as best I could.

To me this dinner, given by this great organization, was one of the distinctive honors of my life.

CHAPTER XXII

Evanston, Illinois, March 6, 1929.

It is at home again, as a private citizen, before the fire in my library, that I record this evening the closing day of my official life at Washington, at the end of which, with the Senate staff, including the pages, bidding us farewell at the depot, Mrs. Dawes and I took the train for Chicago.

The form my farewell address to the Senate should take was a matter of some concern to me. With the Senators individually, my relation in general was that of a sincere friend. That body had adjourned for half an hour Saturday to do me honor, and tributes had been made to me and my conduct of the chair which were unusual and had deeply affected me. Yet I could not, of course, neglect my only remaining opportunity to restate briefly my attitude and convictions as to the defective Senate rules. If I did, it was unconditional surrender. If I did not, and again forced it emphatically upon public attention, at least I should have done my full duty to the issue I myself raised with the Senate.

But after what they had done to express a cordial regard for me, it was psychology neither from the public standpoint nor that of my immediate and most distinguished audience to fail to show the same spirit toward them. To accomplish this without lessening the force and impressiveness of a last attack upon the rules in their Senatorial stronghold was the problem; and, in an attempt to solve this, it seems evident from the press and other comment that I succeeded.

For the first time in the history of the Senate, the microphone for a nationwide broadcasting by radio of the speeches and proceedings there was upon the desk of the President of the Senate.

On the morning of the fourth of March I proceeded to the Vice President's chambers across from the Senate Hall, arriving at ten-thirty o'clock. There I found the new Cabinet of President-elect Hoover — not there to pay their respects to me, though they did so, but because every room around the Senate Chamber was used as a rendezvous for some distinguished official group waiting to make their entry into the Senate Chamber for the exercises attending the inauguration of the new Vice President and the exit of the old one.

At eleven o'clock, I took the chair and convened the Senate which took up the unfinished business of the day before until about quarter to twelve, when the ceremonial procedure commenced.

The insertion here of the printed program for the inaugural ceremonies and an extract from the *Congressional Record* of March 4 will best cover the important events then ensuing, as well as the final exit of President and Mrs. Coolidge and Mrs. Dawes and myself, which occurred at the inauguration stand in front of the Capitol immediately upon the conclusion of the address of President Hoover.

Executive Message from the President

The Vice President. As in Executive Session, the Chair lays before the Senate a certain message in writing from the President of the United States which will lie on the table.

The time has come when the Senate will receive the Speaker and Members of the House of Representatives, and debate is closed.

Guests of the Senate

At 11 o'clock and 45 minutes A.M., the First Assistant Sergeant at Arms of the Senate (Carl A. Loeffler) announced the Speaker of the House of Representatives and the members of the House of Representatives.

The Speaker and the Members of the House occupied the seats reserved for them.

A few minutes later the Ambassadors Extraordinary, Envoys Plenipotentiary, Ministers Plenipotentiary, and Chargé d'Affaires ad interim to the United States were announced and escorted to the seats provided for them.

The members of the President's cabinet were announced by the Second Assistant Sergeant at Arms (Edwin A. Halsey) and shown to the seats assigned to them.

The Chief of Staff of the Army, the Chief of Naval Operations, and the Commandant of the Marine Corps and their aides were announced, respectively, and shown to the seats provided for them.

The Chief Justice of the United States and the Associate Justices of the Supreme Court of the United States were announced and escorted to the seats provided for them.

Soon thereafter the Sergeant at Arms (David S. Barry) announced Charles Curtis, of Kansas, the Vice President-elect, accompanied by the Chairman and members of the Joint Committee on arrangements, consisting of Senator George H. Moses, of New Hampshire, Chairman; Senator Frederick Hale, of Maine; Senator Lee S. Overman, of North Carolina; Representative Bertrand H. Snell, of New York; Representative Leonidas C. Dyer, of

Missouri; and Representative Edward W. Pou, of North Carolina.

The Vice President-elect was seated on the left of the Vice President.

Several minutes before noon the Sergeant at Arms announced the President of the United States, accompanied by the Chairman and Members of the Joint Committee on arrangements. The President of the United States was seated in the space in front of the Secretary's desk.

The Sergeant at Arms then announced Herbert Hoover, of California, President-elect of the United States, accompanied by the chairman and members of the Joint Committee on arrangements.

The President-elect was seated on the left of the President of the United States, the Chairman and members of the Joint Committee on arrangements occupying the seats on either side.

Administration of Oath

The Vice President administered the oath of office prescribed by law to the Vice President-elect.

Address of Vice President Dawes

The Vice President. In a few minutes it will be the last official duty which I am to perform to adjourn the Senate of the Seventieth Congress of the United States.

The passing of a Congress is but an incident in the life of our great Republic, now entering the 140th year of its existence, never stronger in that which is its greatest bulwark, the love and devotion of a united and a happy people. But to many in this Senate Chamber, it means the breaking of close ties formed by the association of years in a common endeavor, human ties, whose strength is never realized until the time of their sundering is at hand.

I want to express my heartfelt gratitude to the members of the Senate, and to the members of the Senate Staff; and especially to Mr. Charles L. Watkins, the parliamentarian of the Senate, for his invaluable aid to me; and for the courtesy and the kindness and the consideration, and the generosity, with which you have all treated me.

I have tried to be worthy as best I could, and in the occupancy of this chair I have never consciously deviated from the duty which inseparably attaches to it, that of impartiality in partisan, personal, and sectional differences.

At the time of parting between friends, there is no place for acrimony, and I assure you there is none in my heart. But I could not be true to myself and to my conception of the duties of this position if as I leave it for the last time, when, if ever, disinterestedness should characterize my convictions, I did not speak again of the collective error of this great and powerful branch of the government. Alone of all the great deliberative bodies of the world, the Senate of the United States, under its rules, has parted with the power to allot its time to the consideration of the subjects before it in accordance with their relative importance. This defect of procedure is fundamental. I take back nothing.

To my successor in office, my dear friend and the dear friend of us all, Senator Curtis, I wish the great success which his fine character, his ability and his long experience in this body makes certain.

I declare the Senate of the Seventieth Congress adjourned sine die.

THE END

INDEX

INDEX

INDEX

6. D3216A

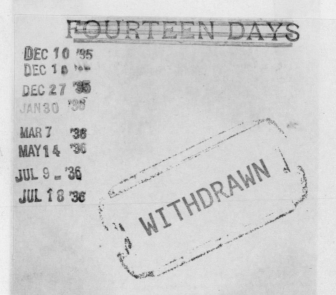